BASIC ECONOMICS

BASIC ECONOMICS

A Citizen's Guide to the Economy

THOMAS SOWELL

BASIC

BOOKS

A Member of the Perseus Books Group

Published by Basic Books,
A Member of the Perseus Books Group

Library of Congress Cataloging-in-Publication Data
Sowell, Thomas, 1930-
    Basic economics : a citizen's guide to the economy/ Thomas Sowell.
        p. cm.
    Includes bibliographical references and index.
    ISBN 0-465-08138-X
        1. Economics. I. Title.

HB171 .S73 2001
330—dc21

                                                                            00-044420

FIRST EDITION

    01 02 03 / 10 9 8 7 6 5 4 3 2

A few lines of reasoning can change the way we see the world.

Steven E. Lansburg

CONTENTS

PART IV: TIME AND RISK

PART V: THE NATIONAL ECONOMY

PART VI: THE INTERNATIONAL ECONOMY

PART VII: POPULAR ECONOMIC FALLACIES

PREFACE

This is an introduction to economics for the general public. The growing sophistication of professional economists has not been accompanied by any greater spread of knowledge about basic economic principles among the population at large. There are, in fact, very few incentives for economists to spend their time explaining the basics of economics to the public. Indeed, even the economic education of college students is not likely to get much attention from economists, if those students are not majoring in economics.

The net result is that complex and high-powered economic analysis within the profession co-exists with utter ignorance and gross fallacies dominating the public, the media and various branches of government. Even scholars with Ph.D.s in other fields are often ill-informed or misinformed about economics, though that seldom deters them from having and voicing opinions on economic issues.

Most of us are necessarily ignorant of many complex fields, from botany to brain surgery. As a result, we simply do not attempt to operate in those fields. However, every voter and every politician that they vote for has something to say about economics. In that case, we need to know the basics. Explaining these basics is the purpose of this book.

It so happens that the first book of mine that was published, back in 1971, was an introductory economics textbook, full of the kinds of graphs and equations that such books are supposed to have. Today, however, *Basic Economics* does not contain a single graph or equation to express the kinds of ideas that economists deal with. Nor does it contain such common jargon among economists as "oligopoly," "marginal revenue product" or "Pareto optimality." This book is about economics, not about the vocabulary or visual aids of economists. Having taught introductory economics more times than I can remember, at colleges and universities across the country, I know how handy those visual aids can be and how easy it is to lapse into familiar jargon. Avoiding these things has made it harder for me to write this book, but the whole point is to make it easier for you to read it.

What I have also learned over the years is that there are many highly intelligent people who want to understand more about the way their country's economy works, but who have no interest in the paraphernalia of the economics profession. This book is written for such people—and also for those high school and college students who are taking introductory economics as part of their efforts to become educated women and men, not necessarily candidates to major in the subject. It is also written with the hope that some economists might discover how much of what they say in ways that are incomprehensible to outsiders could also be said in plain English.

In keeping with the nature of this book as an introduction to economics for the general public, I have left out the usual hundreds of footnotes or end-notes in some of my other books. However, those who wish to check up on some of the surprising facts they will learn about can find the sources listed at the end of the book. This will also be a place for those who simply wish to explore further in some subject that they find intriguing.

While it is advisable to understand the role of prices in a market economy before going on to other subjects, each chapter of this book has been written to stand alone, so that these chapters can be read in any order that your own interest dictates.

Although many of the examples of basic economic principles in action are drawn from market economies, such as that in the United States, many others are not. One of the best ways to understand what a market economy does is by seeing what happens when the same economic activity takes place in a non-market economy, such as that of the late Soviet Union. Economic experiences from every inhabited continent appear in the chapters that follow, for basic economic principles are not limited to any given society or people.

Thomas Sowell
Rose and Milton Friedman Senior Fellow
Hoover Institution
Stanford University

ACKNOWLEDGEMENTS

Strictly speaking, nothing is ever the product of just one worker, as explained in Chapter 9. This book owes much to too many people for me to thank them all. Those who taught me when I was a student, many years ago, deserve great credit, especially for the times when they carefully explained things that should have been obvious without an explanation. I can only hope that I had as much patience with the students I later taught during my academic career at U.C.L.A., Cornell, Rutgers, Howard and Amherst.

Among those who contributed more directly to this book by reading it in manuscript and making comments and suggestions were my wife Mary and my colleagues Professors Walter E. Williams of George Mason University and William R. Allen of U. C. L. A., as well as my friend and New York attorney James Higgins. It goes without saying that they are not to blame for any remaining errors or shortcomings of mine.

Chapter 1

What Is Economics?

To know what economics is, we must first know what an economy is. Perhaps most of us think of an economy as a system for the production and distribution of the goods and services we use in everyday life. That is true as far as it goes, but it does not go far enough. The Garden of Eden was a system for the production and distribution of goods and services, but it was not an economy, because everything was available in unlimited abundance. Without scarcity, there is no need to economize—and therefore no economics. A distinguished British economist named Lionel Robbins gave the classic definition of economics:

> *Economics is the study of the use of scarce resources which have alternative uses.*

What does "scarce" mean? It means that people want more than there is. This may seem like a simple thing, but its implications are often grossly misunderstood, even by highly educated people. For example, a feature article in the *New York Times* of August 1, 1999 laid out the economic woes and worries of middle-class Americans—one of the most affluent groups of human beings ever to inhabit this planet. Although the story includes a picture of a middle-class family in their own swimming pool, the main headline says: "The American Middle, Just Getting By." Other headings in the article include:

> Wishes Deferred and Plans Unmet
> Goals That Remain Just Out of Sight
> Dogged Saving and Some Luxuries

In short, middle-class Americans' desires exceed what they can comfortably afford, even though what they already have would be considered unbelievable prosperity by people in many other countries around the world — or even by earlier generations of Americans. Yet both they and the reporter regard them as "just getting by" and a Harvard sociologist spoke of "how budget-constrained these people really are." However, it is not something as man-made as a budget which constrains them: Reality constrains them. There has never been enough to satisfy everyone completely. That is the real constraint. That is what scarcity means.

Although per capita real income in the United States increased 50 percent in just one generation, these middle-class families "have had to work hard for their modest gains," according to a Fordham professor quoted in the same article. What a shame they could not get manna from heaven! As for the modesty of their gains, this suggests that people not only adjust their expectations upward with growing prosperity, but also adjust their rhetoric as to what it means to be "just getting by." The *New York Times* reporter wrote of one of these middle-class families:

> After getting in over their heads in credit card spending years ago, their finances are now in order. "But if we make a wrong move," Geraldine Frazier said, "the pressure we had from the bills will come back, and that is painful."

To all these people—from academia and journalism, as well as the middle-class people themselves—it apparently seems strange somehow that there should be such a thing as scarcity and that this should imply a need for both productive efforts on their part and personal responsibility in spending. Yet nothing has been more pervasive in the history of the human race than scarcity and all the requirements for economizing that go with scarcity.

Not only scarcity but also "alternative uses" are at the heart of economics. If each resource had only one use, economics would be much simpler. But water can be used to produce ice or steam by itself or innumerable other mixtures and compounds in combination with other things. A virtually limitless number of products can also be produced from wood or from petroleum, iron ore, etc. How much of each resource should be allocated to each of its many uses? Every economy has to answer that question, and each one does, in one way or another, efficiently or inefficiently. Doing so efficiently is what economics is all about.

Whether the people in a given economy will be prosperous or poverty-stricken depends in large part on how well their resources are allocated. Rich resources often exist in very poor countries, simply because the country lacks the economic mechanisms, as well as specific skills, for efficiently turning those resources into abundant output. Conversely, countries with relatively few natural resources—Japan or Switzerland, for example—can have very high standards of living, if their people and their economy are well adapted for allocating and using whatever resources it has or can purchase from other countries.

Among the many misconceptions of economics is that it is something that tells you how to make money or run a business or predict the ups and downs of the stock market. But economics is not personal finance or business administration, and predicting the ups and downs of the stock market has yet to be reduced to a set of dependable principles.

Economics is not about the financial fate of individuals. It is about the material well-being of society as a whole. It shows cause and effect relationships involving prices, industry and commerce, work and pay, or the international balance of trade— all from the standpoint of how this affects the allocation of scarce resources in a way that raises or lowers the material standard of living of the population as a whole.

Money doesn't even have to be involved to make a decision be economic. When a military medical team arrives on a battlefield where soldiers have a variety of wounds, they are confronted with the classic economic problem of allocating scarce resources which have alternative uses. Almost never are there enough doctors, nurses, or paramedics to go around, nor enough medication. Some of the wounded are near death and have little chance of being saved, while others have a fighting chance if they get immediate care, and still others are only slightly wounded and will probably recover whether they get immediate medical care or not.

If the medical team does not allocate its time and medications efficiently, some wounded soldiers will die needlessly, while time is being spent attending to others not as urgently in need of care or still others whose wounds are so devastating that they will probably die in spite of anything that can be done for them. It is an economic problem, though not a dime changes hands.

Most of us hate even to think of having to make such choices. Indeed, as we have already seen, some middle-class Americans are distressed at having to make much milder choices and trade-offs. But life does not ask what we want. It presents us with options. Economics is just one of the ways of trying to make the most of those options.

While there are controversies in economics, as there are in science, this does not mean that economics is just a matter of opinion. There are basic propositions and procedures in economics on which a Marxist economist like Oskar Lange did not differ in any fundamental way from a conservative economist like Milton Friedman. It is these basic economic principles that this book is about.

Much of what follows in the chapters ahead is an analysis of what happens in an economy coordinated by prices and by the resulting flows of money and goods in a competitive market. But it also considers what happens when markets are not permitted to operate in that way, whether because of business, unions, or government. One of the best ways of understanding the role of prices, for example, is by understanding what happens when they are not permitted to play their role in the market. How does an economy respond when prices are set or controlled by the government, rather than being allowed to fluctuate with supply and demand? What happens in an economy that is centrally planned, as distinguished from one in which decisions about how to use resources and distribute goods and services are made by millions of separate individuals, whose decisions are coordinated only by their responses to price movements?

All sorts of economies—capitalist, socialist, feudal, etc.—must determine in one way or another how the available resources are directed toward their various uses. But how well they do it can lead to poverty or affluence for a whole country. That is what the study of economics is all about and that is what makes it important.

PART I:
PRICES

Chapter 2

The Role of Prices

In a market economy, prices play a crucial role in determining how much of each resource gets used where. Yet this role is seldom understood by the public and it is often disregarded entirely by politicians.

Many people see prices as simply obstacles to their getting the things they want. Those who would like to live in a beach-front home, for example, may abandon such plans when they discover how expensive beach-front property is. But high prices are not the reason we cannot all live on the beach front. On the contrary, the inherent reality is that there are not nearly enough beach-front homes to go around and prices are just a way of conveying that underlying reality. When many people bid for a relatively few homes, these homes become very expensive because of supply and demand. But it is not the prices that cause the scarcity, which would exist under whatever other social arrangements might be used instead of prices.

If the government were to come up with a "plan" for "universal access" to beach-front homes and put "caps" on the prices that could be charged for such property, that would not change the underlying reality of the ratio of people to beach-front land. With a given population and a given amount of beach-front property, rationing without prices would now have to take place by bureaucratic fiat, political favoritism or random chance—but the rationing would still have to take place. Even if Congress or the Supreme Court were to decree that beach-front homes were a "basic right" of all Americans, that would still not change the underlying reality in the slightest.

Prices are like messengers conveying news—sometimes bad news, in the case of beach-front property desired by far more people than can possibly live at the beach, but often also good news. For example, computers have been getting both cheaper and better at a very rapid rate, as a result of the development of technological ingenuity. Yet the vast majority of beneficiaries of these high-tech advances, insights, and talents have not the foggiest idea of what these technical changes are specifically. But prices convey to them the end results—which are all that matter for their own decision-making and their own enhanced productivity and well-being from using computers.

Similarly, if vast new rich iron ore deposits were discovered, perhaps no more than one percent of the population would be likely to be aware of it, but everyone would discover that things made of steel were becoming cheaper. People thinking of buying desks, for example, would discover that steel desks had become more of a bargain compared to wooden desks and some would undoubtedly change their minds as to which kind of desk to purchase because of that. The same would be true when comparing various other products made of steel to competing products made of wood, aluminum, plastic or other materials.

In short, price changes would enable a whole society to adjust automatically to a greater abundance of iron ore, even though 99 percent of the people in that society were wholly unaware of the new discovery.

Prices not only guide consumers, they guide producers as well. When all is said and done, producers cannot possibly know what millions of different consumers want. All that automobile manufacturers, for example, know is that when they produce cars with a certain combination of features they can sell these cars for a price that covers their production costs and leaves them a profit, but when they manufacture cars with a different combination of features, they don't sell as well. In order to get rid of the unsold cars, they must cut the prices to whatever level is necessary to get them off the dealers' lots, even if that means taking a loss. The alternative is to take a bigger loss by not selling them at all.

While a free market economic system is sometimes called a profit system, it is really a profit-and-loss system—and the losses are equally important for the efficiency of the economy, because they tell the manufacturers what to stop producing. Without really knowing why consumers like one set of features rather than another, producers automatically produce more of what earns a profit and less of what is losing money. That amounts to producing what the consumers want and stopping the production of what they don't want. Although the producers are only looking out for themselves and their companies' bottom line, nevertheless from the standpoint of the economy as a whole the society is using its scarce resources more efficiently because decisions are guided by prices.

PRICES AND COSTS

The situation we have just examined—where the consumers want A and don't want B—is the simplest example of how prices lead to efficiency in the use of scarce resources. But prices are at least equally important in situation where consumers want both A and B, as well as many other things, some of which require the same ingredients in their production. For example, consumers not only want cheese, they want ice cream and yogurt as well, all of which are made from milk. How do prices help the economy to determine how much milk should go to each of these products?

In bidding for cheese, ice cream, and yogurt, consumers are in effect also bidding for the milk that produces them. The money than comes in from the sales of these products is what enables the producers to buy more milk to use to continue producing their respective products. When the demand for cheese goes up, cheese-makers bid away some of the milk that before went into making ice cream or yogurt, in order to increase the output of their own product to meet the rising demand. In other words, the cost of milk rises to everyone when cheese-makers demand more, so that other users have to cut back on how much milk they buy. As other producers then raise the prices of ice cream and yogurt to cover the higher price of the milk that goes into them, consumers are likely to buy less of these other products at these higher prices.

How will each producer know just how much milk to buy? Obviously they will buy only as much milk as will repay its higher costs from the higher prices of ice cream and yogurt. If consumers who buy ice cream are not as discouraged by rising prices as consumers who buy yogurt are, then very little of the additional milk that goes into making more cheese will come at the expense of ice cream and more will come at the expense of yogurt.

What this all means as a general principle is that the price that one producer is willing to pay for milk (or any other ingredient) is the price that other producers are forced to pay for that same ingredient. Since scarce resources have alternative uses, the value placed on one of these uses by one individual or company becomes a cost that has to be paid by others who want to bid some of these resources away for their own use. What this means, from the standpoint of the economy as a whole, is that *resources tend to flow to their most valued uses*.

This does not mean that one use categorically precludes all other uses. On the contrary, adjustments are incremental. Only that amount of milk which is as valuable to ice cream consumers or consumers of yogurt as it is to cheese purchasers will be used to make ice cream or yogurt. Whether considering consumers of cheese, ice cream, or yogurt, some will be anxious to have a certain amount, less anxious to have additional amounts, and finally—beyond some point—indifferent to having any more, or even unwilling to consume any more after becoming satiated.

Prices coordinate the use of resources, so that only that amount is used for one thing which is equal in value to what it is worth to others in other uses. That way a price-coordinated economy does not flood people with cheese to the point where they are sick of it, while others are crying out in vain for more ice cream or yogurt. Absurd as such a situation would be, it has happened many times in economies where prices do not allocate scarce resources. The Soviet economy, for example, often had unsalable goods piling up in warehouses while people were waiting in long lines trying to get other things that they wanted. The efficient allocation of scarce resources which have alternative uses is not just an abstract notion of economists. It determines how well or how badly millions of people live.

Again, as in the example of beach-front property, prices convey an underlying reality. *From the standpoint of society as a whole, the "cost" of anything is the value that it has in alternative uses.* That cost is reflected in the market when the price that one individual is willing to pay becomes a cost that others are forced to pay, in order to get a share of the same scarce resource or the products made from it. But, no matter whether a particular society has a capitalist price system or a socialist economy or a feudal or other system, the real cost of anything is still its value in alternative uses. The real cost of building a bridge are the other things that could have been built with that same labor and material. This is also true at the level of a given individual, even when no money is involved. The cost of watching a television sitcom or soap opera is the value of the other things that could have been done with that same time.

Different economic systems deal with this underlying reality in different ways and with different degrees of efficiency, but the underlying reality exists independently of whatever particular economic system is used. Once we recognize that, we can then compare how economic systems which use prices to force people to share scarce resources among themselves differ in efficiency from economic systems which determine such things by having kings, politicians or bureaucrats issues orders saying who can get how much of what.

During the brief era of *glasnost* (openness) and *perestroika* (re-structuring) in the last years of the Soviet Union, two Soviet economists named Nikolai Shmelev and Vladimir Popov wrote a book giving a very candid account of how their economy worked and this book was later translated into English. As Shmelev and Popov put it, enterprises in the U.S.S.R. "always ask for more than they need" in the way of raw materials, equipment, and other resources used in production. "They take everything they can get, regardless of how much they actually need, and don't worry about economizing on materials," according to these economists. "After all, nobody 'at the top' knows exactly what the real requirements are," so "squandering" makes sense.

The consequence was that far more resources were used to produce a given output in the Soviet economy as compared to a price-coordinated economic system, such as that in the United States. Citing official Soviet statistics, the Soviet economists lamented:

According to the calculations of the Soviet Institute of World
Economy and International Relations, we use 1.5 times more
materials and 2.1 times more energy per unit of national income
than the United States. . . . We use 2.4 times more metal per unit
of national income than the U.S. . . . This correlation is apparent
even without special calculations: we produce and consume 1.5
to 2 times more steel and cement than the United States, but we
lag behind by at least half in production of items derived from
them. . . . Recently, in Soviet industry the consumption of electri-
cal energy exceeded the American level, but the volume of industrial output in the U.S.S.R. is—by the most generous
estimates—only 80 percent of the American level.

The Soviet Union did not lack for resources, but was in fact
one of the most richly endowed nations on earth. What it lacked
was an economic system that made efficient use of scarce resources. Because Soviet enterprises were not under the same financial constraints as capitalist enterprises, they acquired more
machines than they needed, "which then gather dust in warehouses or rust out of doors," as the Soviet economists put it. In
short, they were not forced to economize—that is, to treat these
resources as both scarce and valuable in alternative uses.

Such a waste of inputs as these economists described could
not of course continue in the kind of economy where these inputs
would have to be purchased and where the enterprise itself could
survive only by keeping its costs lower than its sales receipts. In
such a price-coordinated capitalist system, the amount of inputs
ordered would be based on the enterprise's most accurate estimate of what was really needed, not on how much its managers
could make sound plausible to higher government officials, who
cannot possibly be experts on all the wide range of industries and
products they oversee.

The contrast between the American and the Soviet economies
is just one of many that can be made between economic systems
which use prices to allocate resources and those which have relied
on government control. In other regions of the world as well, and
in other political systems, there have been similar contrasts between places that used prices to ration goods and allocate re-

sources versus places that have relied on hereditary rulers, elected politicians or appointed planning commissions.

When many African nations achieved independence in the 1960s, a famous bet was made between the president of Ghana and the president of the neighboring Ivory Coast as to which country would be more prosperous in the years ahead. At that time, Ghana was not only more prosperous than the Ivory Coast, it had more natural resources, so the bet might have seemed reckless on the part of the president of the Ivory Coast. However, he knew that Ghana was committed to a government-run economy and the Ivory Coast to a freer market. By 1982, the Ivory Coast had so surpassed Ghana that the poorest 20 percent of its people had a higher real income than most of the people in Ghana.

This could not be attributed to any superiority of the country or its people. In fact, in later years, when Ivory Coast politicians eventually succumbed to the temptation to have the government control more of their country's economy, while Ghana finally learned from its mistakes and began to loosen government controls, these two countries' roles reversed—and now Ghana's economy began to grow, while that of the Ivory Coast declined.

Similar comparisons could be made between Burma and Thailand, the former having had the higher standard of living before instituting socialism and the latter a much higher standard of living afterwards. Other countries—Germany, Korea, Sri Lanka, New Zealand—have experienced sharp upturns in their economies when they freed these economies from many government controls and relied more on prices to allocate resources.

In China, government controls were relaxed in particular economic sectors and in particular geographic regions during the reforms of the 1980s, leading to stunning economic contrasts within the same country, as well as rapid economic growth overall. In 1978, less than 10 percent of China's agricultural output was sold in open markets but, by 1990, 80 percent was. The net result was more food and a greater variety of food available to city dwellers in China and a rise in farmers' income by more than 50 percent within a few years. In contrast to China's severe economic problems under heavy-handed government control under Mao, who died in 1976, the subsequent freeing up of prices in the marketplace led to an astonishing economic growth rate of 9 percent per year between 1978 and 1995.

While history can tell us that such things happened, economics helps explain *why* they happened—what there is about prices that allows them to accomplish what political control of an economy can seldom match. There is more to economics than prices, but understanding how prices function is the foundation for understanding the rest of economics.

In a society of millions of consumers, no given individual or set of government decision-makers sitting around a table can possibly know just how much these millions of consumers prefer one product to another, much less thousands of products to thousands of other products. In an economy coordinated by prices, no one has to know. Each producer is simply guided by what price that producer's product can sell for and by how much must be paid for the ingredients that go into making that product.

Knowledge is one of the most scarce of all resources and a pricing system economizes on its use by forcing those with the most knowledge of their own particular situation to make bids for goods and resources based on that knowledge, rather than on their ability to influence other people. However much articulation may be valued by intellectuals, it is not nearly as efficient a way of conveying accurate information as confronting people with a need to "put your money where your mouth is."

Human beings are going to make mistakes in any kind of economic system. In a price-coordinated economy, any producer who uses ingredients that are more valuable elsewhere is likely to discover that the costs of those ingredients cannot be repaid from what the consumers are willing to pay for the product. After all, he has had to bid these resources away from alternative users, paying more than these resources are worth to some of those alternative users. If it turns out that these resources are not more valuable in the uses to which he puts them, he is going to lose money. There will be no choice but to discontinue making that product with those ingredients. For those producers who are too blind or too stubborn to change, continuing losses will force their businesses into bankruptcy, so that the waste of society's resources will be stopped that way.

In a price-coordinated economy, employees and creditors insist on being paid, regardless of whether the managers and owners have made mistakes. This means that businesses can make only so many mistakes for so long before they have to either stop or get stopped—whether by an inability to get the labor and supplies they need or by bankruptcy. In a feudal economy or a socialist economy, leaders can continue to make the same mistakes indefinitely. The consequences are paid by others in the form of a standard of living lower than it would be if there were greater efficiency in the use of scarce resources.

As already noted, there were many products which remained unsold in stores or in warehouses in the Soviet Union, while there were desperate shortages of other things. But, in a price-coordinated economy, the labor, management, and physical resources that went into producing unwanted products would have had to go into producing something that could pay its own way from sales—that is, into producing something that the consumers wanted more than they wanted what was actually produced. In the absence of compelling price signals and the threat of financial losses to the producers that they convey, inefficiency and waste could continue indefinitely or until such time as each waste reached proportions big enough and blatant enough to attract the attention of central planners in Moscow, who were preoccupied with thousands of other decisions.

Ironically, the problems caused by trying to run an economy by fiat or by arbitrarily-imposed prices created by government dictates were foreseen by Karl Marx and Friedrich Engels, whose ideas the Soviet Union claimed to be following. Engels pointed out that price fluctuations have "forcibly brought home to the commodity producers what things and what quantity of them society requires or does not require." Without such a mechanism, he demanded to know "what guarantee we have that necessary quantity and not more of each product will be produced, that we shall not go hungry in regard to corn and meat while we are choked in beet sugar and drowned in potato spirit, that we shall not lack trousers to cover our nakedness while trouser buttons flood us in millions." Marx and Engels apparently understood economics much better than their latter-day followers.

PRICES IN ACTION

There is perhaps no more basic or more obvious principle of economics than the fact that people tend to buy more at a lower price and less at a higher price. By the same token, people who produce goods or supply services tend to supply more at a higher price and less at a lower price. Yet the implications of these two principles, singly or in combination, cover a remarkable range of economic activities and issues—and contradict an equally remarkable range of misconceptions and fallacies.

When people try to quantify the country's "need" for this or that product of service, they are ignoring the fact that there is no fixed or objective "need." The fact that people demand more at a lower price and less at a higher price may be easy to understand, but it is also easy to forget. Seldom, if ever, is there a fixed quantity demanded.

Likewise, there is no fixed supply. Statistics on the amount of petroleum, iron ore, or other natural resources seem to indicate that this is just a simple matter of how much physical stuff there is in the ground. In reality, most natural resources are available at varying costs of discovery, extraction, and processing. There is some oil that can be produced for $10 a barrel and other oil that cannot pay for all its costs at $20 a barrel, but which can at $30 a barrel. *The quantity supplied varies directly with the price*, just as the quantity demanded varies inversely with the price.

When the price of oil falls, certain low-yield oil wells are shut down because the cost of extracting and processing the oil from these wells would exceed the price it would sell for in the market. If the price later rises—or if the cost of extraction or processing is lowered by some new technology—then such oil wells will be put back in operation again. There is no fixed supply of oil—or of most other things.

When people project that there will be a shortage of engineers or teachers or housing in the years ahead, they usually either ignore prices or implicitly assume that there will be a shortage at today's prices. But shortages are precisely what cause prices to rise. At higher prices, it may be no harder to fill vacancies for engineers or teachers than today and no harder to find housing, as rising rents cause more homes and apartment buildings to be built. Price fluctuations are a way of letting a little knowledge go a long way. Price changes guide people's decisions through trial and error adjustments to what other people can and will pay as consumers, as well as what they can and will supply as producers.

The producer whose product turns out to have the combination of features that are closest to what the consumers really want may be no wiser than his competitors. Yet he can grow rich while his competitors who guessed wrong go bankrupt. But the larger result is that society as a whole gets more benefits from its limited resources by having them directed toward where those resources produce the kind of output that millions of people want, instead of producing things that they don't want.

Rationing by Prices

There are all kinds of prices. The prices of consumer goods are the most obvious examples but labor also has prices called wages or salaries, and borrowed money has a price called interest. In addition to prices for tangible things, there are prices for services ranging from haircuts to brain surgery and from astrology to advice on speculating in gold or soybeans.

In so far as these prices result from supply and demand in a free market, they play very similar roles in allocating scarce resources which have alternative uses. So long as people are free to spend their money for what they see fit, price changes in response to supply and demand direct resources to where they are most in demand and direct people to where their desires can be satisfied most fully by the existing supply.

Simple as all this may seem, it contradicts many widely held ideas. For example, high prices are often blamed on "greed" and people often speak of something being sold for more than its "real" value, or of workers being paid less than they are "really" worth.

To treat prices as resulting from greed implies that sellers can set prices where they wish, that prices are not determined by supply and demand. It may well be true that some—or all—sellers prefer to get the highest price that they can. But it is equally true that buyers usually wish to pay the lowest price they can for goods of a given quality. More important, the competition of numerous buyers and numerous sellers results in prices that leave each individual buyer and seller with very little leeway. Any deal depends on both parties agreeing to the same terms. Anyone who doesn't offer as good a deal as a competitor is likely to find himself with nobody willing to make a deal at all.

The fact that prices fluctuate over time, and occasionally have a sharp rise or a steep drop, misleads some people into concluding that prices are deviating from their "real" values. But their usual level under usual conditions is no more real or valid than their much higher or much lower levels under different conditions.

When a large employer goes bankrupt in a small community, or simply moves away to another state or country, many of the business' former employees may decide to move away themselves—and when their numerous homes go on sale in the same small area at the same time, the prices of those houses are likely to be driven down by competition. But this does not mean that they are selling for less than their "real" value. The value of living in this particular community has simply declined with the decline of job opportunities, and housing prices reflect that underlying fact. The new and lower prices reflect the new reality as well as the previous prices reflected the previous reality. A survey of home prices in a number of upstate New York cities that were losing population in the 1990s found that home prices were falling in these communities, while home prices were rising elsewhere in the state and around the country. This is exactly what one should expect on the basis of basic economic principles.

Conversely, when some natural disaster such as a hurricane or flood suddenly destroys many homes in a given area, the price of hotel rooms in that area may suddenly rise, as many people compete for a limited number of rooms, in order to avoid sleeping outdoors or having to double up with relatives and friends, or having to leave the community.

People who charge higher prices for hotel rooms, or for other things in short supply in the wake of some disaster, are especially likely to be condemned for "greed," but in fact the relationship between supply and demand has changed. Prices are simply performing one of their most important functions—rationing scarce resources. When some disaster suddenly makes these resources even more scarce than usual, it is important that prices reflect that underlying reality, so as to reduce the demand that each individual makes on the reduced supply.

Regardless of what hotel owners charge, a sudden and widespread destruction of housing in a given area means that there may be not nearly enough hotel rooms for all the displaced people to get the kinds of accommodations they would like. If prices had remained at their previous levels after the hurricane, a family of four might well rent two rooms—one for the parents and one for the children. But when hotel prices shoot up well beyond their usual level, all four family members may crowd into one room, in order to save money, leaving the other room for other people who have likewise lost their homes and are equally in need of shelter. The more stringent scarcity of housing in the wake of a widespread destruction of homes is inherent, even if temporary, and prices merely reflect that underlying reality. If the government were to impose price controls under these conditions, then those who happened to get to the hotels first would take up more space and leave more latecomers without a place to sleep indoors.

Similarly, if local electric power lines were put out of commission for a few days, the demand for flashlights in that community might suddenly increase, causing prices to rise before new shipments of flashlights could arrive. Had prices remained at their previous level, a family might buy several flashlights, so that each member could have one. But, at the suddenly higher prices, they would more likely buy only one or two, leaving more flashlights for others with a similarly urgent need.

In short, prices force people to share, whether or not they are aware of sharing. Prices perform this function both in normal times and in emergency times. While sharply higher prices may be resented during emergencies, their functions are even more urgently needed at such times.

Prices and Supplies

Prices not only ration existing supplies, they also act as powerful incentives to cause supplies to rise or fall in response to changing demand. When a crop failure in a given region creates a sudden increase in demand for imports of food into that region, food suppliers elsewhere rush to be the first to get there, in order to capitalize on the high prices that will prevail until more supplies arrive to drive food prices back down again. What this means, from the standpoint of the hungry people in that region, is that food is being rushed to them at maximum speed by "greedy" suppliers, probably much faster than if the same food were being transported to them by salaried government employees sent on a humanitarian mission.

Those spurred on by greed may well drive throughout the night or take short cuts through rough terrain, while those operating "in the public interest" are more likely to proceed at a less hectic pace and by safer or more comfortable routes. In short, people tend to do more for their own benefit than for the benefit of others. Freely fluctuating prices can make that turn out to be beneficial to others. In the case of food supplies, earlier arrival can be the difference between temporary hunger and death by starvation.

Where there are local famines in Third World countries, it is not at all uncommon for food supplied by international agencies to the national government to sit spoiling on the docks while people are dying of hunger inland. Much as we may deplore private greed, it is likely to move food much faster, saving far more lives.

In other situations, the consumers may not want more, but less. Prices also convey this. When automobiles began to displace horses and buggies in the early twentieth century, the demand for saddles, horseshoes, carriages and other such paraphernalia declined. As the manufacturers of such products faced losses instead of profits, many began to abandon their occupations for other lines of work in which higher incomes could be had for the same effort, investment, and risk.

In a sense, it is unfair when some people are unable to earn as much as others with similar skills, diligence, and other virtues. Yet this unfairness to particular individuals is what makes the economy as a whole operate more efficiently for the benefit of vastly larger numbers of others.

Chapter 3

Price Controls

Nothing shows the role of price fluctuations in a free market like the *absence* of such price fluctuations. What happens when prices are not allowed to fluctuate freely according to supply and demand, but instead are set by law, as under various kinds of price-control legislation? Price controls have existed, at one time or another, in countries around the world over a period of centuries—in fact, for thousands of years—and have applied to everything from food to housing to gasoline and medical services.

Typically, price controls are imposed in order to keep prices from rising to the levels that they would reach in response to supply and demand. The political rationales for such laws have varied from place to place and from time to time, but there is seldom a lack of rationales whenever it becomes politically expedient to hold down someone's prices in the interests of someone else whose political support seems more important.

Examples include rent control, food price ceilings, and price controls on medical services—all designed to set a limit on how high prices can go. In addition to laws putting a "ceiling" on how high prices will be allowed to rise, there are also laws establishing "floor" prices, which limit how far prices will be allowed to fall.

Many countries have set limits to how low certain agricultural prices will be allowed to fall, sometimes with the government being obligated to buy up the farmer's output whenever free market prices go below the specified levels. Equally widespread are minimum wage laws, which set a lower limit to how low a worker's wage rate may be. Here the government seldom offers to buy up the surplus labor which the free market does not employ, though it usually offers unemployment compensation, covering some fraction of the wages that might otherwise have been earned.

To understand the effects of price control, it is necessary to understand how prices rise and fall in a free market. There is nothing esoteric about it, but it is important to be very clear about what happens. Prices rise because the amount demanded exceeds the amount supplied *at existing prices*. Prices fall because the amount supplied exceeds the amount demanded *at existing prices*. The first case is called a "shortage" and the second is called a "surplus"—but both depend on *existing prices*.

Simple as this might seem, it is often misunderstood—sometimes with disastrous consequences. A closer examination shows why shortages persist when the government sets a maximum price lower than what it would be in a free market and why a surplus persists when the government sets minimum prices for farm products higher than these prices would be in a free market.

PRICE CEILINGS AND SHORTAGES

When there is a "shortage" of a product, there is not necessarily any less of it, either absolutely or relative to the number of consumers. During and immediately after the Second World War, for example, there was a very serious housing shortage in the United States, even though the population and the housing supply had both increased about 10 percent from their prewar levels and there was no shortage when the war began.

In other words, even though the ratio between housing and people had not changed, nevertheless many Americans looking for an apartment during this period had to spend weeks or months in an often vain search for a place to live, or else resorted to bribes to get landlords to move them to the top of waiting lists. Meanwhile, they doubled up with relatives, slept in garages or used other makeshift living arrangements.

Although there was no less housing space per person than before, the shortage was very real *at existing prices*, which were kept artificially lower than they would have been because of rent control laws that had been passed during the war. At these artificially low prices, more people had a demand for more housing space than before rent control laws were enacted. This is a practical consequence of the simple economic principle already noted in Chapter 2 that the quantity demanded varies with how high or low the price is.

Some people who would normally not be renting their own apartments, such as young adults still living with their parents or some single or widowed elderly people living with relatives, were enabled by the artificially low prices created by rent control to move out and into their own apartments. These artificially low prices also caused others to seek larger apartments than they would ordinarily be living in. More tenants seeking both more apartments and larger apartments created a shortage, not any greater physical scarcity of housing relative to the population. When rent control laws expired or were repealed, the housing shortage likewise quickly disappeared.

As rents rose in a free market, some childless couples living in four-bedroom apartments decided that they could live in two-bedroom apartments. Some late teenagers decided that they could continue living with mom and dad a little longer, until their pay rose enough for them to afford their own apartments, now that apartments were no longer artificially cheap. The net result was that families looking for a place to stay found more places available, now that rent-control laws were no longer keeping such places occupied by people with less urgent requirements.

None of this was peculiar to the United States. The same economic principles can be seen in operation around the world and down through history. Rent control had very much the same effects in Sweden. As of 1940, there were 6,330,000 people living in Sweden and there were 1,960,000 dwelling units to house them—about 31 housing units for every 100 people. Over the years, the number of housing units rose relative to the population—to 36 units per 100 people in 1965 and 43 units per 100 people by 1973—and yet the average waiting time for getting a place to live also rose. There was a 9-month wait in 1950, a 23-month wait in 1955 and a 40-month wait by 1958, for example. In short, the longer waits for housing was not due to any less housing in proportion to the population. *There was no greater scarcity but there was a greater shortage.*

As incomes in Sweden rose much faster than rents were allowed to rise under rent control laws, more and more people began to occupy their own independent housing units, making it harder for others to find places to live, even with a massive, government-sponsored program to build more dwelling units. Many unmarried young adults, who would normally still be living with their parents or renting a room from someone else, decided that they could afford to get their own apartments. Before rent control, less than one-fourth of all unmarried adults in Sweden had their own separate housing units in 1940, but that proportion rose until just over half did by 1975.

Not only was the actual physical amount of housing no less than before, Sweden was in fact building more housing per person than any other country in the world during this period. Nevertheless, the housing shortage persisted and got worse. As of 1948, there were about 2,400 people on waiting lists for housing in Sweden but, a dozen years later, the waiting list had grown to ten times as many people, despite a frantic building of more housing. When eventually rent control laws were repealed in Sweden, a housing *surplus* suddenly developed, as rents rose and people curtailed their use of housing as a result. Again, this shows that "shortages" and "surpluses" are matters of *price*, not matters of physical scarcity, either absolutely or relative to the population.

With rent control ended, private developers in Sweden now began building more housing as rents rose—and produced housing more in keeping with what the public wanted, as distinguished from the kind of housing produced by the government under political and bureaucratic incentives. Therefore it was the government-sponsored housing which became vacant—so much so as to become a drain on the public treasury.

Think of all the needless grief and wasted resources that could have been avoided if the Swedish voters had been familiar with basic economic principles and understood that the source of their housing problems were the very attempts to make housing more "affordable" by rent control. No doubt there were Swedish economists who understood this, but there are seldom enough economists in any country to have enough votes to sway decisions made by politicians.

During the period when rent control laws were in effect in Australia, they had the same effect as they had in Sweden—fewer people per dwelling unit and long waits for others seeking housing. Similarly, a study of housing in New York City found 175,000 apartments where one person occupied 4 or more rooms—mostly elderly people in rent-controlled apartments.

In the normal course of events, people's demand for housing space changes over a lifetime. Their demand for space usually increases when they get married and have children. But, years later, after the children have grown up and moved away, the parents' demand for space tends to decline and it often declines yet again after a spouse dies and a widow or widower moves into smaller quarters or goes to live with relatives. In this way, a society's total stock of housing is shared and circulated among people according to their changing individual demands at different stages of their lives.

The individuals themselves do not do this out of a sense of cooperation, but because prices—rents in this case—convey to them the value that other tenants put on housing. Young couples with a growing family are often willing to sacrifice some consumer goods and services in order to have enough money left to pay for more housing space. Parents may go out to restaurants or movies less often, or buy new clothes or new cars at longer intervals, in order that each child may have his or her own bedroom. But, once the children are grown and gone, such sacrifices may no longer make sense, when additional other amenities can now be enjoyed by reducing the housing space being rented.

Given the crucial role of prices in this process, suppression of the process by rent control laws leaves elderly people with little incentive to vacate apartments that they would normally vacate, if that would result in a significant reduction in rent and a corresponding enhancement of their living standards in other respects. Moreover, the chronic housing shortages which accompany rent control greatly increase the time and effort required to search for a new and smaller apartment, while reducing the financial reward for finding one. In short, rent control reduces the rate of housing turnover.

New York City has had rent control longer and more stringently than any other major American city. One consequence has been that the annual rate of turnover of apartments in New York is less than half the national average and the proportion of tenants who have lived in the same apartment for 20 years or more is more than double the national average. As the *New York Times* summarized the situation in 1997:

> New York used to be like other cities, a place where tenants moved frequently and landlords competed to rent empty apartments to newcomers, but today the motto may as well be: No Immigrants Need Apply. While immigrants are crowded into bunks in illegal boarding houses in the slums, upper-middle-class locals pay low rents to live in good neighborhoods, often in large apartments they no longer need after their children move out.

Rent control has effects on supply as well as on demand. Nine years after the end of World War II, not a single new building had been built in Melbourne, Australia, because of rent control laws which made buildings unprofitable. Declines in building construction have likewise followed in the wake of rent control laws elsewhere. After rent control was instituted in Santa Monica, California in 1979, building permits declined to less than a tenth of what they were just five years earlier. In Paris, subject to rent control beginning in the First World War and continuing on past the Second World War, new apartment buildings became so rare that a 1948 survey showed that 90 percent of the city's buildings were built before the *First* World War, more than half before 1880 and more than a quarter before 1850.

Not only is the supply of new apartment construction less after rent control, even the supply of existing housing tends to decline, as fewer people are willing to rent to others after the rents are kept artificially low by law. During 8 years of rent control in Washington during the 1970s, the city's available housing stock declined absolutely, from just over 199,000 units on the market to just under 176,000 units. After rent control was introduced in Berkeley, California, the number of private housing units available to students at the university there declined by 31 percent in five years.

Sometimes the reduction in housing units on the market occurs because people who had been renting rooms or apartments in their homes, or bungalows in their back yards, decide that it is no longer worth the bother at rents kept artificially low under rent control laws. In addition, there are often conversions of apartments to condominiums and an accelerated deterioration of the existing housing stock, as landlords provide less maintenance and repair under rent control, since the housing shortage makes it unnecessary for them to maintain the appearance of their premises in order to attract tenants. Studies of rent control in the United States, England, and France found rent-controlled housing to be deteriorated far more often than non-rent-controlled housing.

Typically, the rental housing stock is relatively fixed in the short run, so that a shortage occurs first because more people want more housing at the artificially low price. Later, there may be a real increase in scarcity as well, as rental units deteriorate more rapidly with reduced maintenance, while not enough new units are being built to replace them as they wear out, because new privately built housing would be unprofitable under rent control. Under rent control in England and Wales, for example, privately-built rental housing fell from 61 percent of all housing in 1947 to 14 percent by 1977. A study of rent control in North America and in Britain, France, Germany, and the Netherlands concluded: "New investment in unsubsidized rented housing is essentially nonexistent in all the European countries surveyed, except for luxury housing."

In short, a policy intended to make housing affordable for the poor has the net effect of shifting resources toward housing affordable only by the affluent, since luxury housing is often exempt from rent control. Among other things, this illustrates the crucial importance of making a distinction between intentions and consequences, which means analyzing economic policies in terms of the incentives created by them, rather than the hopes that inspired them. In terms of incentives, it is easy to understand what happened in England when rent control was extended in 1975 to cover furnished rental units. According to *The Times* of London:

Advertisements for furnished rental accommodations in the *London Evening Standard* plummeted dramatically in the first

week after the Act came into force and are now running about
75 percent below last year's levels.

Since furnished rooms are particularly likely to be in people's
homes, these represent housing units that are easily withdrawn
from the market when the rents no longer compensate for the inconveniences of having renters living with you. However, even
when rent control applies to separate apartment buildings, where
the landlord typically does not live, eventually the point may be
reached where the whole building becomes sufficiently unprofitable to be abandoned. In New York City, for example, many
buildings have been abandoned after their owners found it impossible to collect enough rent to cover the costs of services that
they are legally required to provide. Such owners have simply
disappeared to escape the legal consequences of their abandonment, and such buildings often end up boarded up, though physically sound enough to house people if maintained.

The number of abandoned buildings taken over by the New
York City government runs into the thousands. It has been estimated that there are at least four times as many abandoned housing units in New York City as there are homeless people on the
streets there. Such inefficiency in the allocation of resources
means that people are sleeping outdoors on the pavement on cold
winter nights—some dying of exposure—while the means of
housing them already exist, but are not being used because of
laws designed to make housing "affordable." Once again, this
demonstrates that the efficient or inefficient allocation of scarce
resources is not just some abstract economic notion, but has very
real—and sometimes very painful—consequences, which can
even include matters of life and death. It also illustrates that the
goal of a law—"affordable housing," in this case—is far less important than its consequences.

Just as rent control reduces the housing stock, the end of rent
control often marks the beginning of private building, as it did in
Sweden. In Massachusetts in the 1990s, a state ban on local rent
control laws led to the building of new apartments in formerly
rent-controlled cities for the first time in 25 years.

In short, with housing as with other things, less is supplied at a lower price than at a higher price—less both quantitatively and qualitatively. Polls of economists have found virtually unanimous agreement that declines in product quantity and quality are the usual effects of price controls in general. Of course, there are not enough economists in the entire country for their votes to matter very much to politicians, who know that there are always more tenants than landlords and more people who do not understand economics than there are who do. Politically, rent control is often a big success, however many serious economic and social problems it creates.

Often it is politically effective to represent rent control as a way to keep greedy rich landlords from "gouging" the poor with "unconscionable" rents. In reality, rates of return on investments in housing are seldom higher than on alternative investments and landlords are often people of very modest means. This is especially so for owners of small, low-end apartment buildings that are in constant need of repair, with many of these landlords being handymen who use their own skills and labor to maintain the premises. In short, the kind of housing likely to be rented by the poor often also has owners who are by no means rich.

Where rent control applies to luxury housing, the tenants may be quite affluent, even though their rents are kept down to a fraction of their free-market value. In Manhattan, for example, the chairman of the New York Stock Exchange paid less than $700 a month for a rent-controlled apartment on fashionable Central Park South. Another tenant on Central Park South paid just $400 a month for a six-room apartment. Hollywood star Shelley Winters, who owned a home in Beverly Hills, also rented a two-bedroom apartment in Manhattan for a rent-controlled price of less than $900 a month. New York Mayor Ed Koch paid less than half of that for his rent-controlled apartment in Washington Square, which he kept during the entire 12 years when he lived in Gracie Mansion, the official residence of the mayor. There are numerous other examples of members of the economic, political, and cultural elites renting apartments—sometimes multiple apartments for the same individual —at a fraction of what such apartments cost to someone new to the city who is seeking a place to live in buildings that are not covered by rent control.

Meanwhile, city welfare agencies pay far more rent to house a poverty-stricken family in some cramped and roach-infested apartment in a run-down hotel. The idea that rent control protects poor tenants from rich landlords may be politically effective, but it bears little resemblance to the reality. Where rent control laws apply on a blanket basis to all housing in existence as of the time the law goes into effect, luxurious housing becomes low-rent housing. Then, after it becomes clear that no new housing is likely to be built unless it is exempted from rent control, such exemptions or relaxations of the rent control that still applies to existing apartments means that even new apartments that are very modest in size and quality may rent for far more than older, more spacious and more luxurious apartments. This non-comparability of rents is not peculiar to New York City. It is common in European cities under rent control.

Ironically, cities with strong rent control laws, such as New York, tend to end up with higher average rents than cities without rent control. Where such laws apply only to rents below some specified level, presumably to protect the poor, builders then have incentives to build only apartments luxurious enough to be above the rent-control level. Rich and poor alike who move into the city after rent control has created a housing shortage typically cannot find a rent-controlled apartment, and so have available only housing that costs more than it would in a free market, because of the housing shortage. Not surprisingly, homelessness tends to be greater in cities with rent control.

In order to demonstrate in a different way the crucial distinction between an increased scarcity—where fewer goods are available relative to the population—and a "shortage" as a *price* phenomenon, we can consider a case where the actual amount of housing suddenly declined in a given area without any price control, as happened in the wake of the great San Francisco earthquake and fire of 1906. More than half the city's housing supply was destroyed during this catastrophe in just three days and not a single major hotel remained standing. Yet there was no housing shortage.

When the *San Francisco Chronicle* resumed publication a month after the earthquake, its first issue contained 64 advertisements of apartments or homes for rent, compared to only 5 ads from people seeking apartments to live in. Of the 200,000 people suddenly made homeless by the earthquake, temporary shelters housed 30,000 and an estimated 75,000 left the city. Still, that left nearly 100,000 people to be absorbed into the local housing market. Yet neither the newspapers nor other documents of that time mention any housing shortage or any of the things that accompany housing shortages, such as lengthy searches or bribes paid to landlords. Rising prices not only allocated the existing housing, they provided incentives for rebuilding.

In short, just as there can be a shortage without any greater physical scarcity, so there can be a greater physical scarcity without any shortage. People made homeless by the San Francisco earthquake found housing more readily than people made homeless by New York's rent control laws that took thousands of building off the market.

Similar economic principles apply in other markets. During the gasoline "crisis" of 1972 and 1973, when oil prices were kept artificially low by the federal government, there were long lines of automobiles waiting at filling stations in cities across the United States, but there was in fact 95 percent as much gasoline sold in 1972 as there was in the previous year, when there were no gasoline lines at the filling stations, no shortage and no crisis atmosphere. Similarly, during the gasoline crisis of 1979, the amount of gasoline sold was only 3.5 percent less than in the record-breaking year of gasoline sales in 1978. In fact, the amount of gasoline sold in 1979 was greater than the gasoline consumption in any other previous year in the history of the country except 1978. In short, there was a minor increase in scarcity but a major shortage, with long lines of motorists waiting at filling stations, sometimes for hours, before reaching the pump.

Just as price controls on apartments cause a cutback in painting, maintenance, and other auxiliary services that go with apartments, so price controls on gasoline led to a cutback on such auxiliary services as checking tires, cleaning windshields and—

above all—on the hours that filling stations remained open for their customers' convenience.

Because of the long lines of automobiles waiting to buy gasoline during the shortage, filling stations could sell all the gas they had continuously for a relatively few hours and then shut down for the day when their pumps were empty, instead of having to stay open around the clock to dispense the same amount of gasoline at a normal pace, with cars stopping in at whatever times were convenient to the motorists. In New York City, for example, the average filling station was open 110 hours a week in September 1978, before the shortage, but only 27 hours a week in June 1979, during the shortage. Yet the total amount of gasoline pumped differed by only a few percentage points between these two periods. In short, the problem was not a greater physical scarcity but a shortage at artificially low prices. Shortages mean that the seller no longer has to please the buyer. That is why landlords can let maintenance and other services deteriorate under rent control. In this case, the filling station owners could save on the hours during which they had to pay attendants and the money they had to spend on electricity and other costs of remaining open long hours. No doubt many or most of the motorists whose daily lives and work were disrupted by having to spend hours waiting in line behind other cars at filling stations would gladly have paid a few cents more per gallon of gasoline, in order to avoid such inconveniences and stress, but price control prevents buyers and sellers from making mutually advantageous transactions on terms different from those specified in the law.

Bolder and less scrupulous buyers and sellers make mutually advantageous transactions outside the law. Price controls almost invariably produce black markets, where prices are not only higher than the legally permitted prices, but also higher than they would be in a free market, since the legal risks must also be compensated. While small-scale black markets may function in secrecy, large-scale black markets usually require bribes to officials to look the other way. In Russia, for example, a local embargo on shipment of price-controlled food beyond regional boundaries was dubbed the "150-ruble decree," since this was the cost of bribing police to let the shipments pass through checkpoints.

PRICE FLOORS AND SURPLUSES

Just as a price set below the level that would prevail by supply and demand in a free market tends to cause more to be demanded and less to be supplied, creating a shortage at the imposed price, so a price set above the free market level tends to cause more to be supplied than demanded, creating a surplus. Simple as this principle is, it is often lost sight of in the swirl of more complex events and more politically popular beliefs.

One of the classic examples of a lower limit to prices imposed by government have been the American agricultural price-support programs. As often happens, a real but transient problem led to the establishment of enduring government programs, which long outlived the conditions that initially caused them to be created.

Among the many tragedies of the Great Depression of the 1930s was the fact that many farmers simply could not make enough money from the sale of their crops to pay their bills. The prices of farm products fell much more drastically than the prices of the things that farmers had to buy. As many farmers lost their farms because they could no longer pay the mortgages, and as other farm families suffered privations as they struggled to hang on to their farms and their traditional way of life, the federal government sought to restore "parity" between agriculture and other sectors of the economy by intervening to keep farm prices from falling so sharply.

This intervention took various forms. One approach was to reduce the amount of various crops that could be grown and sold, so as to avoid driving the price below the level the federal government had decided upon. Thus, the supply of peanuts and cotton were restricted by law. The supply of citrus fruit, nuts and various other farm products were regulated by local cartels of farmers, backed up by the authority of the Secretary of Agriculture to issue "marketing orders" and prosecute those who violated these orders by producing and selling more than they were authorized to produce and sell. Such arrangements continued for decades after the poverty of the Great Depression was replaced by the prosperity of the boom following World War II.

These indirect methods of keeping prices artificially high were only part of the story. The key factor in keeping farm prices artificially higher than they would have been under free market supply and demand was the government's willingness to buy up the surpluses created by its control of prices. This they did for such farm products as corn, rice, tobacco, and wheat, among others.

Price control in the form of a "floor" under prices, preventing them from falling further, produced surpluses as dramatic as the shortages produced by price control in the form of a "ceiling" preventing them from rising higher. In some years, the federal government bought more than one-fourth of all the wheat grown in the country and took it off the market, in order to maintain prices at a pre-determined level.

During the Great Depression of the 1930s, agricultural price support programs led to vast amounts of food being deliberately destroyed at a time when malnutrition was a serious problem in the United States and hunger marches were taking place in cities across the country. For example, the federal government bought 6 million hogs in 1933 alone and destroyed them. Huge amounts of farm produce were plowed under, in order to keep it off the market and maintain prices at the fixed level, and vast amounts of milk were poured down the sewers for the same reason. Meanwhile, children were suffering from diseases caused by malnutrition.

Still, there was a food surplus. *A surplus, like a shortage, is a price phenomenon*. It does not mean that there is some excess relative to the people. There was not "too much" food relative to the population during the Great Depression. The people simply did not have enough money to buy everything that was produced at the artificially high prices fixed by the government.

The food surpluses under "floor" prices were as real as the housing shortages under "ceiling" prices. The vast amount of storage space required to keep surplus crops off the market sometimes led to such desperate expedients as storing these farm products in unused warships, when all the storage facilities on land had been filled to capacity. A series of bumper crops could lead to the federal government's having more wheat in storage than was grown by American farmers all year.

How to get rid of all this surplus farm produce was a continuing question for which all sorts of answers were devised over the years. In theory, the surpluses built up during bumper crop years could be sold in the marketplace during years when there were smaller crops, without driving the price down below the price-support level. In practice, however, this provided little relief. Often the surplus food was either sold to other countries at lower prices than the American government had paid for it or it was given away overseas to meet various food emergencies that arose in various countries from time to time.

The cost of agricultural price support programs to the taxpayers reached a peak of more than $16 billion in 1987, before changes in the laws and policies cut that in half by 1991. However, this does not count the additional billions paid by the public in the form of artificially higher food prices. For example, during the mid–1980s, when the price of sugar on the world market was four cents a pound, the wholesale price within the United States was 20 cents a pound.

Although the original rationale for such programs was to save the family farm, in practice more of the money went to big agricultural corporations, some of which received millions of dollars each, while the average farm received only a few hundred dollars.

What is crucial from the standpoint of understanding the role of prices in the economy is that surpluses are as much a result of keeping prices artificially high as shortages are of keeping prices artificially low. Nor were the losses simply the sums of money extracted from the taxpayers or the consumers for the benefit of agricultural corporations and farmers. These are simply internal transfers among Americans, which do not directly reduce the total wealth of the country. The real losses to the country as a whole come from the misallocation of scarce resources which have alternative uses.

Scarce resources such as land. labor, fertilizer, and machinery are needlessly used to produce more than the consumers are willing to consume at the artificially high prices decreed by the federal government. Poor people, who spend an unusually high percent-

age of their income on food, are forced to pay far more than necessary to get the amount of food they receive, leaving them with less
money for other things. Those on food stamps are able to buy less
food with those stamps when food prices are artificially inflated.

From a purely economic standpoint, it is working at cross purposes to subsidize farmers by forcing food prices up and then
subsidize some consumers by bringing their particular costs of
food down with food stamps. However, from a political standpoint, it makes perfect sense to gain the support of two different
sets of voters, especially since most of them do not understand the
full economic implications of the policies.

Setting a "floor" under prices has not been confined to agriculture, nor to the United States. Most of the leading industrial
nations of the world subsidize agricultural prices, largely for the
same political reasons that led the United States to do so. Even
when these subsidies and controls originated during hard times
as a humanitarian measure, they have persisted long past those
times because they developed an organized constituency which
threatened to create political trouble if these subsidies and controls were removed or even reduced. Farmers have blocked the
streets of Paris with their farm machinery when the French government showed signs of scaling back its agricultural programs or
allowing more foreign farm produce to be imported. In Canada,
farmers protesting low wheat prices blocked highways and
formed a motorcade of tractors to the capital city of Ottawa.

It has not been uncommon for governments in the European
Community to spend more than half of their budgets on agricultural subsidies. While roughly one-fifth of farming income in the
United States comes from government subsidies, more than 40
percent of farming income in countries of the European Union
comes from such subsidies, as does an absolute majority of the
farming income in Japan.

THE POLITICS OF PRICE CONTROLS

Simple as basic economic principles may be, their ramifications can be quite complex, as we have seen with the various ef-

fects of rent control laws and agricultural price support laws. However, even this basic level of economics is seldom understood by the public, which often demands political "solutions" that turn out to make matters worse. Nor is this a new phenomenon of modern times in democratic countries. In 1628, a local harvest shortfall in Italy led to reduced supplies of food, which in turn led to this public reaction:

> People implored the magistrates to take measures, measures which the crowd considers simple, just and certain to bring out the hidden, walled-up, buried grain, and to bring back plenty. The magistrates did do something: fixed the maximum price for various foodstuffs, threatened to punish those who refused to sell, and other edicts of the sort. Since such measures, however vigorous, do not have the virtue of diminishing the need for food, growing crops out of season, or attracting supplies from areas of surplus, the evil lasted, and grew. The crowd attributed that effect to the incompleteness and weakness of the remedies, and shouted for more generous and decisive ones.

Since this was a local food shortage, the ordinary effect of supply and demand would have been to cause local prices to rise, attracting more food into the area. Price controls prevented that. Nor was this perverse reaction peculiar to Italy. The same thing has happened in many countries and in many centuries. In eighteenth-century India, for example, a local famine in Bengal brought a government crackdown on food dealers and speculators, imposing price controls on rice, leading to widespread deaths by starvation. However, when another famine struck India in the nineteenth century, under the colonial rule of British officials and during the heyday of classical economics, opposite policies were followed, with opposite results:

> In the earlier famine one could hardly engage in the grain trade without becoming amenable to the law. In 1866 respectable men in vast numbers went into the trade; for the Government, by publishing weekly returns of the rates in every district, rendered the traffic both easy and safe. Everyone knew where to

buy grain cheapest and where to sell it dearest and food was accordingly brought from the districts which could best spare it and carried to those which most urgently needed it.

As elementary as all this may seem, in terms of economic principles, it was made possible politically because the British colonial government was unaccountable to local public opinion. In an era of democratic politics, such actions would require a public familiar with basic economics.

Chapter 4

An Overview

Economics is defined, not just by its subject matter, but by its methods and its purposes. Just as a poetic discussion of the weather is not meteorology, so an issuance of moral pronouncements or political creeds about the economy is not economics. Economics is a study of *cause-and-effect* relationships in an economy. Its purpose is to discern the consequences of various ways of allocating scarce resources which have alternative uses. It has nothing to say about philosophy or values, any more than it has anything to say about music or literature.

CAUSE AND EFFECT

Analyzing economic actions in cause-and-effect terms means examining the logic of the incentives being created, rather than simply the goals being sought. It also means examining the empirical evidence of what actually happens under such incentives. Moreover, the causation at work in an economy is often *systemic* causation, rather than causation determined by personal intention. For example, if the stock market closes at 12,463 on a given day, that is the end result of systemic interactions among innumerable buyers and sellers of stocks, none of whom may have intended for the market to close at 12,463, even though it was their actions in pursuit of other intentions which caused it to do so.

Just as primitive peoples have tended to attribute such things as the swaying of trees in the wind to some intentional action by an invisible spirit, rather than to such systemic causes as variations in atmospheric pressure, so there is a tendency toward intentional explanations of systemic events in the economy, when

people are unaware of basic principles. While rising prices are
likely to reflect changes in supply and demand, people ignorant
of economics may attribute the rises to "greed." Such an intentional explanation raises more questions than it answers. Why
does greed vary so much from one time to another or from one
place to another?

In the Los Angeles basin, for example, homes near the ocean
sell for much higher prices than similar homes located in the
smog-chocked interior. Does this mean that fresh air promotes
greed, while smog makes home sellers more reasonable? To say
that prices are due to greed is to imply that sellers can set prices
by an act of will. If so, no company would ever go bankrupt, since
it could simply raise its prices to cover whatever its costs happened to be.

People shocked by stores in low-income neighborhoods,
high prices in or by the much higher interest rates charged by
pawnbrokers and the small finance companies that operate in
such neighborhoods, as compared to the interest rates charged
by banks, have been quick to blame greed or exploitation on the
part of the people who run such businesses. Yet studies show
that profit rates are no higher in inner city businesses than else
where, and the fact that many businesses are leaving such neighborhoods reinforces that conclusion. The painful fact that poor
people end up paying more than affluent people for many goods
and services has a very plain—and systemic—explanation. It
costs more to deliver goods and services in low-income neighborhoods.

Higher insurance costs and higher costs for various security
precautions, due to higher rates of crime and vandalism, are just
some of many systemic reasons that get ignored by those seeking
an explanation in terms of personal intentions. In addition, the cost
of doing business itself tends to be higher per dollar of business.
Lending $50 each to a hundred low-income borrowers at pawn
shops or local finance companies costs more than lending $5,000 at
a bank to one middle-class customer. An armored car delivering
money in small denominations to a small check-cashing agency in
a ghetto costs just as much as an armored car delivering a hundred
times as much value of money to a Bank of America branch in a

suburban shopping mall. With the cost of business being higher per dollar of business, it is hardly surprising that these higher costs are passed on in higher prices and higher interest rates.

Higher prices for people who can least afford them is a tragic end-result, but its causes are systemic. This is not merely a philosophical distinction. There are major practical consequences to the way causation is understood. Treating the causes of higher prices and higher interest rates in low-income neighborhoods as being personal greed and trying to remedy it by imposing price controls and interest rate ceilings only ensures that even less will be supplied in low-income neighborhoods. Just as rent control reduces the supply of housing, so price controls and interest rate controls can reduce the number of stores, pawn shops, and local finance companies willing to operate in neighborhoods with high costs that cannot be covered by legally permissible prices and interest rates.

If stores and financial institutions close down in low-income neighborhoods, more people in such neighborhoods will then be forced to travel to other neighborhoods to shop for groceries or other goods, paying money for bus fare or taxi fare. Low-income borrowers who no longer have pawnshops or check-cashing agencies and finance companies in their neighborhoods are more likely to be denied loans at banks used to dealing with higher-income people who have less risk of default. If people from poor neighborhoods can get their checks cashed at all at banks in other neighborhood when they are unable to keep large amounts of money in their accounts, their bus or taxi fares there can be more than what they would have paid to a check-cashing agency nearby.

The Hippocratic oath taken by doctors begins: "First, do no harm." Understanding the distinction between systemic causation and intentional causation is one way to do less harm with economic policies. It is especially important to do no harm to people who are already in painful circumstances.

Periods of crisis often generate emotions which seek outlets by blaming personal and intentional causes, rather than systemic causes, which provide no such emotional release for the public or moral melodrama for the media and politicians. Gasoline shortages in the 1970s were blamed on oil company machinations—

which were never substantiated, despite extensive investigations—rather than on gasoline price controls, even though price controls have a record of creating shortages going back for centuries. In addition, personification of "society" introduces the appearance of intention in metaphors about how society distributes its income inequitably or does other things that people don't like, but which are often the results of systemic causes.

Intentional explanations of cause and effect may be more natural, in the sense that less sophisticated individuals and less sophisticated societies tend to turn first to such explanations. In some cases, it has taken centuries for intentional explanations embodied in superstitions about nature to give way to systemic explanations based on science. It is not yet clear whether it will take that long for the basic principles of economics to replace the natural tendency to explain systemic results by someone's intentions.

Although the basic principles of economics are not very complicated, the very ease with which they can be learned also makes them easy to dismiss as "simplistic" by those who do not want to accept analyses which contradict their cherished beliefs. Evasions of the obvious are often far more complicated than the facts. Nor is it automatically true that complex effects must have complex causes. The ramifications of something very simple can become enormously complex. For example, the simple fact that the earth is tilted on its axis causes innumerable very complex reactions in plants, animals, and people, as well as in such inanimate things as ocean currents, weather changes and changes in the length of night and day.

If the earth stood straight up on its axis, night and day would be the same length all year around and in all parts of the world at the same time. Climate would still differ between the equator and the poles but, at any given place, the weather would be the same in winter as in summer. The fact that the earth is tilted on its axis means that sunlight is striking the same country at different angles at different times during the planet's annual orbit around the sun, leading to changing warmth and changing lengths of night and day.

In turn, such changes trigger complex biological reactions in plant growth, animal hibernations and migrations, as well as psychological changes in human beings and many seasonal changes in their economies. Changing weather patterns affect ocean currents and the frequency of hurricanes, among many other phenomena. Yet all of these complications are due to the one simple fact that the earth is tilted on its axis, instead of being straight up.

In short, complex effects may be a result of either simple or complex causes. The specific facts can tell us which. *A priori* pronouncements about what is "simplistic" cannot.

Few things are more simple than the fact that people tend to buy more at lower prices and buy less at higher prices. But, putting that together with the fact that producers tend to supply more at higher prices and less at lower prices, that is enough to predict all sorts of complex reactions to price controls, as for example in the housing market. Moreover, these reactions have been found on all inhabited continents and over thousands of years of recorded history. Economic principles apply across political borders and among wide varieties of peoples and cultures.

The tendency to personalize causation leads not only to charges that "greed" causes high prices in market economies, but also to charges that "stupidity" among bureaucrats is responsible for many things that go wrong in government programs. In reality, many of these things that go wrong are due to perfectly rational actions, *given the incentives* faced by those who run these programs and given the constraints on the amount of knowledge available to any given decision-maker or set of decision-makers.

Where a policy or institution has been established by top political leaders, those subject to their authority may well hesitate to contradict their beliefs, much less to point out the counterproductive consequences that later follow from these policies and institutions. Messengers carrying bad news would be risking their careers or—under Stalin or Mao—their lives. Those carrying out particular policies may be quite rational, however negative these policies prove to be for society at large.

During the Stalin era in the Soviet Union, for example, there was a severe shortage of mining equipment, but the manager of an enterprise producing such machines kept them in storage after they were produced, rather than sending them out to the mines. The reason was that the official orders called for these machines to be painted with red, oil-resistant paint and the producer had on hand only green, oil-resistant paint and red varnish that was not oil-resistant. Disobeying official orders in any respect was a serious offense and "I don't want to get eight years," the manager said.

When the manager appealed to a higher official to use the green, oil-resistant paint, this official's reaction was "Well, I don't want to get eight years either." However, he cabled to his ministry for their permission to give his permission. After a long delay, the ministry granted his request and the mining machinery was finally shipped to the mines. None of these people were behaving irrationally. They were responding quite rationally to the incentives and constraints of the system in which they worked.

INCENTIVES VERSUS GOALS

Because economics is a study of cause and effect, it deals with incentives and their consequences. It has nothing to say about the validity of social, moral, or political goals such as "affordable housing," "a living wage" or "social justice." What it can do is study the incentives and consequences of particular actions taken in the name of these and other goals.

For example, if the desire for "affordable housing" takes the form of rent control, then economics can examine the incentives created for tenants, landlords, and builders by rent control laws—and then see what the empirical consequences of these incentives have been. For tenants, rent control creates incentives to seek to occupy more housing than they would if they had to pay the full value of that housing, as measured by what others would be willing to bid for it. For builders, rent control creates incentives to build less housing, including perhaps none at all. For landlords, it creates incentives for them not to maintain the existing housing as well as they would in a free market, where they would have to compete for tenants, rather than in a rent-controlled market, where there are more applicants than apartments.

Given these incentives, it is not surprising to discover empirically that rent control has been followed by housing shortages, a reduction in the building of new housing, and a faster deterioration of existing housing as it receives less maintenance. It must be emphasized that these are *empirical* consequences, since some people seem to think that the role of prices in the economy is simply a theory by those with "faith in the market." However, it was a Swedish socialist—presumably lacking such "faith" in the market—who said that rent control "appears to be the most efficient technique known to destroy a city—except for bombing." He was an economist familiar with the empirical evidence.

Another comparison between bombing and rent control was made by an official of the Communist government of Vietnam, some years after the Vietnam war. "The Americans couldn't destroy Hanoi," by bombing it during the war, he said, "but we have destroyed our city by very low rents." As a Communist with no bias toward the free market, he had learned the hard way that artificially low rents encouraged demand while discouraging supply—a very simple principle, indeed, but one with major impacts on those who fail to heed it. Bombing does more immediate damage to a city, but many cities have rapidly rebuilt in the postwar world. Rent control does more long-lasting damage because people do not understand the basic economics of it.

In economics, as elsewhere in life, while we are free to do whatever we wish, we are not free to have the consequences be whatever we want them to be. We can leap off the top of a skyscraper, if we wish, but the law of gravity will determine what the consequence will be. In economics as well, the actual consequences of any specific economic policy must be discovered by analysis and evidence, and are wholly independent of what we might wish that these consequences would be. Economics is a study of the consequences of various ways of allocating scarce resources which have alternative uses. It is not a study of our hopes and values.

On the contrary, economics was christened "the dismal science" precisely because its analysis frustrated so many hopes and desires. On the other hand, knowing what was not possible saved many disappointments and disasters.

Our special focus on market economies, in which prices play a key role in the allocation process, is due to two considerations. First, this is the kind of economy with which most Americans are familiar. More important, this is the kind of economy which has produced higher standards of living for most people in countries around the world. What needs to be understood are the particular features of this kind of economy that lead to such results, whether in Europe, Asia, Africa, or the Western Hemisphere.

Incentives matter because most people will do more for their own benefit than for the benefit of others. Incentives link the two concerns together. A waitress brings food to your table, not because of your hunger, but because her salary and tips depend on it. Giant corporations hire people to find out what their customers want, not because of altruism, but because they know that this is the way to make a profit and avoid losses. Producing things that people don't want is a road that leads ultimately to the bankruptcy court.

Prices are important because they convey information in the form of incentives. Producers cannot read consumers' minds but, when automobile manufacturers find it harder to sell station wagons at prices that cover their cost of production and easier to sell sports utility vehicles at cost-covering prices, that is all that the automobile manufacturers need to know in order to decide what to produce.

Prices not only help determine which particular things are produced, they are also one of the ways of rationing the inherent scarcity of all goods and service. However, prices do not create that scarcity, which will require some form of rationing under any other economic system.

Simple as all this may seem, it goes counter to many programs designed to make various goods and services "affordable" or to keep them from becoming "prohibitively expensive." Being prohibitive is precisely how prices limit how much each person uses. If everything were made affordable, there would still not be any more to go around than when things were prohibitively expensive. There would simply have to be some alternative method used to ration the same amount that existed when things were not affordable. Whether that method was through ration coupons, political influence, black markets, or just fighting over things when they go on sale, the rationing would still have to be done, since artificially making things affordable does not create any more total output.

While scarcity is inherent, shortages are not. Scarcity simply means that there is not enough to satisfy everyone's desires. Only in the Garden of Eden was there enough to do that. A shortage, however, means that there are people willing to pay the price of the good but are unable to find it.

Price is an integral part of what a shortage is all about, even though many people mistakenly believe that there is a greater physical scarcity of a good during a shortage. However, as Sweden discovered, even the fastest rate of home-building in the world did not prevent an ever-worsening housing shortage, for the waiting list for housing grew faster, as the artificially low prices of housing under rent control caused many people to use more housing than they would have if they had had to pay the full value of the resources used in producing it.

One of the fundamental problems of price control is defining just what it is whose price is being controlled. Even something as simple as an apple is not easy to define because apples differ in size, freshness, and appearance, quite aside from the different varieties of apples. In a free market, those apples most in demand— for whatever reason—are likely to have higher prices and those least in demand lower prices. Produce stores and supermarkets spend time (and hence money) sorting out different kinds and qualities of apples, throwing away those that fall below a certain quality that their respective customers demand.

Under price control, however, the amount of apples demanded at an artificially low price exceeds the amount supplied, so there is no need to spend so much time and money sorting out apples, as they will all be sold anyway. Some apples that would ordinarily be thrown away under free market conditions may, under price control, be kept for sale to those people who arrive after all the good apples have been sold. As with apartments under rent control, there is no need to maintain high quality when everything will sell anyway during a shortage.

Many apparently humanitarian policies have backfired throughout history because of a failure to understand the role of prices. Attempts to keep food prices down by imposing price controls have led to hunger and even starvation, whether in seventeenth-century Italy, eighteenth-century India, France after the

French Revolution, Russia after the Bolshevik revolution, or in a number of African countries after they obtained independence during the 1960s. Some of these African countries, like some of the countries in Eastern Europe, once had such an abundance of food that they were exporters of food before the era of price control and government planning turned them into countries unable to feed themselves.

The motivation behind price controls on food may have been to make food affordable to the poor, but affordability did not mean any more food. In fact, it led to less food being available when the prices failed to repay the costs and labor required to grow crops or raise animals. Under the changed incentives created by price controls, farmers tended to produce less food and to keep much of what they produced for themselves and their families. Some farmers even gave up farming entirely as unprofitable, and moved to the city, simultaneously reducing the supply of food and adding to the number of urban consumers of food.

None of this is new or peculiar to a modern capitalist economy. Back in the days of the Roman Empire, the emperor Diocletian issued imperial decrees which set the prices of many goods—and "people brought provisions no more to markets," as a contemporary put it. It would be much the same story nearly two thousand years later, when price controls during the Nixon administration led to declining supplies of goods subject to those controls. In Ghana, the country lost its long-standing position as the world's number one producer of cocoa when the government limited how much money would be paid to farmers growing cocoa—and Ghana regained that position after the disastrous decline in the cocoa crop that followed forced the government to change its policy.

Failure to supply goods, as a result of political restrictions, must be sharply distinguished from an inability to produce them. Food can be in short supply in a country with extraordinarily fertile soil, as in post-Communist Russia that had not yet achieved a free-market economy:

> Undulating gently through pastoral hills 150 miles south of Moscow, the Plava River Valley is a farmer's dream come true.

> This is the gateway to what Russians call "Chernozym"—
> "Black Earth Country"—which boasts some of the most fertile
> soil in Europe, within three hours' drive of a giant, hungry me-
> tropolis . . . Black Earth country has the natural wealth to feed
> an entire nation. But it can barely feed itself.

It is hard even to imagine, in a free market economy, a hungry
city, dependent on imports of foreign food, when there is extraordinarily fertile farmland not far away. Yet the people on that very
fertile farmland were as poor as the city dwellers were hungry.
The workers harvesting that land earned the equivalent of about
$10 a week, with even this small amount being paid in kind—
sacks of potatoes or cucumbers—because of a lack of money. As
the mayor of a town in this region said:

> We ought to be rich. We have wonderful soil. We have the scien-
> tific know-how. We have qualified people. But what does it add
> up to?

If nothing else, it adds up to a reason for understanding economics as a means of achieving an efficient allocation of scarce resources which have alternative uses. All that was lacking was a
market to connect the hungry city with the products of the fertile
land and a government that would allow such a market to function freely. In some places, local Russian officials forbad the
movement of food across local boundary lines, in order to assure
low food prices within their jurisdictions and therefore local political support for themselves. Again, it is necessary to emphasize
that this was not a stupid policy, from the standpoint of officials
trying to gain local popularity with consumers by maintaining
low food prices. This protected their own political careers, however disastrous such policies were for the country as a whole.

While systemic causation is in one sense impersonal, in the
sense that its outcomes are not specifically predetermined by
anybody, "the market" is ultimately a way by which people's individual personal desires are reconciled with one another. Too often a false contrast is made between the impersonal marketplace
and the compassionate policies of various government programs.

But both systems face the same scarcity of resources and both systems make choices within the constraints of that scarcity. The difference is that one system involves each individual making choices for himself or herself, while the other system involves a smaller number of people making choices for others.

It may be fashionable for journalists to refer to "the whim of the marketplace," as if that were something different from the desires of people, just as it was once fashionable to refer to "production for use, rather than profit"—as if profits could be made by producing things that people cannot use or do not want to use. The real contrasts is between choices made by individuals for themselves and choices made for them by others who presume to define what these individuals "really" need.

SCARCITY AND COMPETITION

Scarcity means that everyone's desires cannot be satisfied completely, regardless of what economic system or economic policy we choose—and regardless of whether an individual or a society is poor or affluent. Therefore competition among people for these resources is inherent.

It is not a question whether we like or dislike competition. Scarcity means that we do not have the option to *choose* whether or not to have an economy in which people compete. That is the only kind of economy that is possible—and our only choice is among the particular methods that can be used for this competition.

One way in which competition for scarce resources might take place would be for those who hold political power to decide how resources should be allocated to different uses and shared among different people. This has happened in ancient despotisms and under modern communism. Conceivably, the people themselves might decide voluntarily how to share things, as in some tribal societies, though it is hard to imagine how that could happen in societies consisting of millions of people.

Yet another method of sharing resources among competing uses and competing individuals is by having them bid for these resources and the products resulting from them. In this system—a price-coordinated economy—those who want to use wood to produce furniture must bid against those who want to use it to produce houses, paper, or baseball bats. Those who want to use milk to produce cheese must bid against those who want to use it to produce yogurt or ice cream. Most people may be unaware that they are competing and simply see themselves deciding how much of various things to buy at whatever prices they find, but scarcity ensures that they are competing with others, even if they are conscious only of weighing their own purchasing decisions.

One of the incidental benefits of competing and sharing through prices is that different people are not as likely to think of themselves as rivals, nor to develop the kinds of hostility that rivalry can breed. For example, much the same labor and construction material needed to build a Protestant church could be used to build a Catholic church. But, if a Protestant congregation is raising money to build a church for themselves, they are likely to be preoccupied with how much money they can raise and how much is needed for the kind of church they want. Construction prices may cause them to scale back some of their more elaborate plans to fit within what they can afford. But they are unlikely to blame Catholics, even though the competition of Catholics for the same construction materials makes their prices higher than otherwise.

If, instead, the government were in the business of building churches and presenting them to different groups, Protestants and Catholics would be explicit rivals for this largess and neither would have any financial incentive to cut back on their building plans to accommodate the other. Instead, each would have an incentive to make the case, as strongly as possible, for the full extent of their desires and to resent any suggestion that they scale back their plans. The inherent scarcity of materials and labor would still limit what could be built, but that limit would now be imposed politically and seen by each as due to the rivalry of the other. The Constitution of the United States of course prevents the government from building churches for different groups, no doubt to prevent just such political rivalries and the bitterness, and sometimes bloodshed, to which such rivalries have led in other countries.

The same economic principle, however, applies to groups that are not based on religion but on ethnicity, geographical regions,

or age brackets. All are inherently competing for the same resources, simply because those resources are scarce. However,
competing indirectly by having to keep your demands within the
limits of your own pocketbook is very different from seeing your
desires for government benefits thwarted by the rival claims of
some other group.

Because economic resources are not only scarce but have alternative uses, the efficient use of those resources requires both consumers and producers to make trade-offs and substitutions.
Prices provide the incentives for doing so.

When the price of oranges goes up, some consumers switch to
tangerines. When bacon becomes more expensive, some consumers switch to ham. When the cost of a vacation at the beach
rises, some people decide to go on a cruise instead. Note that
what is happening here is not just substitution—it is *incremental*
substitution. Not everybody stops eating oranges when they become more pricey. Some people continue to eat the same number
of oranges they always ate, some cut back a little, some cut back a
lot, and others forget about oranges completely and go to tangerines or some other fruit. Although an orange is physically the
same thing to all, the value that each individual attaches to it obviously differs.

When the price of oranges rises, it is very likely because the
number of oranges demanded at the existing price exceeds the
number of oranges actually available. Something has to give. Incremental substitution, because of price increases, causes the loss
to be minimized by being borne more by those who are relatively
indifferent as between oranges and other substitutes, rather than
by those who are so devoted to oranges that they will simply pay
the higher prices and continue to eat the same number of oranges
as before, cutting back somewhere else in their budget to offset
the additional money spent on oranges.

Incremental substitutions take place in production as well as
consumption. Petroleum, for example, can be used to make heating
oil or gasoline, among other things. More petroleum is turned into
heating oil during the winter, when the demand for heating oil is
greatest, and more into gasoline during the summer, when many
people are doing more driving to vacation spots. This is not a total

substitution, since some petroleum is turned into both products (and many others) throughout the year. It is *incremental* substitution—somewhat more of *A* at the cost of somewhat less of *B*. Prices facilitate this kind of substitution, as they reflect incrementally changing demands, leading to incremental changes in supply.

Trade-offs and substitution can take place either intentionally or systemically. An intentional trade-off has been made by LTV, a steel manufacturer in Cleveland, whose equipment was set to shift automatically from oil to natural gas when the price of oil rose above a given level. Automobiles have also adjusted intentionally by becoming more fuel-efficient. Thus, the average American car drove 2,000 miles more in 1998 than in 1973, but used about 200 gallons less gasoline. This is because of high-tech equipment added to engines, obviously at a cost, but with the cost of this technology substituting for the cost of gasoline.

A systemic trade-off occurs when the economy as a whole uses less oil because the composition of its output changes. As a higher proportion of the output of the American economy has consisted of services, rather than material goods, less fuel is needed in their production. It takes less fuel to create more advanced software than to manufacture steel or automobiles. Over all, the amount of fuel used per dollar of national output has declined steadily since the early 1970s, when prices were raised dramatically by the international petroleum cartel.

As important as it is to understand the role of substitutions, it is also important to keep in mind that the efficient allocation of resources requires that these substitutions be incremental, not total. For example, one may believe that health is more important than amusements but, however plausible that may sound as a political slogan, no one really believes that having a twenty-year supply of band-aids in the closet is more important than having to give up all music in order to pay for it. A price-coordinated economy facilitates incremental substitution, but political decision-making tends toward categorical *priorities*—that is, declaring one thing absolutely more important than another and creating laws and policies accordingly.

When a political figure says that we need to "set national priorities" about one thing or another, what that amounts to is making *A* categorically more important than *B*. That is the opposite of incremental substitution, in which the value of each depends on how much of each we already have and therefore on the changing amount of *A* that we are willing to give up in order to get more *B*. Incremental substitution means that the relative values of each varies with how much of each we already have available.

The Meaning of "Costs"

In light of the role of trade-offs and substitutions, it is easier to understand the real meaning of costs as the foregone opportunities to use the same resources elsewhere. Prices allow each individual to weigh his own changing rates of trade-off, in the light of his own circumstances. Thus a mother may forego a rock concert in order to have her children vaccinated, but will not undergo costly and painful rabies shots to guard against some remote possibility of someday being bitten by an animal with that disease. Because an economy deals with scarce resources which have alternative uses, every benefit has a cost in the alternative uses that could have been made of the same resources that created a particular benefit. We do not simply "put" a price on things. Things have inherent prices and our political choice is only between trying to suppress that fact by laws or allowing these inherent prices to be expressed in the marketplace.

Free-market prices are not mere arbitrary obstacles to getting what people want. Prices are symptoms of an underlying reality that is not nearly as susceptible to political manipulation as the prices are. Prices are like thermometer readings—and a patient with a fever is not going to be helped by plunging the thermometer into ice water to lower the reading. On the contrary, if we were to take the new readings seriously and imagine that the patient's fever was over, the dangers would be even greater, now that the underlying reality was being ignored.

Despite how obvious all this might seem, there are a never-ending stream of political schemes designed to escape the realities being conveyed by prices—whether through direct price controls or by making this or that "affordable" with subsidies or by having the government itself supply various goods and services as a "right." What all these schemes have in common is that they exempt some things from the process of weighing costs and benefits against one another.

Sometimes the rationale for removing particular things from the process of weighing costs against benefits is expressed in some such question as: "How can you put a price on art?"—or education, health, music, etc. The fundamental fallacy underlying this question is the belief that prices are simply "put" on things. So long as art, education, health, music, and thousands of other things all require time, effort, and material resources, the costs of these inputs are the prices that are inherent.

These costs do not go away because a law prevents them from being conveyed through prices in the marketplace. Ultimately, to society as a whole, costs are the other things that could have been produced with the same resources. Money flows and price movements are symptoms of that fact—and suppressing these symptoms will not change the fact.

PART II: INDUSTRY AND COMMERCE

Chapter 5

The Rise and Fall
of Businesses

We tend to think of businesses as simply money-making enterprises, but that can be very misleading, in at least two ways. First of all, most businesses go out of business within a very few years after getting started, so it is likely that at least as many businesses are losing money as are making money. More important, from the standpoint of economics, is not what money the business owner hopes to make or whether he succeeds, but how all this affects the use of scarce resources which have alternative uses—and therefore how it affects the economic well-being of millions of other people in the society at large.

ADJUSTING TO CHANGES

The businesses we hear about, in the media and elsewhere, are usually those which have succeeded, and especially those which have succeeded on a grand scale—General Motors, Microsoft, Kodak, Chase Manhattan Bank. In an earlier era, we would have heard about the A & P grocery chain, once the largest retail chain in any field, anywhere in the world, with sales greater than the combined sales of leading contemporary retail giants Sears, Penney, and Montgomery Ward.

The fact that A & P has shrunk to a fraction of its former size, and is now virtually unknown, suggests that industry and commerce are not static things, but dynamic processes, in which individual companies and whole industries rise and fall, as a result of relentless competition under changing conditions. Half the companies on the "Fortune 500" list of the biggest businesses in 1980 were no longer on that list just a decade later.

At the heart of all of this is the role of profit—and of *losses*. Both are equally important from the standpoint of forcing companies and industries to use scarce resources efficiently. Industry and commerce are not just a matter of routine management, with profits rolling in more or less automatically. Masses of ever-changing details within an ever-changing surrounding economic and social environment mean that the threat of losses hangs over even the biggest and most successful businesses. There is a reason why business executives usually work far longer hours than their employees, and why so many businesses fail within a few years after getting started. Only from the outside does it look easy.

Even companies superbly adapted to a given set of conditions can be left behind when those conditions change suddenly and their competitors are quicker to respond. During the 1920s, for example, the A & P grocery chain was making a phenomenal rate of profit on its investment—never less than 20 percent per year, about double the national average—and it continued to prosper on into the 1930s and 1940s. But all this began to change drastically in the 1950s, when A & P lost more than $50 million in one 52-week period. A few years later, it lost $175 million over the same span of time. Its decline had begun.

A & P's fate, both when it prospered and when it lost out to rival grocery chains, illustrates the dynamic nature of a price-coordinated economy and the role of profits and losses. When A & P was prospering up through the 1940s, it did so by charging *lower* prices than competing grocery stores. It could do this because it kept its costs lower and the resulting lower prices attracted vast numbers of customers. When it began to lose customers to other grocery chains, this was because the latter could now sell for lower prices than A & P. Changing conditions in the surrounding society brought this about—together with differences in the speed with which different companies spotted the changes and realized their implications.

What were these changes? In the years following the end of World War II, suburbanization and the American public's rising prosperity gave huge supermarkets in shopping malls with vast parking lots decisive advantages over neighborhood stores located in the central cities. As the ownership of automobiles, refrigerators and freezers became far more widespread, this completely changed the economics of the grocery industry.

The automobile, which made suburbanization possible, also made possible greater economies of scale for both customers and supermarkets. Shoppers could now buy far more groceries at one time than they could have carried home in their arms from an urban neighborhood store before the war. That was the crucial role of the automobile. Moreover, refrigerators and freezers now made it possible to stock up on perishable items like meat and dairy products. This all added up to fewer trips to the grocery store, with larger purchases each time.

What this meant to the supermarket itself was a larger volume of sales at a given location, which could now draw customers with automobiles from miles around, whereas a neighborhood store in the central city was unlikely to draw customers on foot from ten blocks away. High volume meant savings in delivery costs from the producer to the supermarket, as compared to delivering the same amount of groceries to many neighborhood stores, whose total sales would add up to what one supermarket sold.

It also meant savings in the cost of selling within the supermarket itself, because it did not take ten times as long to check out one customer buying $50 worth of groceries at a supermarket as it did to check out ten customers buying $5 worth of groceries each at a neighborhood store. Because of these and other differences in the costs of doing business, supermarkets could be very profitable while charging prices lower than those in neighborhood stores that were struggling to survive.

All this not only lowered the costs of delivering groceries to the consumer, it changed the relative economic advantages and disadvantages of different locations for stores. Some supermarket chains, such as Safeway, responded to these radically new conditions faster and better than A & P which, for example, lingered in the central cities longer and did not follow the shifts of population to California and other sunbelt areas, as well as being reluctant to sign long leases or pay high prices for new locations where the customers and their money were now moving. After years of being the lowest-price grocery chain, A & P suddenly found itself being undersold by rivals with even lower costs of doing business.

Lower costs reflected in lower prices is what made A & P the world's leading retail chain in the first half of the twentieth century. And lower costs reflected in lower prices is what enabled other supermarket chains to take A & P's customers away in the second half of the twentieth century. While A & P succeeded in one era and failed in another, what is more important is that the economy as a whole succeeded in both eras in getting its groceries at the lowest prices possible at the time—from whichever company happened to have the lowest prices.

Many other corporations that once dominated their fields have likewise fallen behind in the face of changes or have even gone bankrupt. For decades, the Graflex Corporation produced most of the cameras used by press photographers. Movies and newsreels of the 1930s and 1940s almost invariably showed news photographers using a big, bulky camera with a bellows called a Speed Graphic, produced by Graflex. Then, in the early 1950s, outstanding photographs of the Korean war were made with a 35mm Leica camera, using lenses produced by a Japanese manufacturer that also made a new camera called the Nikon.

Advances in lens design and optical technology now made it possible for newspaper and magazine photographers to take pictures with smaller cameras that had enough sharpness and detail to compete with pictures taken by much bulkier cameras. Within a decade, smaller cameras rapidly replaced Speed Graphics and other large cameras made by the Graflex Corporation. The last Speed Graphic was produced in 1973 and the Graflex Corporation itself became extinct, after decades of dominating its field.

Similar stories could be told in industry after industry. Pan American Airlines, which pioneered in commercial flights across the Atlantic and the Pacific, went out of business in the wake of the deregulation of the American airline industry in the 1970s. Famous newspapers like the *New York Herald-Tribune*, with a pedigree going back more than a century, stopped publishing in a new environment, after television became a major source of news and newspaper unions made publishing more costly.

Smith-Corona dominated the typewriter industry for decades, but then laptop computers appeared on the scene and displaced portable typewriters, while desktop computers began displacing other typewriters. Like A & P before it, Smith-Corona began losing millions of dollars under changed conditions. It went five years in a row without making a profit during the 1980s. Only by beginning to produce word processors, a sort of half-way house between typewriters and computers, was Smith-Corona able to survive and begin making money again.

The great industrial and commercial firms that have declined or become extinct are a monument to the unrelenting pressures of competition. So is the rising prosperity of the consuming public. The fate of particular companies or industries is not what is most important. Consumers are the principal beneficiaries of lower prices made possible by the more efficient allocation of scarce resources which have alternative uses.

The key roles in all of this are played not only by prices and profits, but also by losses. These losses force businesses to change with changing conditions or find themselves losing out to competitors who spot the new trends earlier or who understand their implications better. Knowledge is one of the scarcest of all resources in any economy, and the insight distilled from knowledge is scarcer still. An economy based on prices, profits, and losses gives decisive advantages to those with greater knowledge and insight.

Put differently, knowledge and insight can guide the allocation of resources, even if most people, including the country's political leaders, do not share that knowledge or do not have the insight to understand what is happening. Clearly this is not true in the kind of economic system where political leaders control economic decisions, for then the limited knowledge and insights of those leaders become decisive barriers to the progress of the whole economy. Even when leaders have more knowledge and insight than the average member of the society, they are unlikely to have nearly as much knowledge and insight as exists scattered among the millions of people subject to their governance.

Knowledge and insight need not be technological or scientific for it to be economically valuable and decisive for the material well-being of the society as a whole. Something as mundane as

retailing has changed radically over the past century, revolution-
izing both department stores and grocery stores—and raising the
standard of living of millions of Americans by lowering the costs
of delivering goods to them.

Today, names like Sears and Ward's mean department store
chains to most people. However, neither of these enterprises began as department store chains. Montgomery Ward—the original
name of today's Ward's department stores—began as a mail-order
house in the nineteenth century. Under the conditions of that
time, before automobiles or trucks and with most Americans living in small rural communities, the cost of delivering consumer
goods to widely-scattered local stores was very high and that fact
was reflected in the high prices that were charged. These high
costs, in turn, meant that ordinary people could seldom afford
many of the things that we today regard as necessities.

Montgomery Ward cut these costs by operating as a mail-order house, selling directly to consumers all over the country from
its warehouse in Chicago. Its high volume of sales reduced its cost
per sale and allowed it to cut its prices below those charged by local stores in small communities. Under these conditions, it became the world's largest retailer in the late nineteenth century.
Sears then arose as a competing mail-order house and eventually
surpassed Montgomery Ward in sales and size.

More important than the fates of these two businesses was the
fact that millions of people were able to afford a higher standard
of living than if they had to be supplied with goods through cost-
lier channels. Meanwhile, there were gradual changes in American society, with more and more people beginning to live in urban
communities. This was not a secret, but not everyone noticed it
and even fewer had the insight to understand its implications for
retail selling. It was 1920 before the Census showed that, for the
first time in the country's history, there were more Americans living in urban areas than in rural areas.

One man who liked to pore over such statistics was Robert
Wood, an executive at Montgomery Ward. Now, he realized, selling merchandise through a chain of urban department stores
would be more efficient and more profitable than selling exclusively by mail order. Not only were his insights not shared by the
head of Montgomery Ward, Wood was fired.

Meanwhile, a man named James Cash Penney had the same insight and was already setting up his own chain of department stores, almost 300 by 1920 and more than a thousand by the end of the decade. Their greater efficiency in delivering goods to urban consumers was a boon to consumers—and a big economic problem for the mail order giants Sears and Montgomery Ward, both of which began losing money. The fired Robert Wood went to work for Sears and convinced their top management to begin building department stores of their own. After they did, Montgomery Ward had no choice but to do the same belatedly, though it was never able to catch up to Sears again.

Rather than get lost in the details of histories of particular businesses, we need to look at this from the standpoint of the economy as a whole and the standard of living of the people as a whole. One of the biggest advantages of an economy coordinated by prices and operating under the incentives created by profit and loss is that it can tap scarce knowledge and insights, even when most of the people do not share such knowledge and insights. The competitive advantages of those who are right can overwhelm the numerical, or even financial, advantages of those who are wrong.

James Cash Penney began as just a one-third partner in a store in a little town in Wyoming when Sears and Montgomery Ward were unchallenged giants of nationwide retailing. Yet his insights into the changing conditions of retailing and chain-store operations eventually forced these giants into doing things his way, on pain of extinction. Robert Wood failed to convince Montgomery Ward to change, but competition and red ink on the bottom line convinced them. In a later era, a clerk in a J.C. Penney store named Sam Walton would learn retailing from the ground up and put his knowledge and insights to work in his own store, which would eventually expand to become the Wal-Mart chain, with sales larger than those of Sears and J. C. Penney combined.

One of the great handicaps of government-run economies, whether under medieval mercantilism or modern communism, is that insights which arise among the masses have no such powerful leverage as to force those in authority to change the way they do things. Under any form of economic or political system, those at the top tend to become complacent, if not arrogant. Convincing them of anything is not easy, especially when it is some new way of doing things that is very different from what they are used to. The big advantage of a free market is that you don't have to con-vince anybody of anything. You simply compete with them in the marketplace and let that be the test of what works best.

Imagine a system in which J. C. Penney had to verbally con-vince the heads of Sears and Montgomery Ward to expand beyond mail-order retailing and build a nationwide chain of stores. Their response might well have been: "Who is this guy Penney—a part-owner of some little store in a hick town nobody ever heard of—to tell us how to run the largest retail companies in the world?"

In a market economy, Penney did not have to convince any-body of anything. All he had to do was deliver the merchandise to the consumers at a lower price. His success and their own red ink left Sears and Montgomery Ward no choice but to imitate this up-start, in order to become profitable again and regain their leader-ship of the retail merchandise industry. The firing of Robert Wood at Montgomery Ward is all too typical of what can happen to those who tell people things they do not want to hear. Years later, during the post-World War II era, a similar fate awaited execu-tives at Montgomery Ward who tried to tell its chief executive of-ficer, Sewell Avery, that the company needed to establish stores in suburban shopping malls.

Many things that we take for granted as features of the Amer-ican economy were resisted when first proposed and had to fight uphill to establish themselves by the power of the marketplace. Even something as widely used today as credit cards were ini-tially resisted. When Mastercard and Bankamericard first ap-peared in the 1960s, leading New York department stores such as Macy's and Bloomingdale's said that they had no intention of honoring credit cards, even though there were already millions of people with such cards in the New York metropolitan area. Only after the success of credit cards in smaller stores did the big de-partment stores finally relent and begin accepting credit cards— and eventually issuing their own.

What is important is not the success or failure of particular in-dividuals or companies, but the success of particular knowledge and insights in prevailing despite the blindness or resistance of others. Given the scarcity of such mental resources, an economy in which they have such decisive advantages is an economy which itself has great advantages in creating a higher standard of living for the population at large. A society in which only members of a hereditary aristocracy, a military junta, or a ruling party can make major decisions is a society that has thrown away much of the knowledge, insights, and talents of most of its people.

Contrast that with a society in which a farm boy who walked eight miles to Detroit to look for a job could end up creating the Ford Motor Company and changing the face of America with mass-produced automobiles—or a society in which a couple of young bicycle mechanics could create the airplane and launch the aviation industry. Neither a lack of pedigree nor a lack of academic degrees nor even a lack of money could stop ideas that worked, for investment money is always looking for a winner to back and cash in on. A society which can tap all kinds of talents from all kinds of sources has obvious advantages over societies in which only the talents of a preselected few are allowed to determine its destiny.

No economic system can depend on the continuing wisdom of its existing leaders. A price-coordinated economy with competition in the marketplace does not have to, because those leaders can be forced to change course—or be replaced—whether because of red ink, irate stockholders, outside investors ready to take over, or because of a bankruptcy court. Given such economic pressures, it is hardly surprising that economies under the thumbs of kings or commissars have seldom matched the track record of capitalist economies.

THE COORDINATION OF KNOWLEDGE

In medieval times, when craftsmen produced everything from swords to plowshares on a direct order from the customer, there was no problem of knowing what was wanted by whom. But a modern economy—whether capitalist or socialist—faces an entirely different situation. Today's supermarket or department store stocks an incredible variety of goods without knowing who will buy how much of what. Automobile dealers, bookstores, florists, and other businesses likewise keep a stock on hand to sell, without really knowing what the consumers will turn out to want. In a capitalist economy, wrong guesses can lead to anything from clearance sales to bankruptcy.

Under both capitalism and socialism, the scarcity of knowledge is the same, but the way these different economies deal with it can be quite different. The problem is not simply with the overall scarcity of knowledge, but also with the fact that this knowledge is often fragmented into tiny bits and pieces, the totality of which is not known to anybody.

Imagine the difficulties of an oil company headquartered in Texas trying to decide how much gasoline—and what kinds—will be needed in a filling station at the corner of Market and Castro Streets in San Francisco during the various seasons of the year, as well as in thousands of other locations across the country. The people who actually own and operate the filling stations at all these locations have far better knowledge of what their particular customers are likely to buy at different times of the year than anybody in a corporate headquarters in Texas can hope to have.

Variations can be great, even within a single city at a single time. If people who live in the vicinity of Market and Castro Streets in San Francisco own more sports cars than people who live near the filling station at 19th Avenue and Irving Street, then the filling station owner at Market and Castro is likely to order more premium gasoline than the filling station owner who sells to people with cheaper cars that use cheaper gasoline or to truckers who want diesel fuel. No single person at any given location—whether at a filling station or in corporate headquarters—can possibly have all this information for the whole country at his fingertips, much less keep updating it for thousands of filling stations from coast to coast as the seasons and the neighborhoods change. But that is wholly unnecessary in an economy where each kind of fuel simply goes wherever the money directs it to go.

The amount of such highly localized information, known to thousands of individual filling station owners scattered across the United States, is too enormous to be transmitted to some central point and then be digested in time to lead to government allocations of fuel with the same efficiency as a price-coordinated market can achieve. No oil company knows or cares about all this information. All they know is that orders are pouring in for diesel fuel in North Dakota this month, while Massachusetts is buying lots of premium gasoline and Ohio is buying mostly regular unleaded. Next month it may be a totally different pattern and the oil company may not have any more clue about the reasons for the new pattern than about the reasons for the old. But all that the oil company has to do is to supply the demand, wherever it is and for whatever reason.

The significance of prices in the allocation of resources can be seen most clearly by looking at situations where prices are not allowed to function. Two Soviet economists described a situation in which their government raised the price it would pay for moleskins, leading hunters to sell more of them:

> State purchases increased, and now all the distribution centers are filled with these pelts. Industry is unable to use them all, and they often rot in warehouses before they can be processed. The Ministry of Light Industry has already requested Goskomsten twice to lower the prices, but "the question has not been decided" yet. This is not surprising. Its members are too busy to decide. They have no time: besides setting prices on these pelts, they have to keep track of another 24 million prices.

However overwhelming it might be for a government agency to try to keep track of millions of prices, a country with hundreds of millions of people can far more easily keep track of these prices individually, because no one individual or business enterprise has to keep track of more than the relatively few prices relevant to their own decision-making. The situation as regards pelts was common during the days of the Soviet Union's centrally planned economy, where a recurrent problem was a piling up of unsold goods in warehouses at the very time when there were painful shortages of other things that could have been produced with the same resources. Like oil company executives in the United States, the executives who ran Soviet enterprises had no way to keep track of all the thousands of local conditions and millions of individual desires in a country that stretched all the way across the Eurasian land mass from Eastern Europe to the Pacific Ocean. Unlike American executives, however, their Soviet counterparts did not have the same guidance from prices or the same incentives from profits and losses. The net result was that many Soviet enterprises kept producing things in quantities beyond what anybody wanted, unless and until the problems became so huge and so blatant as to attract the attention of central planners in Moscow, who would then change the orders they sent out to manufacturers. But this could be years later and enormous amounts of resources would be wasted in the meantime.

The wastefulness of a centrally planned economic system translated into a painfully low standard of living for millions of Soviet citizens, living in a country with some of the richest natural resources in the world. Their standard of living was low, not only by comparison with that in the United States, but also compared to the standard of living in countries with far fewer natural resources, such as Japan and Switzerland. Efficiency is more than just an abstract concept of economists and accountants. It directly translates into the well-being of hundreds of millions of human beings.

The problems faced by the Soviet economy were not due to deficiencies peculiar to Russians or the other peoples of the Soviet Union. Americans faced very similar problems when the federal government was controlling the price of gasoline and its allocation during the 1970s. While both individuals and businesses had to drastically curtail their use of gasoline in some locations, such as New York and Washington, in some other places—mostly rural areas—there was a surplus of unsold gasoline.

This was not due to stupidity on the part of government allocators, but to the fact that a process that is relatively simple, when prices direct resources and products where millions of individuals want them to go, is enormously complex when a set of central planners seeks to substitute their necessarily very limited knowledge for the knowledge scattered among all those vast numbers of people in highly varying circumstances. The federal government issued 3,000 pages of regulations, supplemented by various official "clarifications," but none of this allocated gasoline as smoothly as the ordinary operations of a free market price system.

To know how much gasoline should be sent where and when requires an enormous amount of knowledge of when and where it is most in demand at any given moment—and that changes throughout the year, as well as varying from place to place. People drive more to particular vacation spots during the summer and more diesel-powered trucks carry produce to and from other places at harvest time, in addition to other changing uses of motor vehicles for all sorts of other reasons.

Nobody in any kind of economic or political system can possibly know the specifics of all these things. The advantage of a price-coordinated economy is that nobody has to. The efficiency of such an economy comes from the fact that vast amounts of knowledge do not ever have to be brought together, but are coordinated automatically by prices that convey in summary and compelling form what innumerable people want. The difference between the limited knowledge of a business executive and the similarly limited knowledge of a government official is that the business executive is *receiving* instructions from others on what to do—whom to supply, and when, with what kinds of fuel, in this case—while the government official is *giving* instructions to others and compelling them to obey.

In short, economic decisions are ultimately being directed or controlled by those who have specific knowledge in a price-coordinated economy, while those decisions move in the opposite direction—from those with less knowledge, who are giving orders to those with more knowledge—in a centrally planned economy. The difference is fundamental and profound in its implications for the material well-being of the population at large.

During the episodic gasoline shortages of the 1970s, Americans experienced in one industry for a limited period of time the severe economic problems that were common across the board in the Soviet Union for more than half a century. Because such an experience was so rare and shocking to Americans, they were receptive to all sorts of false political explanations and conspiracy theories for such an extraordinary situation, when in fact such situations were common in other countries using government allocation.

What was uncommon was for such methods to be used in the United States. The rationale was that reduced oil supplies from the Middle East required government intervention to prevent chaos in American oil markets. Needless to say, politicians were not about to admit that it was precisely this intervention which brought chaos, since the reduction in the total amount of gasoline in the country was just a few percentage points—the kind of reduction in supply that is routinely handled in all sorts of industries by a small price increase in a free market.

Indeed, a previous Arab oil embargo in 1967 had caused no such dislocations because it was not accompanied by the kinds of price controls instituted by the Nixon administration and continued by the Ford and Carter administrations. Nor were there long lines of cars waiting for hours at filling stations in other Western industrial nations or Japan, even though most of these other nations produced a far smaller percentage of their own petroleum than the United States did. These other countries did not have price controls on gasoline, so they did not have the shortages that go with price controls.

When government control of gasoline prices was ended in 1981—amid widespread warnings that this would lead to drastically higher prices—what followed was virtually a lesson in elementary economics. Higher prices brought a greater supply of gasoline and a smaller demand. Oil exploration shot up and existing wells whose costs could not have been covered at the controlled prices began pumping oil again. Within months, gasoline prices fell below what they had been under complex government controls. This fall continued over the years until gasoline prices reached an all-time low in real terms. Additional taxes were piled onto the prices at the pump, but the gas itself was cheaper than ever—and there were no waiting lines.

Chapter 6

The Role of Profits— and Losses

People often refer to an enterprise system as a profit system. This is a great mistake. It is a profit and loss system, and the loss part, in my opinion, is more important than the profit part. The crucial difference is not in what ventures are undertaken. The crucial difference is in what ventures are continued and which ones are abandoned . . . The crucial requirement for maintaining growth and progress is that successful experiments be continued and unsuccessful experiments be terminated.

- Milton Friedman

While part of the efficiency of a price-coordinated economy comes from the fact that goods can simply "follow the money," without the producers really knowing just why people are buying one thing here and something else there and yet another thing during a different season. However, it is necessary for them to keep track not only of the money coming in from the customers, it is equally necessary to keep track of how much money is going out to those who supply raw materials, labor, parts, and other inputs. Keeping careful track of these numerous flows of money in and out can make the difference between profit and loss.

PROFITS

Profits are perhaps the most misconceived subject in economics. Socialists have long regarded profits as simply "overcharge,"
as Fabian socialist George Bernard Shaw called it, or a "surplus
value" as Karl Marx called it. From their perspectives, profits
were simply unnecessary charges added on to the costs of producing goods and services, driving up the cost to the customer.
One of the great appeals of socialism, especially when it was just
an idealistic theory without any concrete examples in the real
world, was that it would eliminate these unnecessary charges,
making things generally more affordable, especially for people
with lower incomes. Only after socialism went from being a theory to being an actual economic system in various countries did it
become painfully apparent that people in socialist countries had a
harder time trying to afford things that most people in capitalist
countries could afford with ease and took for granted.

With profits eliminated, prices should have been lower in socialist countries, according to theory. Why then was it not that
way in practice?

Profits as Incentives

Let us go back to square one. The hope for profits and the
threat of losses is what forces a business owner in a capitalist
economy to produce at the lowest cost and sell what the customers are most willing to pay for. In the absence of these pressures, those who manage enterprises under socialism have far less
incentive to be as efficient as possible under given conditions,
much less to keep up with changing conditions and respond to
them quickly, as capitalist enterprises must do if they expect to
survive.

It was a Soviet premier who said that his country's managers
shied away from innovation "as the devil shies away from in-
cense." But, given the incentives of a socialist economy, why
should these managers have stuck their necks out by trying new

methods, when they stood to gain little or nothing if it succeeded. and might have lost their jobs (or worse) if it failed?[1]

Under capitalism, even the most profitable business can lose its market if it doesn't keep innovating, in order to avoid being overtaken by its competitors. For example, in the 1970s Intel replaced IBM computers that were 3,000 cubic feet in size with a chip smaller than a fingernail—and yet Intel itself was then constantly forced to improve that chip at an exponential rate, as rivals like Advanced Micro Devices, Cyrix, and others kept closing in on them technologically. More than once Intel poured such huge sums of money into the development of improved chips as to risk the financial survival of the company itself. But the alternative was to allow itself to be overtaken by rivals, which would have been an even bigger risk to Intel's survival.

In short, while capitalism has a visible cost—profit—that does not exist under socialism, socialism has an invisible cost—inefficiency—that gets weeded out by losses and bankruptcy under capitalism. The fact that most goods are available more cheaply in a capitalist economy implies that profit is less costly than inefficiency. Put differently, profit is a price paid for efficiency. Clearly the greater efficiency must outweigh the profit or else socialism would in practice have the lower prices and greater prosperity that its theorists expected, but which did not materialize in practice.

While capitalists have been conceived of as people who make profits, what a business owner really gets is a legal claim to whatever residual is left over after the costs have been paid out of the money received from customers. That residual can turn out to be positive, negative or zero. Workers must be paid and creditors

---

[1]During an earlier era, when Stalin ruled the Soviet Union by sheer terror, there was even less initiative by managers of enterprises in the U.S.S.R., because disobedience of orders could land a manager in a prison camp in Siberia or in front of a firing squad. At one point, there was a severe shortage of mining machinery, while the manager of a firm that produced such machines was keeping them in storage after they were produced, rather than sending them out to the mines. The reason was that the official orders called for these machines to be painted with red, oil-resistant paint—and the producer had on hand only green, oil-resistant paint and red paint that was not oil-resistant. Pending the arrival of the kind of paint he needed, he would just keep the machinery in storage because, as he explained, "I don't want to get eight years" for disobeying orders.

must be paid or they will take legal action to seize the company's assets. The only person whose payment is contingent on how well the business is doing is the owner of that business. This is what puts unrelenting pressure on the owner to monitor everything that is happening in the business and everything that is happening in the market for the business' products.

In contrast to the layers of authorities monitoring the actions of those under them in a government-run enterprise, the business owner is essentially an *unmonitored monitor* as far as the economic efficiency of the business is concerned. Self-interest takes the place of external monitors, and forces far closer attention to details and far more expenditure of time and energy at work than any set of rules or authorities is likely to be able to do. That simple fact gives capitalism its enormous advantages. More important, it gives the people living in price-coordinated market economies visibly higher standards of living.

It is not just ignorant people, but also highly educated people like George Bernard Shaw and Karl Marx, who have misconceived profits as arbitrary charges added on to the prices of goods and services. To many people, even today, high profits are often attributed to high prices charged by those motivated by "greed." In reality, most of the great fortunes in American history have resulted from someone's figuring out how to charge *lower* prices and therefore gain a mass market for the product. Henry Ford did this with automobiles, Rockefeller with oil, A & P with groceries, Alcoa with aluminum, and Sears, Wal-Mart and other department stores with a variety of products.

A supermarket chain in a capitalist economy can be very successful charging prices that allow about a penny of clear profit on each dollar of sales. Because several cash registers are usually bringing in money simultaneously all day long in a big supermarket, those pennies can add up to a very substantial rate of return on the supermarket chain's investment, while adding very little to what the customer pays. If the entire contents of the store get sold out in about two weeks, then that penny on a dollar becomes more like a quarter on the dollar (26 cents, to be exact) over the course of a year, when that same dollar comes back to be re-used 26 times a year.

Under socialism, that penny would be eliminated, but so too would be all the economic pressures on the management to keep costs down. A customer in a socialist country paying two dollars for what a customer under capitalism would get for one dollar could have the satisfaction of knowing that none of his two dollars went for profits, but that might be small comfort for someone with a lower standard of living.

When most people are asked how high they think the average rate of profit is, they usually suggest some number much higher than the actual rate of profit. From 1978 through 1998, American corporate profit rates fluctuated between a low of just above 6 percent to a high of about 13 percent. As a percentage of national income, corporate profits after taxes never exceeded 9 percent and was often below 6 percent over a thirty-year period ending in 1998. However, it is not just the numerical rate of profit that most people misconceive. Many misconceive its whole role in a price-coordinated economy, which is to serve as incentives—and it plays that role wherever its fluctuations take it. Moreover, some people have no idea that there are vast differences between profits on sale and profits on investments.

Profit Rates

Profits on sales are very different from profits on investment. If a store buys widgets for $10 each and sells them for $15 each, some might say that it makes $5 in profits on each widget. But, of course, the store has to pay the people who work there, the utility company that supplies the electricity for the lights, cash registers and other electrical devices in the store, as well as other suppliers of other goods and services needed to keep the store running. What is left over after all these people have been paid is the net profit, usually a lot less than the gross profit. But that is still not the same as profit on investment.

When someone invests $10,000, what that person wants to know is what annual rate of return it will bring, whether it is invested in stores, real estate, or stocks and bonds. Profits on particular sales are not what matter most. It is the profit on the total capital that has been invested in the business that matters. Things can be sold at prices that are much higher than what the seller paid for them and yet, if those items sit in the store for months before being sold, they may be less profitable than other items that have less of a markup but which sell out within a week. A store that sells pianos undoubtedly makes a higher percentage profit on each sale than a supermarket makes selling bread. But a piano sits in the store for a much longer time waiting to be sold than a loaf of bread does. Bread would go stale waiting for as long as a piano to be sold.

When a supermarket chain buys $10,000 worth of bread, it gets its money back much faster than when a piano dealer buys $10,000 worth of pianos. The piano dealer must charge a higher percentage mark-up on the sale of each piano than a supermarket charges on each loaf of bread, if the piano dealer is to make the same annual percentage rate of return on a $10,000 investment. When the supermarket gets its money back in a shorter period of time, it can turn right around and re-invest it, buying more bread or other grocery items. In the course of a year, the same money turns over many times in a supermarket, earning a profit each time, so that a penny of profit on the dollar can produce a total profit for the year on the initial investment equal to what a piano dealer makes charging a much higher percentage markup on an investment that turns over much more slowly.

Profits on sales and profits on investment are not merely different concepts. They can move in opposite directions. One of the keys to the rise to dominance of the A & P grocery chain in the 1920s was a conscious decision by the head of the company to cut profit margins on sales, in order to increase the profit rate on investment. With the new and lower prices made possible by selling with lower profits per item, A & P was able to attract greatly increased numbers of customers, making far more total profit because of the increased volume of sales. Making a profit of only a few cents on the dollar on sales, but with the inventory turning over nearly 30 times a year, A & P's profit rate on investment soared. This low price and high volume strategy set a pattern that spread to other grocery chains and to other kinds of enterprises as well. In a later era, huge supermarkets were able to shave the profit margin on sales still thinner, because of even higher volumes, enabling them to displace A & P from industry leadership by charging still lower prices.

COSTS OF PRODUCTION

Since profits are the difference between what consumers pay and what the products cost to produce and distribute, it is important to be very clear about these costs. Unfortunately, costs are misconceived almost as much as profits.

First of all, there is no such thing as "the" cost of producing a given product or service. Henry Ford proved long ago that the cost of producing an automobile was very different when you produced 100 cars a year than when you produced 100,000. With a mass market for automobiles, it paid to invest in expensive production machinery, whose cost per car would turn out to be modest when spread out over a huge number of automobiles. But, if you sold only half as many cars as you expected, then the cost of that machinery per car would be twice as much. It is estimated that the minimum amount of automobile production required to achieve efficient production levels today runs into the hundreds of thousands. Back in 1896, the largest automobile manufacturer in the United States produced just six cars a year. At that level of output, only the truly rich could afford to buy an automobile. It was Henry Ford whose mass production brought cars within the price range of ordinary Americans.

Similar principles apply in other industries. It does not cost as much to deliver a hundred cartons of milk to one supermarket as it does to deliver ten cartons of milk to each of ten different neighborhood stores. When building a beer brewery, construction costs are about one-third less per barrel of beer when the brewery's capacity is 4.5 million barrels per year than when its capacity is 1.5 million barrels. Moreover there are other economies in large-scale beer production. Although Annheuser-Busch spends millions of dollars advertising Budweiser and its other beers, its huge volume of sales means that its advertising costs per barrel of beer are about two dollars less than that of its competitors Coors and Miller.

In short, the cost of producing a given product or service varies with the volume being produced. This is what economists call "economies of scale." But that is only half the story. If economies of scale were the whole story, the question would then have to be asked: Why not produce cars in even more gigantic enterprises? If General Motors, Chrysler, and Ford all merged, would they not be able to produce cars even more cheaply and thereby make more profit than when they produce separately?

Probably not. There comes a point, in every industry, beyond which the cost of producing a unit of output no longer declines as the amount of production increases. In fact, costs per unit actually rise after an enterprise becomes so huge that it is difficult to monitor and control, when the right hand doesn't know what the left hand is doing. The coordination of knowledge within an organization is as big a problem as it is in the economy. Moreover, within the organization there are usually no such efficient devices as prices to convey information, so that coordination and control must take place through more cumbersome methods, such as articulation and monitoring, both of which have serious limitations.

Back when the American Telephone and Telegraph Company was the world's largest corporation, its own chief executive officer said: "A.T. & T. is so big that, when you give it a kick in the behind today, it takes two years before the head says, 'Ouch!'"[2] General Motors is the largest manufacturer of automobiles in the world, but its cost of production per car is estimated to be hundreds of dollars more than the costs of Ford, Chrysler, or leading Japanese manufacturers.

In short, while there are economies of scale, there are also what economists call "diseconomies of scale." Economies and diseconomies exist simultaneously at many different levels of output. That is, there may be things the business could do better if it were larger and other things it could do better if it were smaller. Eventually, the diseconomies begin to outweigh the economies, so it does not pay a firm to expand beyond that point. That is why industries usually consist of many firms, instead of one giant, super-efficient monopoly.

---

[2] I was an economist working for A.T.&T. at the time and heard him say it.

In the Soviet Union, where there was a fascination with economies of scale and a disregard of diseconomies of scale, both the industrial and agricultural enterprises in the U.S.S.R. were the largest in the world. The average Soviet farm, for example, was ten times the size of the average American farm and employed more than ten times as many workers. But Soviet farms were notoriously inefficient. Among the reasons for this inefficiency cited by Soviet economists was "deficient coordination."

Economies and diseconomies take many forms. Moreover, these economies and diseconomies mean that there may be no given cost for doing a given thing. In the American airline industry, for example, it would be cheaper to fly passengers directly from city A to city B than to have them fly to city C and then transfer to another plane to complete their journey—*other things being equal.* However, the reason other things are not equal is that it is also usually cheaper to fly 200 passengers on a 200-passenger plane than on two 100-passenger planes or by flying them in two half-empty 200-passenger planes.

By incurring the extra cost of flying passengers to an intermediate "hub" city, where they join other passengers from other cities going to the same ultimate destinations, the airlines are able to fill more of the seats on a bigger plane flying out of the hub, reducing their costs per passenger. In other words, there are both economies and diseconomies of scale here, as in many other situations. Whether one outweighs the other in a given situation depends on the volume of traffic between different cities and the cost differences per passenger between airplanes of different sizes. If there are enough passengers flying between city A and city B to fill the larger planes, then direct flights between those cities would cost the airline less per passenger than sending them to a hub city to transfer. Again, there is no such thing as "the" cost of flying passengers from one city to another, nor is one way cheaper than another under all circumstances. That is why most major airlines have both hub cities and direct flights.

The point at which the disadvantages of size begin to outweigh the advantages differs from one industry to another. That is why restaurants are smaller than steel mills. A well-run restaurant usually requires the presence of an owner with sufficient incentives to continuously monitor all the things necessary for successful operation, in a field where failures are all too common. Not only must the food be prepared to suit the tastes of the restaurant's clientele, the waiters and waitresses must do their jobs in a way that encourages people to come back for another pleasant experience, and the furnishings of the restaurant must also be such as to meet the desires of the particular clientele that it serves.

Moreover, these are not problems that can be solved once and for all. Food suppliers must be continuously monitored to see that they are still sending the kind and quality of produce, fish, meats, and other ingredients needed to satisfy the customers. Cooks and chefs must also be monitored to see that they are continuing to meet existing standards—as well as adding to their repertoires, as new foods and drinks become popular and old ones are ordered less often by the customers.

The normal turnover of employees also requires the owner to be able to select, train, and monitor new people on an on-going basis. Moreover, changes outside the restaurant—in the kind of neighborhood around it, for example—can make or break its business. All these factors, and more, must be kept in mind and weighed by the owner, and continuously adjusted to, if the business is to survive, much less be profitable.

Such a spectrum of details, requiring direct personal knowledge and control by someone on the scene with incentives going beyond a fixed salary, limits the size of restaurants, as compared to the size of steel companies, airplane manufacturers, or mining companies. Even where there are nationwide restaurant chains, often these are run by separate owners operating franchises from some national organization that supplies such things as advertising and general guidance and standards, leaving the numerous monitoring tasks to local owners. Howard Johnson pioneered in restaurant franchising in the 1930s, supplying half the capital, with the local manager supplying the other half. This gave the local franchisee a vested interest in the restaurant's profitability, rather than simply a fixed salary.

Costs vary not only with the volume of output, and to varying degrees from one industry to another, they also vary according to the extent to which existing capacity is being used. When an airplane with 200 seats is about to take off with 180 passengers on board, the cost of letting 20 "standby" passengers get on the flight is negligible. That is one reason for radically different prices being charged to people flying on the same plane. Some passengers bought guaranteed reservations and others essentially bought a chance of getting on board. Different levels of probability have different costs in airline tickets, as elsewhere. The passengers themselves also differ in how important it is for them to be at a particular place at a particular time. Those on urgent business may want a guaranteed reservation, even at a higher price, while others may be in a position where saving money is more important than being on one particular flight rather than another.

In many industries and enterprises, capacity must be built to handle the peak volume—which means that there is excess capacity at other times. The cost of accommodating more users of the product or service during the times when there is excess capacity is much less than the cost of handling those who are served at peak times. A cruise ship, for example, must receive enough money from its passengers to cover not only such current costs as paying the crew, buying food, and using fuel, it must also be able to pay such overhead costs as the purchase price of the ship and the expenses at the headquarters of the cruise line. To handle twice as many passengers at the peak season may mean buying another ship, as well as hiring another crew and buying twice as much food and fuel.

However, if the number of passengers in the off season is only one-third of what it is at the peak, then a doubling of the number of off-season passengers will not require buying another ship. Existing ships can simply sail with fewer empty cabins. Therefore, it pays the cruise line to try to attract economy-minded passengers by offering much reduced fares during the off season. Groups of retired people, for example, can schedule their cruises at any time of the year, not being tied down to the vacation schedules of their jobs or their children's schools. It is common for seniors to get large discounts in off-season travel, both on land and at sea. Businesses in general can afford to do this because their costs are lower—and each particular business is forced to do it because their competition will take customers away from them if they don't.

SPECIALIZATION AND DISTRIBUTION

A business firm is limited, not only in its over-all size, but also in the range of functions it can perform efficiently. General Motors makes millions of automobiles, but not a single tire. It buys them from Goodyear, Michelin, Firestone, and others tire manufacturers. Nor do automobile manufacturers own their own automobile dealerships across the country. Typically, automobile producers sell cars to local people who in turn sell to the public. In short, the automobile manufacturer specializes in manufacturing automobiles, leaving other functions to people who develop different knowledge and different skills needed to specialize in those particular functions.

The perennial desire to "eliminate the middleman" is perennially thwarted by economic reality. The range of human knowledge and expertise is limited for any given person or for any manageably-sized collection of people, so that only a certain number of links in the great chain of production and distribution can be mastered and operated efficiently by the same set of managers. Beyond some point, there are other people who can perform the next step in the sequence more cheaply or more effectively—and, at that point, it pays a firm to sell its output to some other businesses that can carry on the next part of the operation more efficiently. Newspapers seldom, if ever, own and operate their own news stands, nor do furniture manufacturers typically own or operate furniture stores. Most authors do not do their own publishing, much less own their own bookstores.

Prices play a crucial role in all of this, as in other aspects of a market economy. Any economy must not only allocate scarce resources which have alternative uses, it must determine how long the resulting products remain in whose hands before being passed along to others who can handle the next stage more efficiently. Profit-seeking businesses are guided by their own bottom line, but this bottom line is itself determined by what others can do and at what cost. When an oil company discovers that it can make more money by selling gasoline to local filling stations than by owning and operating its own filling stations, then the gasoline passes out of its hands and is then dispensed to the public by others. In other words, the economy as a whole operates more efficiently when the oil company turns the gasoline over to others at this point, though the oil company itself does so only out of self-interest. What connects the self-interest of a company with the efficiency of the economy as a whole are prices. When a product becomes more valuable in the hands of somebody else, that somebody else will bid more for the product than it is worth to its current owner. The owner then sells, not for the sake of the economy, but for his own sake. However, the end result is a more efficient economy, where goods move to those who value them most.

Despite superficially appealing phrases about "eliminating the middleman," middlemen continue to exist because they can do their phase of the operation more efficiently than others. It should hardly be surprising that people who specialize in one phase can do that phase better than others.

As in other cases, one of the best ways of understanding the role of prices and profits is to see what happens in their absence.

Socialist economies not only lack the kinds of incentives which force individual enterprises toward efficiency and innovation, they also lack the kinds of financial incentives that lead each given producer in a capitalist economy to limit its work to those stages of production at which it has lowest production costs than alternative producers. Capitalist enterprises buy components from others who have lower costs in producing those particular components, and sell their own output to whatever middlemen can most efficiently carry out its distribution. But a socialist economy may forego these advantages of specialization.

In the Soviet Union, for example, many enterprises produced their own components, even though specialized producers of such components could manufacture them at lower cost. Two Soviet economists estimated that the costs of components needed for a machine-building enterprise in the U.S.S.R. were two to three times as great as the costs of producing those same components in specialized enterprises. But what does cost matter in a system where profits and losses are not decisive?

This was not peculiar to machine-building enterprises. According to these same Soviet economists, "the idea of self-sufficiency in supply penetrates all the tiers of the economic and administrative pyramid, from top to bottom." Just over half the bricks in the U.S.S.R. were produced by enterprises that were *not* set up for that purpose, but which made their own bricks in order to build whatever needed building to house their main economic activity. That was because these Soviet enterprises could not rely on deliveries from the Ministry of Construction Materials, which had no financial incentives to be reliable in delivering bricks on time or of the quality required.

For similar reasons, far more Soviet enterprises were producing machine tools than were specifically set up to do so. Meanwhile, specialized plants set up for this purpose worked below their capacity—which is to say, at higher costs than if their overhead had been spread out over more output—because so many other enterprises were producing these things for themselves. Capitalist producers of bricks or machine tools have no choice but to produce what is wanted by the customer, and to be reliable in delivering it, if they intend to keep those customers in competition with other producers of bricks or machine tools. A socialist monopoly has no such pressures.

By contrast, General Motors can produce millions of automobiles without producing a single tire to go on them, because they can rely on Goodyear, Michelin, or whoever else supplies their tires to have those tires waiting to go on the cars when they come off the production lines. To leave General Motors high and dry, with no tires to go on their cars, would be financially suicidal to a tire company, since it would lose a customer for millions of tires each year.

Reliability is an inherent accompaniment of the physical product when keeping customers is a matter of economic life and death under capitalism, whether at the manufacturing level or the retail level. Back in the early 1930s, when refrigerators were just beginning to become widely used, there were many technological and production problems with the first mass-produced refrigerators sold by Sears. The company had no choice but to honor its money-back guarantee by taking back 30,000 refrigerators, at a time when they could ill afford to do so. This provided enormous pressure on Sears to either stop selling refrigerators (which is what some of its executives and many of its store managers wanted) or else greatly improve their reliability, which is what they eventually did, becoming one of the leading sellers of refrigerators in the country.

None of this was painless. Nor is it likely that a socialist monopoly would have been forced to undergo such economic trauma to please its customers. There was a reason why Soviet enterprises could not rely on their suppliers and chose instead to make many things for themselves, even though they were not specialists in making those things. The suppliers did not have to please their customers. All they had to do was follow orders from the central planning commission in Moscow.

Chapter 7

Big Business
and Government

Thus far, we have been considering what happens when businesses compete freely with one another in the marketplace. But this is not always the case. Sometimes one company produces the total output of a given good or service. For many years, each local telephone company was a monopoly in its region of the country. For about half a century before World War II, the Aluminum Company of America (Alcoa) produced all the virgin ingot aluminum in the United States. Such situations are unusual, but they are important enough to deserve some serious attention.

Most big businesses are not monopolies and not all monopolies are big business. Nor is this distinction a technicality. Many policies designed to deal with monopolistic behavior end up restricting the competitive advantages of large-scale enterprises and thereby restricting consumers' ability to benefit from economies of scale that produce lower prices.

MONOPOLIES AND CARTELS

Just as we can understand the function of prices better after we have seen what happens when they are not allowed to function, so we can understand the role of competition in the economy better after we contrast what happens in competitive markets with what happens in markets that are not competitive.

Thus far, we have considered prices as they emerge in a free market with many competing businesses. Such markets tend to cause goods and services to be produced at the lowest costs possible under existing technology and with existing resources. Take something as simple as apple juice. It undoubtedly costs something to produce apple juice, but how do we know that the price being charged is not far above those costs of production? After all, most of us do not grow apples, much less process them into juice and then bottle the juice and transport and store it, so we have no idea how much any or all of this costs.

Competition in the marketplace makes it unnecessary for us to know. Those few among us who do know such things, and who are in the business of making investments, have every incentive to invest wherever there are higher rates of return and to reduce their investments where the rates of return are lower or negative. If the price of apple juice is higher than necessary to compensate for the costs incurred in producing it, then high rates of profit will be made—and will attract ever more investment into this industry until the competition of additional producers drives prices down to a level that just compensates the costs with the same average rate of return on similar investment available elsewhere. Only then will the in-flow of investments from other sectors of the economy stop, with the incentives for these in-flows now being gone.

If, however, there were a monopoly in producing apple juice, this whole process would not take place. Chances are that monopoly prices would remain at levels higher than necessary to compensate for the costs and efforts that go into producing apple juice. Many people object to the fact that a monopolist can charge higher prices than a competitive business could. That is certainly true, but its ability to transfer money from other members of the society to itself is not the sole harm done by a monopoly. From the standpoint of the economy as a whole, these internal transfers do not change the total wealth of the society, even though this redistributes that wealth in a manner that may be objectionable. What adversely affects the total wealth in the economy as a whole is the effect of a monopoly on the allocation of scarce resources which have alternative uses.

When a monopoly charges a higher price than it could charge if it had competition, consumers tend to buy less of the product than they would at a lower competitive price. In short, a monopolist produces less output than a competitive industry would produce with the same available resources, technology and cost conditions. The monopolist stops short at a point where consumers are still willing to pay enough to cover the cost of production (including a normal profit) of more output because the monopolist is charging more than the usual cost of production and making more than the usual profit. In terms of the allocation of resources which have alternative uses, the net result would be that some resources which could have been used to produce more apple juice would instead go into producing other things elsewhere in the economy, even if those other things were not as valuable as the apple juice that could and would have been produced in a free competitive market. In short, the economy's resources are used inefficiently when there is monopoly, because these resources would be transferred from more valued uses to less valued uses.

Fortunately, monopolies are very hard to maintain without laws to protect the monopoly firms from competition. The ceaseless search of investors for the highest rates of return virtually ensures that such investments will flood into whatever segment of the economy is earning higher profits, until the rate of profit in that segment is driven down by the increased competition caused by that flood of investment. It is like water seeking its own level. But, just as dams can prevent water from finding its own level, so government intervention can prevent a monopoly's profit rate from being reduced by competition.

In centuries past, government permission was required to open businesses in many parts of the economy, especially in Europe and Asia, and monopoly rights were granted to various businessmen, who either paid the government directly for these rights or bribed officials who had the power to grant such rights, or both. However, by the end of the eighteenth century, the development of economics had reached the point where increasingly large numbers of people understood how this was detrimental to society as a whole and counter-pressures developed toward freeing the economy from monopolies and government control. Monopolies have therefore become much rarer, at least at the national level, though it remains common in many cities where restrictive licensing laws limit how many taxis are allowed to operate, causing fares to be artificially higher than necessary and cabs less available than they would be in a free market.

Again, the loss is not simply that of the individual consumers. The economy as a whole loses when people who are perfectly willing to drive taxis at fares that consumers are willing to pay are nevertheless prevented from doing so by artificial restrictions on the number of taxi licenses issued, and thus either do some other work of lesser value or remain unemployed. If the alternative work were of greater value, and were compensated accordingly, then such people would never have been potential taxi drivers in the first place.

From the standpoint of the economy as a whole, this means that consumers of the monopolist's product are foregoing the use of scarce resources which would have a higher value to them than in alternative uses. That is the inefficiency which causes the economy as a whole to have less wealth under monopoly than it would have under free competition.

It is sometimes said that a monopolist "restricts output," but this is not the intent. The monopolist would love to have the consumers buy more at its inflated price, but the consumers stop short of the amount that they would buy at a lower price under free competition. It is the monopolist's higher price which causes the consumers to restrict their own purchases and therefore causes the monopolist to restrict production to what can be sold. But the monopolist may be advertising heavily to try to persuade consumers to buy more.

Similar principles apply to a cartel—that is, a group of businesses which agree among themselves to charge higher prices or otherwise avoid competing with one another. In theory, a cartel could operate collectively the same as a monopoly. In practice, individual members of cartels tend to cheat on one another secretly—lowering the cartel price to some customers in order to take business away from other members of the cartel. When this becomes widespread, the cartel becomes irrelevant, whether or not it formally ceases to exist.

Because cartels were once known as "trusts," legislation designed to outlaw monopolies and cartels became known as "antitrust laws." However, such laws are not the only way of fighting monopolies and cartels. Private businesses that are not part of the cartel have incentives to fight them in the marketplace. Moreover, private businesses can take action much faster than the years required for the government can bring an anti-trust case to a successful conclusion.

In the nineteenth-century heyday of the trusts, Montgomery Ward was one of their biggest opponents. Whether the trust involved agricultural machinery, bicycles, sugar, nails or twine, Montgomery Ward would seek out manufacturers that were not part of the trust and buy from them below the cartel price, reselling to the general public below the retail price of the goods produced by members of the cartel. Since Montgomery Ward was the number one mail-order business in the country at that time, it was also big enough to set up its own factories and make the product itself if need be.

The later rise of other huge retailers like Sears and A & P likewise confronted the big producers with financial giants able to either produce their own competing products to sell in their own stores or to buy enough from some small enterprise outside the cartel to enable that enterprise to grow into a big competitor. Sears did both. It produced stoves, shoes, guns, and wallpaper, among other things, in addition to subcontracting the production of other products. A & P imported and roasted its own coffee, canned its own salmon, and baked half a billion loaves of bread a year for sale in its own stores.

While giant firms like Sears, Montgomery Ward and A & P were unique in being able to compete against a number of cartels simultaneously, smaller companies could also take away sales from cartels in their respective industries. Their incentive is the same as that of the cartel—profit. Where a monopoly or cartel maintains prices that produce higher than normal profits, other businesses are attracted to the industry. This additional competition then tends to force prices and profits down. In order for a monopoly or cartel to succeed, it must find ways to prevent others from entering the industry. This is easier said than done. One way to keep out potential competitors is to have the government make it illegal for others to operate in particular industries. Kings granted or sold monopoly rights for centuries, and modern governments have restricted the issuance of licenses for various in-dustries and occupations, ranging from airlines to taxicabs to trucking to the braiding of hair. Political rationales are never lack-ing for these restrictions, but their net economic effect is to protect existing enterprises from additional potential competitors and therefore to maintain prices at artificially high levels.

In the absence of government prohibition of entry, various clever schemes can be used privately to try to erect barriers to keep out competitors and protect monopoly profits. But other businesses have incentives to be just as clever at evading these barriers. Accordingly, the effectiveness of barriers to entry have varied from industry to industry and from one era to another in the same industry. The computer industry was once difficult to enter, back in the days when a computer was a huge machine tak-ing up a major part of a room, and the costs of manufacturing such machines was huge. But the development of microchips meant that smaller computers could do the same work and could be manufactured by smaller companies. One small and largely unknown computer manufacturer—MSE Engineering—supplies computers to the Hoover Institution at Stanford University.

In addition to private responses to monopoly and cartels which arise more or less spontaneously in the marketplace, the federal government began to respond to monopolies and cartels in the late nineteenth century. These responses included both di-rectly regulating the prices which the monopolist were allowed to charge and taking legal action against these monopolies and car-tels under the Sherman Anti-Trust Act of 1890 and other later an-titrust legislation.

When railroads were first built in the nineteenth century, there were many places where only one rail line existed, leaving these railroads free to charge whatever prices would maximize their profits where they had a monopoly. Complaints about this situa-tion led to the creation of the Interstate Commerce Commission in 1887, the first of many federal regulatory commissions to control the prices charged by monopolists. During the era when tele-phone companies were monopolies in their respective regions, the Federal Communications Commission controlled the price of phone service.

Another approach has been to pass laws against the creation or maintenance of a monopoly or against various practices, such as price discrimination, growing out of monopolistic behavior. These anti-trust laws were intended to allow businesses to operate without the kinds of detailed government supervision which exist under regulatory commissions, but with a sort of general surveillance, like that of traffic police, with intervention occurring only when there are specific violations of laws.

REGULATORY COMMISSIONS

Although the functions of a regulatory commission are fairly straightforward in theory, in practice its task is far more complex and, in some respects, impossible. Moreover, the political climate in which regulatory commissions operate often lead to policies and results directly the opposite of what was expected by those who created such commissions.

Ideally, a regulatory commission would set prices where they would have been if there were a competitive marketplace. In practice, there is no way to know what those prices would be. Only the actual functioning of a market itself could reveal such prices, as the less efficient firms were eliminated by bankruptcy and only the most efficient survived. No outside observers can know what the most efficient ways of operating a given firm or industry are. Indeed, many managements within an industry discover the hard way that what they thought was the most efficient way to do things was not efficient enough to meet the competition. The most that a regulatory agency can do is accept what appear to be reasonable production costs and allow the monopoly to make what seems to be a reasonable profit over and above such costs.

Regulatory agencies are often set up after some political crusaders have successfully launched investigations or publicity campaigns that convince the authorities to establish a permanent commission to oversee and control a monopoly or some group of firms few enough in number to be a threat to behave in collusion as if they were one monopoly. However, after a commission has been set up and its powers established, crusaders and the media tend to lose interest over the years and turn their attention to other things. Meanwhile, the firms being regulated continue to take a keen interest in the activities of the commission and to lobby the state or federal legislature for favorable regulations and favorable appointments of individuals to these commissions.

The net result of these asymmetrical outside interests on these agencies is that commissions set up to keep a given firm or industry within bounds, for the benefit of the consumer, often metamorphose into agencies seeking to protect the existing regulated firms from threats arising from new firms with new technology or new organizational methods. Thus the Interstate Commerce Commission responded to the rise of the trucking industry, whose competition in carrying freight threatened the economic viability of the railroads, by extending their control over trucking.

The original rationale for regulating railroads was that these railroads were often monopolies in particular areas of the country. But now that trucking undermined that monopoly, the response of the I.C.C. was not to say that the need for regulating transportation was now less urgent or perhaps even unnecessary. Instead, it sought—and received from Congress—broader authority under the Motor Carrier Act of 1935, in order to restrict the activities of truckers. This allowed railroads to survive under new economic conditions, despite truck competition that was more efficient for various kinds of freight hauling. Trucks were now permitted to operate across state lines only if they had a certificate from the Interstate Commerce Commission declaring that the trucks' activities served "public necessity and convenience" as defined by the I.C.C.

In short, freight was no longer hauled in whatever way required the use of the least resources, as it would be under open competition, but only by whatever way met the arbitrary requirements of the Interstate Commerce Commission. The I.C.C. might, for example, authorize a particular trucking company to haul freight from New York to Washington, but not from Philadelphia to Baltimore, even though these cities are on the way. If the certificate did not authorize freight to be carried back from Washington to New York, then the trucks would have to return empty, while other trucks carried freight from D.C. to New York. From the standpoint of the economy as a whole, enormously greater costs were incurred than were necessary to get the work done. What this accomplished politically was to allow far more companies—both truckers and railroads—to survive and make a profit than if there were an unrestricted competitive market, where the transportation companies would have no choice but to use the most efficient ways of hauling freight.

While open and unfettered competition would have been economically beneficial to the society as a whole, such competition would have been politically threatening to the regulatory commission. Firms facing economic extinction because of competition would be sure to resort to political agitation and intrigue against the survival in office of the commissioners and against the survival of the commission and its powers. Labor unions also had a vested interest in keeping the status quo safe from the competition of technologies and methods that might require fewer workers to get the job done.

After the I.C.C.'s powers to control the trucking industry were reduced by Congress in 1980, freight charges declined substantially and shippers reported a rise in the quality of the service. This was made possible by greater efficiency in the industry, as there were now fewer trucks driving around empty and more truckers hired workers whose pay was determined by supply and demand, rather than by union contracts. Because truck deliveries were now more dependable in a competitive industry, businesses using their services were able to carry smaller inventories, saving in the aggregate tens of billions of dollars.

The inefficiencies created by regulation were indicated not only by such savings after federal deregulation, but also by the difference between the costs of interstate shipments and the costs of *intrastate* shipments, where strict state regulation continued after federal regulation was cut back. For example, shipping blue jeans within the state of Texas from El Paso to Dallas cost about 40 percent more than shipping the same jeans internationally from Taiwan to Dallas.

Gross inefficiencies under regulation were not peculiar to the Interstate Commerce Commission. The same was true of the Civil Aeronautics Board, which kept out potentially competitive airlines and kept the prices of airfares high enough to insure the survival of existing airlines, rather than force them to face the competition of other airlines that could carry passengers cheaper or with better service. Once the CAB was abolished, airline fares came down, some airlines went bankrupt, but new airlines arose and in the end there were far more passengers being carried than at any time under the constraints of regulation. Savings to airline passengers ran into the billions of dollars. These were not just zero-sum changes, with airlines losing what passengers gained. The country as a whole benefitted from deregulation, for the industry became more efficient. Just as there were fewer trucks driving around empty after trucking deregulation, so airplanes began to fly with a higher percentage of their seats filled after airline deregulation and passengers had more choices of carriers on a given route than before.[1]

The original rationale for regulation was to keep prices from rising excessively but, over the years, this turned into regulatory restrictions against prices *falling* to a level that would threaten existing firms. Political crusades are based on plausible rationales but, even when those rationales are sincerely believed and honestly applied, their actual consequences may be completely different. When major mistakes are made in a competitive economy, those who were mistaken can be forced from the marketplace. But, in politics, those who were mistaken can often continue to survive by doing things that were never contemplated when their positions and their powers were created.

ANTI-TRUST LAWS

With anti-trust laws, as with regulatory commissions, a sharp distinction must be made between their original rationales and

---

[1]One of the continuing problems of the airline industry—airport congestion—occurs because landing fees have *not* been deregulated. Instead of being determined by supply and demand for landing rights at airports, landing fees are determined by arbitrary formulas which allow small private planes to use a scarce resource at less than its value to jumbo jets carrying hundreds of passengers. The predictable net result is that small private planes carrying a handful of people are able to land at overcrowded major airports when they could just as easily land at smaller airports where they would not either delay vastly larger numbers of other passengers or preclude the scheduling of more flights in bigger planes.

what they actually do. The basic rationale for anti-trust laws is to prevent monopoly and other conditions which allow prices to rise above where they would be in a free and competitive marketplace. In practice, most of the great anti-trust cases have involved some business that charged *lower* prices than its competitors. Often it has been complaints from these competitors which caused the government to act.

The basis of many government prosecutions under the anti-trust laws is that some company's actions threatens competition. However, the most important thing about competition is that it is a *condition* in the marketplace. This condition cannot be measured by the number of competitors existing in a given industry at a given time, though politicians, lawyers and assorted others have confused the existence of competition with the number of surviving competitors. But competition as a condition is precisely what eliminates many competitors.

Obviously, if it eliminates all competitors, then the surviving firm would be a monopoly and could charge far higher prices than in a competitive market. But that is extremely rare. However, the specter of monopoly is often used to justify government policies of intervention where there is no serious danger of a monopoly.

Back when the A & P grocery chain was the largest retail chain in the world, it still sold less than one-fifth of the groceries in the country. Yet the Justice Department brought an anti-trust action against it, using the company's low prices, and the methods by which it achieved those low prices, as evidence of unfair competition against competitors. Throughout the history of anti-trust prosecutions, there has been an unresolved confusion between what is detrimental to competition and what is detrimental to competitors. In the midst of this confusion, the question of what is beneficial to the consumer has often been lost sight of.

What has also been lost sight of is the question of the efficiency of the economy as a whole, which is another way of looking at the benefits to the consuming public. Fewer scarce resources are used when products are bought and sold in carload lots, as large chain stores are often able to do, than when the shipments are sold and delivered in much smaller quantities to numerous smaller stores. Both delivery costs and selling costs are less per unit of product when the product is bought and sold in large enough amounts to fill a railroad boxcar.

Production costs are also lower when the producer has a large enough order to be able to schedule production far ahead, instead of finding himself forced to pay overtime to fill many small and unexpected orders that happen to arrive at the same time.

Despite such economies of scale, the government took action against the Morton Salt Company in the 1940s for giving discounts to buyers who bought carload lots of their product. Businesses that bought less than a carload lot of salt were charged $1.60 a case, those who bought carload lots were charged $1.50 a case, and those who bought 50,000 cases or more in a year's time were charged $1.35. Because there were relatively few companies that could afford to buy so much salt and many more that could not, "the competitive opportunities of certain merchants were injured," according to the Supreme Court, which upheld the Federal Trade Commission's actions against Morton Salt.

The government likewise took action against the Standard Oil Company in the 1950s for allowing discounts to those dealers who bought oil by the tank car. The Borden company was similarly brought into court in the 1960s for having charged less for milk to big chain stores than to smaller grocers. In all these cases, the key point was that such price differences were considered "discriminatory" and "unfair" to those competing firms unable to make such large purchases.

While the sellers were allowed to defend themselves in court by referring to cost differences in selling to different classes of buyers, the apparently simple concept of "cost" is by no means simple when argued over by rival lawyers, accountants and economists. Where neither side could prove anything conclusively about the costs—which was common—the accused lost the case. In a fundamental departure from the centuries-old traditions of Anglo-American law, the government need only make a superficial or *prima facie* case, based on gross numbers, to shift the burden of proof to the accused. This same principle and procedure was to reappear later in employment discrimination cases under the civil rights laws. As with anti-trust case, these employment discrimination cases likewise produced many consent decrees and large out-of-court settlements by companies well aware of the virtual impossibility of proving their innocence, regardless of what the facts might be.

The rarity of genuine monopolies in the American economy has led to much legalistic creativity, in order to define various companies as monopolistic or as potential or "incipient" monopolies. How far this could go was illustrated when the Supreme Court in 1966 broke up a merger between two shoe companies that would have given the new combined company less than 7 percent of the shoe sales in the United States. It likewise that same year broke up a merger of two local supermarket chains which, put together, sold 7.5 percent of the groceries in the Los Angeles area.

A standard practice in the courts and in the literature on anti-trust laws is to describe the percentage of sales made by a given company as the share of the market it "controls." By this standard, such now defunct companies as Graflex and Pan American "controlled" a substantial share of their respective markets, when in fact the passage of time showed that they controlled nothing, or else they would never have allowed themselves to be forced out of business. The severe shrinkage in size of such former giants as A & P and Smith-Corona likewise suggests that the rhetoric of "control" bears little relationship to reality. But such rhetoric remains effective in courts of law and in the court of public opinion.

Even in the rare case where a genuine monopoly exists on its own—that is, has not been created or sustained by government policy—the consequences in practice have tended to be much less dire than in theory. During the decades when the Aluminum Company of America (Alcoa) was the only producer of virgin ingot aluminum in the United States, its annual profit rate on its investment was about 10 percent after taxes. Moreover, the price of aluminum went down to a fraction of what it had been before Alcoa was formed. Yet Alcoa was prosecuted under the anti-trust laws and lost. Why were aluminum prices going down under a monopoly, when in theory they should have been going up? Despite its "control" of the market for aluminum, Alcoa was well aware that it could not jack up prices at will, without risking the substitution of other materials—steel, tin, wood, plastics—for aluminum by many users.

This raises a question that applies far beyond the aluminum industry. Percentages of the market "controlled" by this or that company ignore the role of substitutes that may be classified as products of other industries, but which can nevertheless be used by many buyers, if the price of the monopolized product rises significantly. A technologically very different product may serve as a substitute, as laptop computers did when they replaced portable typewriters, or as television did when it replaced many newspapers as sources of information and entertainment. A 100 percent monopoly of Valencia oranges would mean little if people were free to buy navel oranges, tangerines, and other similar fruit. In a sense, every company that sells brand-name merchandise has a monopoly of that particular merchandise. But a monopoly of Canon cameras means little when photographers are free to buy Nikon, Minolta, Pentax, and other cameras.

An extreme example of how misleading market share statistics can be was the case of a local movie chain that showed 100 percent of all the first-run movies in Las Vegas. It was prosecuted as a monopoly but, by the time the case reached the 9th Circuit Court of Appeals, another movie chain was showing more first-run movies in Las Vegas than the "monopolist" that was being prosecuted. Fortunately, sanity prevailed in this instance. Judge Alex Kozinski of the 9th Circuit pointed out that the key to monopoly is not market share—even when it is 100 percent—but the ability to keep others out. A company which cannot keep competitors out is not a monopoly, no matter what percentage of the market it may have at a given moment.

Focusing on market shares at a given moment has also led to a pattern in which the government has prosecuted leading firms in an industry just when they were about to lose that leadership. In a world where it is common for particular companies to rise and fall over time, anti-trust lawyers can take years to build a case against a company that is at its peak—and about to head over the hill. For example, an anti-trust case against the A & P grocery chain ended in 1949, just three years before A & P lost $50 million and began a long and catastrophic economic decline.[2] The "control," "power," and "dominance" of A & P, which the government lawyers depicted so convincingly in court proved to be of little consequence in the marketplace, when other supermarket chains were able to provide better service at lower prices.

A major anti-trust case can take a decade or more to be brought to a final conclusion. Markets often react much more quickly than this against monopolies and cartels, as early twentieth century trusts found when giant retailers like Sears, Montgomery Ward and A & P outflanked them long before the government could make a legal case against them.

Perhaps the most clearly positive benefit of anti-trust laws has been a blanket prohibition against collusion to fix prices. This is an automatic violation, subject to heavy penalties, regardless of any justification that might be attempted. Whether this outweighs the various negative effects of other anti-trust laws on competition in the marketplace is another question.

---

[2]Why did A & P not adjust to the new conditions as fast as Safeway? Partly, the answer may be that there are always differences among individuals in how fast they notice changes and how quickly they respond. Another factor in the case of A & P was that the company was owned and operated [for more than half a century] by two brothers, and the death of the last brother in 1951 brought to leadership a man who had served faithfully under the old system. Was such a man at such a time, in the wake of his leader's death, likely to turn the company upside down and throw away the managerial legacy he had received?

Chapter 8

An Overview

Perhaps the most overlooked fact about industry and commerce is that they are run by people who differ greatly from one another in insight, foresight, leadership, organizational ability, and dedication—just as people do in every other walk of life. If the economy is to achieve the most efficient use of its scarce resources, there must be some way of weeding out those business owners or managers who do not get the most from those resources.

Losses accomplish that. Bankruptcy shuts down the entire enterprise that is failing to come up to the standards of its competitors or is producing a product that has been superseded by some other product. Before reaching that point, however, losses can force a firm to make internal reassessments of its policies and personnel. These include the chief executive, who can be replaced by irate stockholders who are not receiving the dividends they expected. The whole management team can also be replaced when outside financial interests realize that the business would be worth more if managed by someone else, and who therefore take over the business, in order to run it better and more profitably with a different set of managers.

Because assets tend to move through a competitive market to those who value them most, and who are therefore willing to bid the most for these assets, a poorly managed company is more valuable to outside investors, who are convinced that they can improve its performance, than to existing owners. These outside investors can therefore offer existing stockholders more for their stock than it is currently worth and still make a profit, if that stock's value later rises to the level expected when existing management is replaced by better managers.

For example, if the stock is worth $80 a share under inefficient management, outside investors can start buying it up at $90 a share until they have a controlling interest in the corporation. After using that control to fire existing managers and replace them with a more efficient management team, the value of the stock might rise to $150 a share. While this profit is what motivates the investors, from the standpoint of the economy as a whole, what matters is that such a rise in stock prices usually means that either the business is now serving more customers, or offering them better quality or lower prices, or is operating at lower cost—or some combination of these things.

Thus profits and losses work together in a market economy to replace personnel, products and whole companies and industries with better alternatives. The net effect of achieving higher levels of efficiency is higher standards of living for the consuming public. Moreover, this process is never-ending because its problems can never be solved once and for all. Changes in technology, in the company's internal personnel and in the surrounding economy and society present ever-changing challenges to be dealt with, all under the constant threat of losses, as well as opportunities for profit.

As noted in Chapter 5, in the predominantly rural America of the late nineteenth and early twentieth centuries, the most efficient way to distribute many goods to a widely scattered population was by mail. Montgomery Ward and then Sears became the biggest retailers in the country by selling through their mail-order catalogs from their respective headquarters in Chicago, at prices below those charged by local stores, whose distribution costs were higher. However, the growing urbanization of the country slowly but surely changed all that.

A more concentrated urban population could now be more cheaply served by building chains of stores in their midst. By the early 1920s, both Montgomery Ward and Sears were struggling to survive financially, while chain stores like J. C. Penney were springing up and prospering, taking away their customers. It was only when these two giants of the mail-order catalog business built chain stores themselves that their fortunes revived and they surged to the top again.

Just as the urbanization of early twentieth-century America radically changed the relative costs of distributing general merchandise by mail and through stores, so the postwar suburbanization and rising prosperity of America changed the relative costs of distributing groceries through neighborhood stores and through supermarkets located in shopping malls. Again, some individuals and businesses grasped this sooner than others, allowing Safeway to ride the crest of the new wave to leadership of the industry, while the previous leader—A & P—sank into virtual oblivion, though it had been more than twice the size of Safeway as late as 1962.

The Great Depression of the 1930s left many business leaders very cautious about expanding their operations, especially if this required borrowing money that might be hard to repay if the economy turned down. Even highly profitable businesses could decide to save their money for a rainy day, rather than risk it in new ventures. Against this background, it is not surprising that the dramatic change in the American economy and society between the Great Depression of the 1930s and the booming prosperity that began after World War II was perceived very differently by different business leaders.

Fear that a new depression might be coming caused the managements of Montgomery Ward and A & P to be reluctant to pay high prices for suburban locations for new stores, while Sears and Safeway plunged ahead with expansion into such areas, to which much of the most affluent population was now moving. In this case, those who gambled won and those who played it safe lost. In other cases under other circumstances, those who expanded met disaster. The W. T. Grant variety store chain, once one of the biggest retailers in America during the first half of the twentieth century, became in the 1970s one of the biggest bankruptcies in the history of the country, after financing a costly expansion which did not work out.

Grocery stores and department stores were not the only businesses presented with a radically changed environment as a result of the rapid increase of automobile ownership during the post-World War II boom and suburbanization. McDonald's fast-food restaurants were entirely a postwar phenomenon, going from one hamburger stand in southern California operated by the

McDonald brothers in 1955 to 4,000 nationwide just 20 years later and 8,000 a decade after that. Many of these McDonald's were built on highways or at other locations from which they could draw customers in automobiles from miles around.

In previous decades—from the 1920s into the 1950s—White Castle was the dominant hamburger chain in the country. People walked to White Castle hamburger stands, which meant that these stands had to be located in places with high population densities, so as to generate a large volume of pedestrian traffic into the restaurant, so that White Castle could sell to many people who came from a limited distance. Accordingly, White Castles were often located near factories or in crowded working class neighborhoods in central cities. And they stayed open around the clock.

Financing was also very different in this different era. Unlike later fast-food chains, White Castle did not have franchises. The company owned each restaurant and built new ones only when it had the money on hand to pay cash to do so. This enabled White Castle to ride out the Great Depression of the 1930s, when many other businesses, homes, and farms were lost because mortgages could not be paid at a time when money was so scarce. Indeed, White Castle expanded during the Depression. It was almost ideally adapted to the world in which it existed. But it lost its unchallenged leadership of the industry and began a decline into obscurity when the American economy and society changed around them in the middle of the century.

As middle-class and even working class people became more prosperous and moved out of the central cities into the suburbs, White Castle could no longer count on the heavy urban pedestrian traffic on which it had thrived. Its conservative financing policies meant that it could not expand as rapidly into the suburbs as other businesses which went into debt to do so or raised capital by requiring their franchisees to put up part of the money needed. The rising crime and violence of the central cities in the 1960s was more of a problem for White Castle than for other hamburger chains located on highways or in suburban shopping malls. Staying open all night in low-income urban neighborhoods was no longer safe, financially or otherwise.

At the heart of the changed environment for fast-food chains was the automobile. Unlike White Castle, McDonald's did not have to adapt to the world of the automobile, because Mcdonald's began in the part of the country where automobile ownership was most widespread—southern California—and was geared to that environment from the beginning. As automobile ownership and suburbanization spread across the country, so did McDonald's. By 1988, half of McDonald's sales were made at drive-through windows, which were capable of handling a car every 25 seconds, or well over a hundred per hour. As with the supermarkets, this represented extremely low costs of selling, enabling prices to be kept down to levels that were highly competitive. Drive-through restaurants in general require far less land per customer served than does a sit-down restaurant. This of course lowers the cost of doing business. Such economies enable prices to be kept down, while competition forces them to be kept down.

Just as neighborhood grocery stores, catering to pedestrian customers in central cities during the prewar era, were eclipsed in the postwar world by suburban supermarkets serving customers coming from miles around in their cars, so local fast food restaurants serving customers walking in off the street were surpassed—and sometimes forced out of business—by competition from drive-in fast food restaurants, serving people arriving in automobiles. By 1996, White Castle's sales were just one percent of McDonald's.

In a society that is constantly evolving, the conditions surrounding a given company or industry are always changing and not all business leaders are equally quick to spot the changes or grasp their implications. For example, the changing age-structure of the American population created a huge market for hamburgers as the baby boom generation reached adolescence and young adulthood. The number of Americans aged 18 to 24 years nearly doubled between 1960 and 1980, but then began to drop. Accordingly, the total number of hamburgers sold in the United States dropped for the first time in 1989.

LEADERSHIP

Given the importance of the human factor and the variability among people—or even with the same person at different times—it can hardly be surprising that dramatic changes in the relative positions of businesses have been the norm. In the nineteenth century, Montgomery Ward was the biggest retailer in the country at a time when Richard Sears was just a young railroad agent who sold watches on the side. Yet the small company that Sears founded grew over the years to eventually become several times the size of Montgomery Ward. Differences in management had much to do with the different fates of these two companies, long after both Aaron Montgomery Ward and Richard Warren Sears were gone.

Some business leaders are very good at some aspects of management and very weak in other aspects. The success of the business then depends on which aspects happen to be crucial at the particular time. Sometimes two executives with very different skills and weaknesses combine to produce a very successful management team, whereas either one of them might have failed completely if alone. Some executives are very successful during one era in the country's evolution, or during one period in their own lives, and very ineffective at a later time.

Sewell Avery, for example, was for many years a highly successful and widely praised leader of U. S. Gypsum and then of Montgomery Ward. Yet his last years were marked by public criticism and controversy over the way he ran Montgomery Ward, and by a bitter fight for control of the company that he was regarded as mismanaging. When he resigned as chief executive officer, the value of Montgomery Ward's stock rose immediately.

Neither individuals nor companies are successful forever. Death alone guarantees turnover in management. An A & P executive during its declining phase summarized its problems by saying: "The simple fact is that A & P had only one major management problem—the company was unable to replace Mr. John," the name long used inside the company for John Hartford, the last member of the founding family to run A & P. The decline of A & P began with his death. His successors could not simply continue his policies, for the whole retail grocery industry and the society around it were changing rapidly. "You cannot run a retail business from memory," John Hartford himself once remarked. What was needed after his death were not the particular policies and practices that were geared to his day. What was needed was the same kind of foresight, dedication, and imagination that had raised A & P to its pinnacle in the first place—and such talents are not readily available, certainly not continuously and indefinitely in one company.

Like so many other things, running a business looks easy from the outside. On the eve of the Bolshevik revolution, V. I. Lenin declared that "accounting and control" were the key factors in running an enterprise and that capitalism had already "reduced" management to "extraordinarily simple operations" that "any literate person can perform"—that is, "supervising and recording, knowledge of the four rules of arithmetic, and issuing appropriate receipts." Such "exceedingly simple operations of registration, filing and checking" can, according to Lenin, "easily be performed" by people receiving ordinary workmen's wages.

After just a few years in power, however, Lenin confronted a very different—and very bitter—reality. He himself wrote of a "fuel crisis" which "threatens to disrupt all Soviet work," of economic "ruin, starvation, and devastation" in the country and even admitted that peasant uprisings had become "a common occurrence" under Communist rule. In short, the economic functions which had seemed to easy and simple before having to perform them now loomed menacingly difficult. Now Lenin saw a need for people "who are versed in the art of administration" and admitted that "there is nowhere we can turn to for such people except the old class"—that is, the capitalist businessmen. In his address to the 1920 Communist Party Congress, Lenin warned his comrades: "Opinions on corporate management are all too frequently imbued with a spirit of sheer ignorance, an anti-expert bias." The apparent simplicities of just three years earlier now required experts. Thus began Lenin's New Economic Policy, which allowed more market activity, and under which the economy began to revive.

KNOWLEDGE AND DECISIONS

Knowledge is one of the scarcest of all resources. Glib generalities abound, but specific hard facts that are relevant to economic decisions are something entirely different. In some respects, governments are able to assemble vast amounts of knowledge, but the kind of knowledge involved is often in the form of statistical generalities or verbal generalities known as "expertise," while many economic decisions depend crucially on highly specific knowledge of particular things.

Central Planning

While many examples of the difficulties faced by government planning of economic activity have come from the Soviet Union, similar results have marked the history of similar efforts in other countries. One of the classic disasters of government planning involved the British government's attempts to grow peanuts in colonial Rhodesia after World War II. Yet ordinary farmers around the world had been deciding for generations where and how to grow peanuts, each on his own particular land, whose individual characteristics were known directly from personal experience. Even a single acre of land usually has variations in its chemical composition and its slope, which determines how water runs off after a rainfall, and may vary as well in the degree to which is it shaded by trees, hills, or other things. All this affects what will grow best where.

No officials sitting in London could know land in Africa so intimately. Even a trip to Rhodesia by "experts" could not find out the widely varying qualities of the soil from place to place the way each farmer could on his own plot of land, much less understand all the insects, birds, animals, and rainfall patterns in various localities and what effect they might have on the peanut crop. Yet even an illiterate farmer would almost automatically know such things from experience on his own farm.

Theoretically, the experts could ask each individual farmer in Rhodesia about such things. But, aside from the improbability of experts with university degrees deferring to farmers with much less formal schooling, the accurate transmission of knowledge would depend crucially on how articulate and precise these farmers were in what they said. Since verbal precision is hardly universal, even among highly educated people, this would be a very chancy way to gather information.

A price-coordinated economy does not depend on anything so fragile. Each farmer decides individually whether or not to grow peanuts—and how many—at the prices that peanuts can be sold for in the marketplace. These prices are a much more accurate means of communication because each farmer and each buyer of peanuts knows that one mistake in weighing all the various factors can spell economic disaster. When it is no longer a question of talking to strangers, but of protecting your own economic future, there should be no surprise that markets generally work better than government planning.

In the Soviet Union as well, what was lacking was not expertise but highly specific knowledge. There were Soviet economists who were as much aware of the same general principles as Western economists. What the U.S.S.R. did not have were decision-making individuals with the same range of hard facts at their disposal. Power and knowledge were separated in the Soviet Union, as in all centrally planned economies.

Enterprise managers knew what the specific equipment, personnel, and supplies at their disposal could and could not do, but central planners in Moscow did not—and it was the central planners who held the power to make the ultimate decisions. Nor could the central planners possibly be sufficiently knowledgeable about all the industries, technologies, and products under their command to be able to determine what would be best for each, independently of what the respective enterprise managers told them. Central planners could be skeptical of the self-serving statements and demands of the enterprise managers, but skepticism is not knowledge. Moreover, changing circumstances would almost inevitably be known first to the local managers on the scene and often much later, if at all, to the central planners, who had far too many industries and products to oversee to be able keep up with day-to-day changes for them all.

A price-coordinated economy may have no more total knowledge over all than a centrally-planned economy, but that knowledge is distributed very differently, as is decision-making power. When the owner of gas station located on a highway sees that the highways is being torn up for repairs, he knows to order less gasoline than usual from his supplier, because there will not be nearly as much traffic going past his station as before, at least until the repair is completed. This local gas station owner does not need the permission of anybody to change how much gasoline he orders or what hours he will stay open. The knowledge and the power are combined in the same person. Moreover, that person is operating under the incentives and constraints inherent in the prospect of profits and the threat of losses, rather than under orders from distant bureaucrats. Nor is this peculiar to gas stations. The same instant and local decision-making power by those with the facts before their eyes is common throughout a price-coordinated market economy. That is one of its advantages over a centrally-planned economy and one of the factors behind the enormous differences in results between the two kinds of economies.

Agents

As a scarce resource, knowledge can be bought and sold in various ways in a market economy. The hiring of agents is essentially the purchase of the agent's knowledge to guide one's own decisions. Real estate agents commonly charge 6 percent of the sale price of a home and literary agents typically charge 15 percent of a writer's royalties. Why would a writer surrender 15 percent of his royalties, unless 85 percent of what the agent can get for him is worth more than 100 percent of what he can get for himself? And why would a publisher be willing to pay more to an agent than to a writer for the same manuscript? Similarly, why would a home-owner accept 6 percent less for his house when sold through a real estate agent, unless the agent could either get a higher price or a quicker sale, both of which amount to the same thing, since delay and its accompanying stresses are both costs to the home-owner?

Let's go back to a basic principle of economics: The same physical object does not necessarily have the same value to different people. This applies to an author's manuscript as well as to a house, a painting or an autograph from a rock star. What a literary agent knows is where a particular manuscript is likely to have its greatest value. If it is a cookbook, the agent knows which publishers and which editors have the knowledge and the connections to promote such a book in places that are very interested in such things—gourmet magazines, cooking programs on television, and the like. This cookbook would be far more valuable to such editors and publishers than to others who specialize in technology, social issues, or other subjects, or to editors whose knowledge of food does not extend much beyond hamburgers and fried chicken. Even if an agent is not able to get any more money out of a given publisher than a writer could have gotten, the agent knows which publishers are most likely to pay top dollar for a given book, because that particular publisher can probably sell more copies.

A real estate agent is similarly more knowledgeable than the average home-owner as to the channels through which a given home can be marketed most quickly and for the highest sale price. Often there are little defects in the home that need to corrected, or cosmetic changes that need to be made, before the house goes on the market. An agent who keeps up with changing fashions in houses is not only more likely to know what these things are but also whether or to what extent money spent upgrading the house will be recouped in a higher sale price or whether it is better to sell the house "as is" as a bargain "fixer-upper." The agent is also more likely to be knowledgeable as to which particular contractors are more reliable or more reasonable in price for doing whatever repairs or remodelling are called for, as well as which financial institutions are best to deal with for the buyer and seller of this particular house. Therefore, the same house is likely to bring in more money when sold through a real estate agent, just as a writer's manuscript is likely to sell for more through a literary agent.

Franchises

Knowledge is shared in both directions when hotels, restaurants and other businesses are franchised. The knowledge offered by the chain that does the franchising is based on its experience with similar businesses in various locations around the country. It is also likely to be more knowledgeable about where and how to advertise and how to deal with suppliers. However, the local franchisee is likely to be more knowledgeable about things that only someone on the scene can know—the local labor market, changes in the surrounding community and of course all the details that have to be monitored on the premises day to day.

Chains and franchises are not synonymous. The first great hamburger chain—the chain that put the hamburger on the map in the 1920s—was the White Castle chain, which owned all of its hundreds of restaurants. Its top management, however, had much local experience before going regional and then national—and they made many visits to their local outlets to keep in touch. The era of the franchised restaurant chain began with Howard Johnson in the 1930s and the heyday of franchised hamburger stands began with McDonald's in the 1950s. By and large, franchises have been more successful in these fields. By 1990, more than one-third of all revenues from retail sales of goods and services in the United States went to franchise outlets. Nearly three-quarters of all revenues from hotels and motels were earned by those affiliated with chains.

EFFICIENCY AND ITS IMPLICATIONS

Economics is not about the fate of particular companies. It is about the fate of the economy and of the standard of living that depends on that economy's performance. Competition in a price-coordinated economy ends up with most people getting most of their goods and services from whatever companies best supply what they want at prices they are willing to pay—whether those companies happen to be Sears and A & P in one era or Wal-Mart and Safeway in another era.

Keeping prices down usually means keeping costs of production and distribution down. Huge volumes of sales help do both. Production costs are reduced when the fixed overhead costs can be spread out over a large volume of output, adding little to the cost of each individual item. Scheduling also affects production costs. When a high-volume retailer signs a contract for a large order from a given manufacturer, that manufacturer can then schedule the work evenly throughout the year. This avoids the additional costs that go with ups and downs in the orders that come in unpredictably from the market, leaving the manufacturer's workforce idle during some weeks and working overtime during others. When there are long lay-offs during a slack period, some of the workers may take other jobs and not come back when business picks up again, making it necessary to hire replacements and spend time training them—all of which costs money and adds to the costs of the goods being produced.

Because of the savings made possible by advance scheduling of large orders, high-volume retailers have been able to sign contracts on terms that enable them to buy goods from the manufacturer at prices lower than those charged to others. This is a net benefit to both the producer and the retailer. More importantly, it is a benefit to the economy as a whole, by getting the most output from scarce resources which have alternative uses.

The fact that profits are contingent on efficiency in producing what consumers want, at a price that consumers are willing to pay—and that losses are an ever-present threat if a business fails to do provide that—explains much of the economic prosperity found in economies that operate under free market competition. Profits as a realized end-result are crucial to the individual business, but it is the *prospect* of profits—and the threat of losses—that is crucial to the functioning of the economy as a whole. For the economy as a whole, profits are a minor item, about 10 percent of what the American economy produces. But it is a major item as an incentive to efficiency in producing the other 90 percent.

People in other countries with different economic systems may work very hard for longer hours than most Americans and yet end up with far less to show for their efforts. The back-breaking toil of Third World farmers seldom produces the prosperity enjoyed by Americans working in air-conditioned offices with a relaxed work pace and coffee breaks. Efficiency is the difference between having the necessities, comforts and amenities of high-income countries and suffering the hunger and deprivations too often found in poorer countries.

Some of these economic differences are due to technology, to education or to other favorable or unfavorable geographic or historical conditions, but much of it is due to having a price-coordinated economy with strong financial incentives to decision-makers to be right and ruthless elimination of those whose decisions turn out to be mistaken too often.

MARKET VERSUS NON-MARKET ECONOMIES

Although economics is often thought of as dealing with how individuals and businesses make money, in reality it is the study of how a whole society uses scarce resources that have alternative uses. Economics is about how a society economizes and how individuals share, without even being aware of sharing. However important money may be to individuals, to society as a whole money is just green pieces of paper printed by the government and used to enable markets to allocate resources through prices.

There are many other possible ways of allocating resources, and many of these alternatives are particularly attractive to those with political power. However, none of these alternative ways of organizing an economy has matched the track record of economies where prices direct what resources go where and in what quantities.

The collapse of communism in Eastern Europe was only the most dramatic example of the failure of economies where resources are allocated by those with political power, rather than through market prices determined by what millions of other people know and want. Anyone who saw East Berlin and West Berlin, during the years when communism prevailed in the eastern part of the city and a market economy in the rest of it, could not help noticing the sharp contrast between the prosperity of West Berlin and the poverty in East Berlin. Indeed, it was hard to avoid being shocked by it, especially since people of the same race, language, culture and history lived in both parts of this city.

Perhaps the most decisive evidence of the role of profit as an incentive is the record of socialist economies which have eliminated it. The sums of money saved by eliminating profits have failed to lower prices and make the consuming public better off, because the absence of incentives has allowed many inefficiencies to go unchecked and technological and organizational changes to lag.

Monopoly is the enemy of efficiency, whether under capitalism or socialism. The difference between the two systems is that monopoly is the norm under socialism. Even in a mixed economy, with some economic activities being carried out by government and others being carried out by private industry, the government's activities are typically monopolies, while those in the private marketplace are typically activities carried out by rival enterprises.

Thus, when a hurricane, flood, or other natural disaster strikes an area, emergency aid usually comes both from the Federal Emergency Management Agency (FEMA) and from private insurance companies whose customers' homes and property have been damaged or destroyed. FEMA has been notoriously slower and less efficient than the private insurance companies. Allstate cannot afford to be slower in getting money into the hands of its policy-holders than State Farm is in getting money to the people who hold its policies. Not only would existing customers in the disaster area be likely to switch insurance companies if one dragged its feet in getting money to them, while their neighbors received substantial advances from a different insurance company to tide them over, word of any such difference would spread like wildfire across the country, causing millions of people elsewhere to switch billions of dollars worth of insurance business from the less efficient company to the more efficient one.

A government agency, however, faces no such pressure. No matter how much FEMA may be criticized or ridiculed for its failure to get aid to disaster victims in a timely fashion, there is no rival government agency that these people can turn to for the same service. Moreover, the people who run these agencies are paid according to a fixed salary schedules, not by how quickly or how well they serve people hit by disaster.

Inertia is common to people under both capitalism and socialism. In the early twentieth century, both Sears and Montgomery Ward were reluctant to begin operating out of stores, after decades of great success selling from their mail order catalogs. It was only when the 1920s brought competition from chain stores that cut into their profits and caused red ink to start appearing on the bottom line that they had no choice but to become chain stores themselves. (In 1920, Ward lost nearly $10 million and Sears was $44 million in debt.) Under socialism, they could have remained mail order retailers and there would have been little incentive for the government to pay to set up rival chain stores to complicate everyone's life.

Henry Ford likewise wanted to keep on doing what he had always done—producing the same standard model car, year after year, painted just one color (black). But, when a new company named General Motors started changing the styling of their cars and painting them different colors, the Ford Motor company started losing customers and GM replaced Ford as the number one auto maker in the industry. Only then did Ford automobiles begin to change their styling and become available in whatever colors the customers wanted.

Socialist and capitalist economies differ not only in the quantity of output they produce but also in the quality. Everything from cars and cameras to restaurant service and airline service were of notoriously low quality in the Soviet Union. Nor was this a happenstance. The incentives are radically different when the producer has to satisfy the consumer, in order to survive financially, than when the test of survivability is carrying out production quotas set by central planners. The consumer is going to look not only at quantity but quality. But a central planning commission is too overwhelmed with the millions of products they oversee to be able to monitor much more than gross output.

That this low quality is a result of incentives, rather than being due to traits peculiar to Russians or other Eastern Europeans, is shown by the quality deterioration that has taken place in the United States or Western Europe when free market prices are replaced by rent control or other forms of price controls and government allocation. While some businesses can and do cut corners on quality in a free market, they do so at the risk of their survival. The great financial success stories in American industry have often involved companies almost fanatical about maintaining the reputation of their products, even when these products have been quite inexpensive.

McDonald's built its reputation on a standardized hamburger and maintained quality by having its own inspectors make unannounced visits to its meat suppliers in the middle of the night, to see what was being put into the meat it was buying. Colonel Sanders was notorious for showing up unexpectedly at Kentucky Fried Chicken restaurants. If he didn't like the way the chickens were being cooked, he would dump them all into a garbage can, put on an apron, and proceed to cook some chickens himself, to demonstrate how he wanted it done. His protegé Dave Thomas later followed similar practices when he created his own chain of Wendy's hamburger stands. Although Colonel Sanders and Dave Thomas could not be everywhere in a nationwide chain, no local franchise owner could take a chance on seeing his profits being thrown into a garbage can by the head honcho of the chain.

Quality control is of course even more important to financial success with more expensive products and services. The producers of Linhof cameras—costing thousands of dollars each—not only buy their lenses from the world's leading optical companies, they also subject each individual lens put on one of their cameras to their own tests and standards, even though these lenses have already passed tests made by the manufacturers. Linhof's standards are sufficiently more stringent that an identical make and model of lens on a Linhof camera sells for a higher price, both new and used, than the same lens sells for when bought independently. Even if the lens is being bought to be put on another camera, the fact that it came off a Linhof brings a higher price than the identical model of lens by the identical manufacturer that did not come from a Linhof.

Behind all of this is the basic fact that a business is selling not only a physical product, but also the reputation which surrounds that product. Motorists traveling in an unfamiliar part of the country are more likely to turn into a hamburger stand that has a McDonald's or Wendy's sign on it than one that does not. That reputation translates into dollars and cents—or, in this case, millions and billions of dollars. People with that kind of money at stake are unlikely to be very tolerant of anyone who would compromise their reputation. Ray Kroc, the founder of the McDonald's chain, would explode in anger if he found a McDonald's parking lot littered.

When speaking of quality in this context, what matters is the kind of quality that is relevant to the particular clientele being served. Hamburgers and fried chicken may not be regarded by others as either gourmet food or health food, nor can a nationwide chain mass-producing such meals reach quality levels achievable by more distinctive, fancier, and pricier restaurants. What the chain can do is assure quality within the limits expected by their particular customers.

What is called "capitalism" might more accurately be called consumerism. It is the consumers who call the tune, and those capitalists who want to remain capitalists have to learn to dance to it. The twentieth century began with high hopes for replacing the competition of the marketplace by a more efficient and more humane economy, planned and controlled by government in the interests of the people. However, by the end of the century, all such efforts were so thoroughly discredited by their actual results in countries around the world that even Communist nations abandoned central planning, while socialist governments in democratic nations began selling off government-run enterprises, whose losses were a heavy burden to the taxpayers.

Privatization was embraced as a principle by such conservative governments as those of Prime Minister Margaret Thatcher in Britain and President Ronald Reagan in the United States. But the most decisive evidence for the efficiency of the marketplace was that even those who were philosophically opposed to capitalism turned back towards it after seeing what happens when industry and commerce operate without the guidance of prices, profits and losses.

WINNERS AND LOSERS

Many people who appreciate the prosperity created by market economies may nevertheless lament the fact that particular individuals, groups, industries, or regions of the country do not share in the general economic advances, or some may even be worse off than before. Political leaders or candidates are especially likely to deplore the inequity of it all and to propose various government actions to "correct" the situation.

Whatever the merits or demerits of various political proposals, what must be kept in mind when evaluating them is that the good fortunes and misfortunes of different sectors of the economy may be closely related as cause and effect—and that preventing bad effects may prevent good effects. It was not accidental that Smith Corona was losing millions of dollars on its typewriters while Dell was making millions on its computers. It was not accidental that Safeway surged to the top of the grocery business while A & P fell from its peak to virtual oblivion. It was not accidental that coal-mining regions suffered economic declines with the rise of alternative fuel sources.

The efficient allocation of scarce resources which have alternative uses means that some must lose their ability to use those resources, in order that others can gain the ability to use them. Smith-Corona had to be *prevented* from using scarce resources, including both materials and labor, to make typewriters, when those resources could be used to produce computers that the public wanted more. Nor was this a matter of anyone's fault. No matter how fine the typewriters made by Smith-Corona and or how skilled and conscientious its employees, typewriters were no longer what the public wanted after they had the option to achieve the same end result—and more—with computers.

Scarcity implies that resources must be taken from some places, in order to go to other places. Few individuals or businesses are going to want to give up what they have been used to doing, especially if they have been successful at it, for the greater good of society as a whole. But, in one way or another, under any economic or political system, they are going to have to be forced to relinquish resources and change what they themselves are doing, if rising standards of living are to be achieved and sustained.

The financial pressures of the free market are just one of the ways in which this can be done. Kings or commissars could instead simply order individuals and enterprises to change from doing *A* to doing *B*. No doubt other ways of pursuing the same goals are possible, with varying degrees of effectiveness and efficiency. What is crucial, however, is that it must be done. Put differently, the fact that some people, regions, or industries are being "left behind" or are not getting their "fair share" of the general prosperity is not necessarily a problem with a political solution, as abundant as such proposed solutions may be, especially in election years.

PART III:
WORK AND PAY

Chapter 9

Productivity and Pay

Do you pay your secretaries less than your engineers because you like the engineers better, or because the secretaries don't need the dough?

-Thomas W. Hazlett

So far, we have been discussing the prices of goods—present and future, consumer goods and capital goods. But people are part of the economy too, and not just as consumers. People are a key part of the inputs which produce output. Since most people are not volunteers, they must either be forced to work or paid to work, since the work has to be done in any case, if we are to live at all, much less enjoy the various amenities that go into our modern standard of living. In a free society, people are paid to work.

Simple as this may seem, its implications are often not fully understood or accepted. The very idea of buying and selling human labor is vaguely unsettling. The Clayton Act declared in its preamble: "The labor of a human being is not a commodity or article of commerce." Perhaps the long history of slavery, which has plagued the human race on every inhabited continent, has left this uneasiness with the idea of selling human labor, or even renting it. Nevertheless, most Americans earn their livings by renting their time and talents—and live much better than people in many other countries where most adults own their own land and work only for themselves.

Stories about the astronomical pay of athletes, movie stars, or chief executives of corporations often cause journalists and others to question how much this or that person is "really" worth.

Fortunately, since we know from Chapter 2 that there is no such thing as "real" worth, we can save all the energy that others put into such unanswerable questions. Instead, we can ask a more down-to-earth question. What determines how much people get paid for their work? To this question there is a very down-to-earth answer: Supply and Demand. However, that is just the beginning. Why does supply and demand cause one individual to earn more than another?

Workers would obviously like to get the highest pay possible and employers would like to pay the least possible. Only where there is overlap between what is offered and what is acceptable can anyone be hired. But why does that overlap take place at a pay rate that is several times as high for an engineer as for a messenger?

Messengers would of course like to be paid what engineers are paid, but there is too large a supply of people capable of being messengers to force the employer to raise his offer to that level. Because it takes a long time to train an engineer and not everyone is capable of mastering such training, there is no such abundance of engineers relative to the demand. That is the supply side of the story. But what determines the demand for labor? What determines the limit of what an employer is willing to pay?

It is not merely the fact that engineers are scarce that makes them valuable. It is what an engineer can add to a company's earnings that makes an employer willing to bid for his services—and sets the limit to how high the bids can go. An engineer who added $100,000 to a company's earnings and asked for a $200,000 salary would not be hired. On the other hand, if the engineer added a quarter of a million dollars to a company's earnings, it would pay to hire him at $200,000.

The term "productivity" is sometimes used loosely to describe an employee's contribution to a company's earnings. The problem is that this word is also defined in other ways and sometimes the implication is left that each worker has a certain "productivity" that is inherent in that worker, rather than being dependent on surrounding circumstances as well. A worker using the latest modern equipment can produce more output than the very same worker employed in another firm whose equipment is not quite as up-to-date or whose management does not have things organized as well.

The same principle applies outside what we normally think of as economic activities. In baseball, a slugger gets more chances to hit home runs if he is batting ahead of another slugger. But, if the batter hitting after him is not much of a home run threat, pitchers are more likely to walk the slugger in a tight situation, so that he will get fewer opportunities to hit home runs over the course of a season.

Ted Williams, for example, had one of the highest percentages of home runs—in proportion to his times at bat—in the history of baseball, but he had only one season when he hit as many as 40 homers, because he was walked as often as 162 times a season—averaging more than one walk per game, during the era of the 154-game season. By contrast, when Roger Maris hit 61 home runs in 1961, breaking the existing record, he was walked less than a hundred times because Mickey Mantle was batting right after him and Mantle hit 54 home runs that season. There was no percentage in walking Maris to pitch to Mantle with one more man on base. Maris' productivity as a home-run hitter was greater because he batted with Mickey Mantle in the on-deck circle.

In virtually all jobs, the quality of the equipment, management and other workers goes into determining a given worker's productivity. Movie stars like to have good supporting actors, good make-up artists and good directors, all of whom enhance the star's performance. Scholars depend heavily on their research assistants and generals rely on their staffs, as well as their troops, to win battles.

Whatever the source of a given individual's productivity, that productivity determines the upper limit of how far an employer will go in bidding for that person's services. That is the demand side of the equation.

Employers seldom bid as much as they would if they had to, because there are other individuals willing and able to supply the same services for less. By the same token, consumers would pay a lot more for their food than they do, if there were no competing sellers and their only choice was to pay what a monopolist charged or starve. In short, it is the *combination* of supply and demand which determines pay, as it determines the prices of goods and services in general.

Just as we can better understand the role of prices in general when we see what happens when prices are not allowed to function, so we can understand the role of workers' pay by seeing what happens when that pay is not allowed to vary with supply and demand. In Europe, for example, minimum wage laws set pay scales much higher than such laws do in the United States. The net result is that only those workers whose productivity is at this higher level are likely to be hired or retained. Younger, less experienced and otherwise less productive workers simply are not hired to the extent that they are in the United States. Just as government-imposed higher prices for agricultural produce under New Deal farm programs (designed to help farmers) led to a surplus of unsold farm products, so today's government-imposed higher prices for labor in Europe has led to unsold labor—that is, unemployment rates roughly double those in the United States.

FORMS OF PAYMENT

When we think of people being paid for their work, we usually think of someone drawing a paycheck every week or month for putting in a certain amount of hours on the job. But that is only one of the ways people get paid.

Shoeshine boys get paid every time they shine a pair of shoes and doctors get paid every time a patient visits their offices. Farmers get paid when they sell their crops. Business owners get whatever is left over from their sales after they have paid their employees, creditors, tax collectors, etc.—and the amount left can be either positive or negative. Oil prospectors may lose money far more times than they make any, but the size of the profits when they strike oil can cover all the losses before then. If not, people would stop prospecting for oil.

These and other ways of compensating people's efforts can be broken down into two broad categories—fixed guarantees of payment and variable chances of payment. Wages and salaries are usually fixed guarantees. Those who work for an employer expect to be paid what they were promised, regardless of whether the business is operating at a profit or a loss. If the business issues stocks and bonds, then those who buy bonds expect to receive a fixed amount, just like the employees, regardless of how well or how badly the business is going, while those who buy stocks may get nothing if things are going badly and can get very lucrative dividends if business is booming.

By and large, those with guarantees receive less money than those who take their chances. If the business goes bankrupt, not only does the stockholder not get any dividends, he also loses whatever money he paid for the stock, which now becomes worthless paper. The bondholder, however, is legally entitled to a share of whatever assets the bankrupt business has left when it closes down. It is hardly surprising then that, in normal times, stockholders usually receive a higher rate of return than bondholders. They are taking a bigger risk and are being compensated for that risk. Otherwise, no one would buy stocks when bonds are safer.

As in other areas of economics, the facts are fairly simple and straightforward, but the fallacies get very complicated. One of the most widespread fallacies is that only fixed payments are "real" costs of producing goods and services. There is thought to be something illegitimate about the money earned by such risk-bearing people as speculators. Profits in general have been seen by some people as something arbitrarily added on to the "real" costs of producing things.

However, the fact that a payment is variable and risky does not mean that it is any less necessary to cause things to get produced. While someone may go into business and work long and hard with no income to show for it, that will continue to happen only in so far as enough people make enough money in such activities to attract others willing to put forth the efforts and take the risks.

Even if profits are a necessary cost of producing things, how do we know that the amount of those profits is not "too much"? The same way we know that a worker is not receiving "too much"—namely that, if someone else were willing to do his job for less, the employer would not be paying him as much as he gets.

Although profit levels are not decided by anyone—it is simply what is left over after paying other costs—the same principle applies. If one company can manufacture widgets for $10 each and sell them for $12, making $2 gross profit on each, anybody who can manufacture them for $9 dollars each will be able to make more gross profit, whether by selling them for the same $12 and having more gross profit left over or by selling the same product for $11 and making more gross profit by taking away some of their competitor's customers with lower prices. In either case, they earn their money by satisfying customers at lower costs of production. What this means from the standpoint of the economy as a whole is that they are using fewer of society's resources to get the same job done.

If profits were nothing more than an arbitrary overcharge, then things produced by organizations that do not make a profit would be cheaper than things produced by organizations that do. In reality, one of the largest organizations that does not make a profit—government—usually produces things at a higher cost than private, profit-making businesses. Many activities engaged in by state, local, or national governments have been contracted out in recent years to private businesses precisely because these businesses do the job cheaper, whether that job is collecting garbage or running prisons.

There are fairly straightforward reasons for this. A private entrepreneur whose own income depends on how much is left over after paying the costs of production has far more incentive to operate efficiently, in order to keep those production costs low, than does a government official on a fixed salary. Often, government officials are paid according to their level of responsibility—which is to say, according to how many people they supervise and how large a budget they administer. Under these circumstances, the more people they use and the more money they spend to achieve a given goal, the easier it will be for them to obtain promotion to a level with higher pay. Since the incentives facing a private business owner and those facing a government official are so different, it should not be surprising that the results likewise tend to be very different.

PAY DIFFERENCES

Wages and salaries serve the same economic purposes as other prices—that is, they guide the utilization of scarce resources which have alternative uses. Yet because these scarce resources are human beings, we tend to look on wages and salaries differently. Often we ask questions that are quite emotionally powerful, even if they are logically meaningless. For example: Are the wages "fair"? Are the workers "exploited."? Is this "a living wage"?

Such questions seldom get asked about the prices of inanimate things, such as a can of peas or a share of stock in General Motors. But people are believed to be entitled to pay that is "fair," even if no one can define what that means. "Exploitation" and "a living wage" are likewise emotionally powerful expressions without concrete meanings. If a worker is living, how can he be receiving less than "a living wage"—unless he is, as some have said thoughtlessly, "living below subsistence"?

No one likes to see fellow human beings living in poverty and squalor, and many are prepared to do something about it, as shown by the vast billions of dollars that Americans donate to a wide range of charities every year, on top of the additional billions spent by federal, state, and local governments in an attempt to better the condition of less fortunate people. These socially important activities occur alongside an economy coordinated by prices, but the two things serve different purposes.

Attempts to make prices, including the prices of people's labor and talents, be something other than signals to guide resources to their most valued uses, make those prices less effective for their basic purpose, on which the prosperity of the whole society depends. Ultimately, it is economic prosperity that makes it possible for hundreds of billions of dollars to be devoted to helping the less fortunate. It is also economic prosperity which allows people born into poverty to rise to economic heights undreamed of by their parents or perhaps even by themselves.

INCOME "DISTRIBUTION"

Nothing is more straightforward and easy to understand than the fact that some people earn more than others, for a variety of reasons. Some people are simply older than others, for example, and their additional years have given them opportunities to acquire more experience, skills, formal education and on-the-job-training—all of which allows them to do a given job more efficiently or to take on more complicated jobs that would be overwhelming for a beginner or for someone with limited experience or training. With the passing years, older individuals may also become more knowledgeable about job opportunities, while more other people may become more aware of them and their abilities. These and other commonsense reasons for income differences among individuals are often lost sight of in abstract discussions of the ambiguous term "income distribution."

Most income is of course not distributed at all, in the sense in which newspapers, milk, or Social Security checks are distributed from some central place. Most income is distributed only in the statistical sense in which there is a distribution of heights in a population—some people being 5 foot 4 inches tall, others 6 foot 2 inches, etc.—but none of these heights were sent out from some central location. Yet it is all too common to read journalists and others discussing how "society" *distributes* its income, rather than saying in plain English that some people make more money than others.

More is involved than a misleading metaphor. Often the very units in which income differences are discussed are as misleading as the metaphor. Family income or household income are not like individual income. An individual always means the same thing—one person—but the sizes of families and households differ substantially from one time period to another, from one racial or ethnic group to another, and from one income bracket to another. For example, there are 39 million people in the bottom 20 percent of households, but 64 million people in the top 20 percent of households. Although many people assume that these quintiles represent dividing the country into "five equal layers," as two economists have misstated it, there is nothing equal about these layers. They represent grossly different numbers of people.

These differences in the sizes of families and households are not incidental. They radically change the meaning of "income distribution" statistics that are thrown around in the media and in politics. For example, real income per American household rose only 6 percent over the entire period from 1969 to 1996, but real per capita income rose 51 percent over the same period. The average size of families and households was simply declining, so that smaller households were now earning about the same as larger households had earned a generation earlier.

As so often happens, the facts are not complicated, but misunderstandings abound nevertheless. A *Washington Post* writer, for example, declared in 1998 that "the incomes of most American households have remained stubbornly flat over the past three decades." It would be more accurate to say that some writers have remained stubbornly blind to economic facts. When two people in one household today earn the same total amount of money that three people were earning in that household in the past, that is a 50 percent increase in income per person—even when household income remains the same.

It is equally misleading to compare high-income families or households with low income families and households. There are more people per family in upper income families compared to lower income families—and more of those people work. That is part of the reason for some families having higher incomes than others. It is not uncommon for families in the top 20 percent of income-earners to supply several times as many man-hours of work per year as families in the bottom 20 percent. Many of the latter work very little or not at all, whether due to illness, retirement, single mothers raising children on welfare, or for other reasons. Yet plain facts like these are often omitted by those who speak and write of how "society" unequally or unfairly "distributes" its income. A closer look at these households reveals that those in the top quintile contain more than 40 million people of working age—18 to 64 years of age —while the bottom quintile contains fewer than 20 million people in such age brackets.

Perhaps the most radical difference between individual and family or household statistics are those used when comparing different American racial or ethnic groups. For example, real income per black household rose only 7 percent in the two decades from 1967 to 1988, but real per capita income among blacks rose 81 percent over those very same years. Average black household size was simply declining during these decades, so that a substantial increase in real income per person appeared statistically as a trivially small increase per household. Moreover, because black household size was declining more sharply than white household size, black incomes appeared to be falling behind white incomes when household statistics were used, but were in fact rising faster than white incomes when individual statistics are examined.

For both blacks and whites, rising prosperity was one reason for more people to be able to go set up their own individual households, instead of continuing to live with parents or as roomers or by sharing an apartment with a roommate. Yet these consequences of prosperity generate household statistics that are widely used to suggest that there has been no real economic progress.

Among individuals in the general population, age makes a big difference is income—and a huge difference in wealth. Inexperienced young people beginning their careers in their twenties seldom make as much money as their parents who are in their forties and fifties. Having just begun to work, these younger workers are usually not as valuable as older and more experienced people. Having just begun to save, they are likely to have much less money in the bank or in a pension fund, as compared to their parents, who have been saving for decades and acquiring other assets for decades.

Although people in the top income brackets and the bottom income brackets—"the rich" and "the poor," as they are commonly called —may be discussed as if they were different classes of people, often they are the very same people at different stages of their lives. An absolute majority of the people in the bottom 20 percent in income in 1975 were also in the top 20 percent at some point over the next 17 years.

This is not surprising. After 17 years, people usually have had 17 years more experience, perhaps including on-the-job training or formal education. It would be surprising if they were not able to earn more money as a result. It is not uncommon for most of the people in the top 5 percent of income-earners to be 45 years old and up.

Although people in upper income brackets are often characterized as "rich," in reality a family or household can reach the top 10 percent with incomes that fall far short of what truly wealthy people make. As of 1998, a household income of $75,000 a year was enough to put the people in that household in the top 10 percent. A couple making $38,000 each hardly seems like "the rich." Even the top 5 percent of households could be reached with a combined income of $133,000—comfortable, but hardly in the same category as millionaires and billionaires.

Even people in the top one percent in wealth bear little resemblance to "the idle rich" conjured up in popular legend or ideological rhetoric. The average person in the top one percent works 52 hours a week. At the other end of the scale, more than half of all those in the bottom 20 percent do not have a full-time job.

Another common statistical illusion comes from determining whether "inequality" is increasing or decreasing by comparing the incomes of those in the top 20 percent with the incomes of those in the bottom 20 percent. Nothing is easier to find than media and academic proclamations that the difference between incomes in these top and bottom brackets has grown wider over the years. Even when the changes are only of a few percentage points, there may be much hand-wringing and moral indignation. However, if our concern is not with statistical categories but with flesh-and-blood human beings, then we must focus not on brackets but on the people who are constantly moving in and out of those brackets.

Fewer than 3 percent of those in the bottom 20 percent in 1975 were still there in 1991, while 39 percent of them were now in the top 20 percent. Most of "the poor" of the 1970s had reached higher real income levels in the 1990s than most of the whole American population had in the 1970s. To compare the current incomes of these now "rich" people with the current incomes of the currently "poor" ignores the likelihood that today's "poor" will continue to repeat this pattern and be even more prosperous in 2010 than our current top 20 percent are today.

Time has an even stronger effect on the accumulation of wealth. The average amount of wealth held by people in the older age brackets is usually several times the amount held by people in their twenties. But these are not the kind of enduring economic differences we usually have in mind when we talk about classes. People in their forties or fifties are not a different class from people in their twenties, because all forty-year-olds were once twenty-year-olds and all twenty-year-olds are going to be forty-year-olds, unless they die prematurely. Not only are most of them likely to be both "rich" and "poor" at different stages of their lives, even at a given moment many of the low-income people are the children of high-income people—and their heirs.

Genuinely rich and genuinely poor people exist—people who are going to be living in luxury or in poverty all their lives—but they are much rarer than gross income statistics would suggest, when these statistics are not broken down by age. The turnover was huge in all income brackets in just 17 years, less than half of most people's working life.

Just as most American "poor" do not stay poor, so most rich Americans were not born rich but only achieved wealth at some point in their own lifetimes. Moreover, the genuinely rich are nearly as rare as the genuinely poor. Even if we take a million dollars in net worth as our criterion for being rich, only about 3.5 percent of Americans are at that level at a given time. This is in fact a fairly modest level, given that net worth counts everything from household goods and clothing to the total amount of money in an individual's pension fund. Nevertheless, the genuinely rich and the genuinely poor, put together, add up to less than 7 percent of the American people, even though political rhetoric might suggest that we are all either "haves" or "have nots."

While, in some senses, those who are called "the poor" are not as badly off as instantaneous statistics might suggest, in other respects they are worse off. They must often pay higher prices for inferior goods and services, because of the higher costs of delivering those goods and services to low-income neighborhoods. As already noted in Chapter 6, a suburban supermarket has lower costs of delivering groceries to its customers than does a typical neighborhood store in the inner city, and that translates into higher prices charged to low-income customers than to high-income customers. Similarly, banks serving middle-class people have lower costs per transaction than institutions serving people in poverty, such as pawnshops or check-cashing agencies.

It does not cost a hundred times as much to process a $5,000 loan to an affluent person as it does to make a $50 loan to someone in poverty. Cashing a check for an affluent person whose employment and credit history is known to the bank, and who has had an account in the bank for years, is much less risky than cashing a check for someone who walks in off the street into a check-cashing agency in a low-income neighborhood and who probably does not have a bank account or perhaps even a permanent job. Thus affluent people have their checks cashed free of charge in their banks and receive bank loans at a lower interest rate than those charged the poor by pawn shops of other sources of credit that will take a chance on them. Being poor is expensive. Fortunately, most Americans do not remain poor very long.

JOB DISCRIMINATION

While pay differences often reflect differences in skills, experience, or willingness to do hard or dangerous work, they may also reflect discrimination against particular segments of society, such as ethnic minorities, women, lower castes, or other groups. However, in order to determine whether there is discrimination or how severe it is, we need to define what we mean.

Sometimes discrimination is defined as judging individuals from different groups by different standards when hiring, paying or promoting. In its severest form, this can mean refusal to hire at all. "No Irish Need Apply" was a stock phrase in advertisements for many desirable jobs in nineteenth- and early twentieth-century America. Before World War II, many hospitals in the United States would not hire black doctors or Jewish doctors, and some prestigious law firms would not hire anyone who was not a white Protestant male from the upper classes. In other cases, people might be hired from a number of groups, but individuals from different groups were channeled into different jobs.

None of this has been peculiar to the United States or to the modern era. On the contrary, members of different groups have been treated differently in laws and practices all around the world and for thousands of years of recorded history. It is the idea of treating individuals the same, regardless of what group they come from, that is relatively recent as history is measured.

Overlapping with discrimination, and often confused with it, are employment differences based on very substantial differences in skills, experience, and work habits from one group to another. Mohawk Indians, for example, have long been sought after to work on the construction of skyscrapers, for they walk around high up on the steel frameworks with no apparent fear of distraction from their work. Italian workers were in such demand in nineteenth century Brazil that its government subsidized their importation. During the industrialization of the Soviet Union in the 1920s and 1930s, large numbers of German, American, and other foreign workers, technicians, and engineers were imported at attractive salaries. More than 10,000 Americans alone went to work in the U.S.S.R. during a one-year period beginning in September 1920.

While preferences for some groups and reluctance or unwillingness to hire others have often been described as due to "bias," "stereotypes" or "perceptions," third-party observers cannot so easily dismiss the first-hand knowledge of those who are backing their beliefs with their own money. Even in the absence of different beliefs about different groups, application of the same employment criteria to different groups can result in very different proportions of these groups being hired, fired, or promoted.

Distinguishing discrimination from differences in qualifications and performances is not easy in practice, though the distinction is fundamental in principle. Seldom do statistical data contain sufficiently detailed information on skills, experience, performance, or absenteeism, much less work habits and attitudes, to make possible comparisons between truly comparable individuals from different groups.

Women, for example, have long had lower incomes than men, but most women give birth to children at some point in their lives and many stay out of the labor force until their children reach an age where they can be put into some form of day care while their mother works. These interruptions of their careers cost women workplace experience and seniority, which in turn inhibit the rise of their incomes over the years relative to that of men who have been working continuously. However, as far back as 1972, women who worked continuously from high school through their thirties earned slightly *more* than men of the same description, even though women as a group earned substantially less than men as a group.

This suggests that employers are willing to pay women of the same experience the same as men, and that women with the same experience may even outperform men, but that differences in domestic responsibilities prevent the sexes from having identical workplace experience or identical incomes based on that experience. In 1991, women without children earned 95 percent of what men earned, while women with children earned just 75 percent of what men earned. Moreover, the very possibility of having children makes different occupations have different attractions to women. Occupations like librarians or teachers, which one can resume after a few years off to take care of small children, are more attractive than occupations such as computer engineers, where a few years off can leave you far behind in this rapidly changing field. In short, women and men make different occupational choices and prepare for many of these occupations by specializing in a very different mix of subjects while being educated.

The question as to whether or how much discrimination women encounter in the labor market is a question about whether there are substantial differences in pay between women and men in the same fields with the same qualifications. The question as to whether there is or is not income parity between the sexes is very different, since differences in occupational choices, educational choices, and continuous employment all affect incomes. Men also tend to work in more hazardous occupations, which tend to pay more than similar occupations that are safer. As one study notes, "although 54 percent of the workplace is male, men account for 92 percent of all job-related deaths."

Similar problems in trying to compare comparable individuals make it difficult to determine the presence and magnitude of discrimination between groups that differ by race or ethnicity. It is not uncommon, both in the United States and in other countries, for one racial or ethnic group to differ in age from another by a decade or more—and we have already seen how age makes a big difference in income. While gross statistics show large income differences between American racial and ethnic groups, finer breakdowns usually show much smaller differences. For example, black, white, and Hispanic males of the same age (29) and

IQ (100) all have average annual incomes within a thousand dollars of one another.

Whatever the amount and magnitude of discrimination, it is important to be aware of what economic factors tend to cause it to be larger or smaller. While it is obvious that discrimination imposes a cost on those being discriminated against, in the form of lost opportunities for higher incomes, it is also true that discrimination can impose costs on those who do the discriminating, where they too lose opportunities for higher incomes. For example, when a landlord refuses to rent an apartment to people from the "wrong" group, that can mean leaving the apartment vacant longer.

Clearly, that represents a loss of rent—if this is a free market. However, if there is rent control, with a surplus of applicants, then such discrimination costs the landlord nothing.

Similar principles apply in job markets. An employer who refuses to hire qualified individuals from the "wrong" groups risks leaving his jobs unfilled longer in a free market. That means that he must either leave work undone and orders unfilled or else pay overtime to existing employees to get it done, losing money either way. However, in a market where wages are set artificially above the level that would exist through supply and demand, the resulting surplus of applicants can mean that discrimination costs the employer nothing. Whether these artificially higher wages are set by a labor union or by a minimum wage law does not change the principle. Empirical evidence strongly indicates that racial discrimination tends to be greater when the costs are lower and lower when the costs are greater.

Even in South Africa under apartheid, where racial discrimination was required by law, white employers in competitive industries hired more blacks and in higher occupations than they were permitted to do by the government, and were often fined when caught doing so. This was because it was in the employers' economic self-interest to hire blacks. Similarly, whites who wanted homes built in Johannesburg typically hired illegal black construction crews, often with a token white nominally in charge to meet the requirements of the apartheid laws, rather than pay the higher price of hiring a white construction crew as the government wanted them to do. Landlords likewise often rented to blacks in areas where only whites were legally allowed to live.

The cost of discrimination to the discriminators is crucial for understanding such behavior. Employers who are spending other people's money—government agencies or non-profit organizations, for example—are much less affected by the cost of discrimination. In countries around the world, discrimination by government has been greater than discrimination by businesses operating in competitive markets. Understanding the basic economics of discrimination makes it easier to understand why American blacks were starring on Broadway in the 1920s, at a time when they were not permitted to enlist in the U. S. Navy and were kept out of many civilian government jobs as well. Broadway producers were not about to lose big money that they could make by hiring black entertainers, but the costs of government discrimination was paid by the taxpayers, whether they realized it or not.

CAPITAL, LABOR, AND EFFICIENCY

While everything requires some labor for its production, practically nothing can be produced by labor alone. Farmers need land, taxi drivers need cars, artists need something to draw on and something to draw with. Even a stand-up comedian needs an inventory of jokes, which is his capital, as much as hydroelectric dams are the capital of utility companies that supply electricity.

Capital complements labor in the production process, but it also competes with labor for employment. Many goods and services can be produced either with much labor and little capital or much capital and little labor. When transit workers' unions force bus drivers' pay rates much above what they would be in a competitive labor market, transit companies tend to add more capital, in order to save on the use of the more expensive labor. Busses grow longer, sometimes becoming essentially two busses with a flexible connection between them, so that one driver is using twice as much capital as before and is capable of moving twice as many passengers.

Some may think that this is more "efficient" but efficiency is not so easily defined. If we arbitrarily define efficiency as output per unit of labor, as the U.S. Department of Labor sometimes does, then it is merely circular reasoning to say that having one bus driver moving more passengers is more efficient. It may in fact cost more money per passenger to move them, as a result of the additional capital needed for the expanded busses and the more expensive labor of the drivers.

If bus drivers were not unionized and were paid no more than was necessary to attract qualified people, then undoubtedly their wage rates would be lower and it would then be profitable for the transit companies to hire more of them and use shorter busses. This would in turn mean that passengers would have less time to wait at bus stops because of the shorter and more numerous busses. This is not a small concern to people waiting on street corners on cold winter days or in high-crime neighborhoods at night.

"Efficiency" cannot be meaningfully defined without regard to human desires and preferences. Even the efficiency of an automobile engine is not simply a matter of physics. All the energy generated by the engine will be used in some way—either in moving the car forward, overcoming friction among the moving parts, or shaking the automobile body in various ways. It is only when we define our goal—moving the car forward—that we can regard the percentage of the engine's power that is used for that task as indicating its efficiency and the other power dissipated in various other ways as being "wasted."

Europeans long regarded American agriculture as "inefficient" because output per acre was much lower in the United States than in much of Europe. On the other hand, output per agricultural worker was much higher in the United States than in Europe. The reason was that land was far more plentiful in the U.S. and labor was more scarce. An American farmer would spread himself thinner over far more land and would have correspondingly less time to devote to each acre. In Europe, where land was more scarce, and therefore more expensive because of supply and demand, the European farmer concentrated on the more intensive cultivation of what land he could get, spending more time clearing away weeds and rocks, or otherwise devoting more attention to ensuring the maximum output per acre.

Similarly, Third World countries often get more use out of given capital equipment than do wealthier and more industrialized countries. Such tools as hammers and screw-drivers may be plentiful enough for each worker in an American factory or shop to have his own, but that is much less likely to be the case in a much poorer country, where such tools are more likely to be shared, or shared more widely, than among Americans making the same products. Looked at from another angle, each hammer in a poor country is likely to drive more nails per year, since it is shared among more people and has less idle time. That does not make the poorer country more "efficient." It is just that the relative scarcities are different. Capital tends to be scarcer and more expensive in poorer countries, while labor is more abundant and cheaper. Such countries tend to economize on the more expensive factor, just as richer countries economize on a different factor that is more expensive scarce there, namely labor. It is just that, in richer countries, capital is more plentiful and cheaper, while labor is more scarce and more expensive.

When a freight train comes into a railroad yard or onto a siding, workers are needed to unload it. When a freight train arrives in the middle of the night, it can either be unloaded then and there, so that the train can proceed on its way, or the boxcars can be left on a siding until the workers come to work the next morning. In a country where such capital as railroad box cars are very scarce and labor is plentiful, it makes sense to have the workers available around the clock, so that they can immediately unload box cars and this very scarce resource does not remain idle. But, in a country that is rich in capital, it may often be better to let box cars sit idle on a siding, waiting to be unloaded, rather than to have expensive workers sitting around idle waiting for the next train to arrive.

It is not just a question about these particular workers' paychecks or this particular railroad company's expenses. From the standpoint of the economy as a whole, the more fundamental question is: What are the alternative uses of these workers' time and the alternative uses of the railroad boxcars? In other words, it is not just a question of money. The money only reflects underlying realities that would be the same in a socialist, feudal or other non-market economy. Whether it makes sense to leave the boxcars idle waiting for the workers to arrive or to leave the workers idle waiting for trains to arrive depends on the relative scarcities of labor and capital and their relative productivity in alternative uses.

During the era of the Soviet Union and Cold War competition, the Soviets used to boast of the fact that an average Soviet box car moved more freight per year than an average American box car. But, far from indicating that their economy was more efficient, this showed that Soviet railroads lacked the abundant capital of the American railroad industry, and that Soviet labor had less valuable alternative uses of its time than did American labor. Similarly, a study of West African economies in the mid-twentieth century noted that trucks there "are in service twenty-four hours a day for seven days a week and are generally tightly packed with passengers and freight."

For similar reasons, automobiles tend to have longer lives in poor countries than in richer countries. Remember that economics is the study of scarce resources which have alternative uses. The alternative uses of American labor are too valuable for it to be used keeping ten-year-old cars repaired—except for those Americans wealthy enough to be able to indulge a hobby of collecting vintage automobiles or those poor enough that the alternative uses of their time are not very remunerative and they are unable to afford a new car.

By and large, it pays Americans to junk their cars, refrigerators, trolleys, and other capital equipment in a shorter time than it would pay people in poorer countries to do so. Nor is this a matter of being able to afford "waste." It would be a waste to keep repairing this equipment, when the same efforts elsewhere in the American economy would produce more than enough wealth to buy replacements. But it would not make sense for poorer countries, whose alternative uses of time are not as productive, to junk their equipment at the same times when American junk theirs. Accordingly, many older American cars, trolleys, and sewing machines may be bought second-hand and used for years longer in Third World countries after they have been junked in the United States. This can be an efficient way of handling the situation for both kinds of countries.

A book by two Soviet economists pointed out that in the U.S.S.R. "equipment is endlessly repaired and patched up," so that the "average life of capital stock in the U.S.S.R. is forty-seven years, as against seventeen in the United States." They were not bragging. They were complaining.

Chapter 10
Controlled Labor Markets

Pay and employment conditions are not always a result of free market competition. Either or both may be controlled by law, custom, or organizations of employers or employees. Among the major factors behind such controls have been desires for job security and for collectively-set limits on how high or how low pay scales will be allowed to go in particular occupations or industries.

Here as elsewhere, we are concerned not so much with the goals or rationales of such policies, but with the incentives created by these arrangements and the consequences to which such incentives lead. These consequences extend beyond the workers themselves to the economy as a whole, where labor is one of the scarce resources which have alternative uses.

JOB SECURITY

Virtually every modern industrial economy has faced issues of job security, whether they have faced these issues realistically or unrealistically, successfully or unsuccessfully. At the most simplistic level, some people advocate that every worker be guaranteed a job, with the government if necessary. In some countries, laws make it difficult and costly for a private employer to fire anyone. Labor unions try to do this in many industries and in many countries around the world. Teachers' unions in the United States are so successful at this that it can easily cost a school district tens of thousands of dollars—or even hundreds of thousands in some places—to fire just one teacher, even if that teacher is grossly incompetent.

The very thing that makes a modern industrial society so efficient and so effective in raising living standards—the constant
quest for newer and better ways of getting work done and more
goods produced—also makes it impossible to keep on doing
things the same old familiar ways with the same workers doing
the same jobs. For example, back at the beginning of the twentieth
century, the United States had about 10 million farmers and farm
laborers to feed a population of 76 million people. By the end of
the twentieth century, there were less than one-fifth this many
farmers and farm laborers, feeding a population more than three
times as large. Yet, far from having less food, Americans' biggest
problems now included obesity and trying to find export markets
for their surplus food. All this was made possible because farming became a radically different enterprise, using machinery,
chemicals and methods unheard of when the century began—and
requiring far fewer people.

Farming is of course not the only sector of the economy to be
revolutionized during the twentieth century. Whole new industries have sprung up, such as aviation and computers, and even
old industries like retailing have seen radical changes in which
companies and which methods have survived. In little over a
decade, between 1985 and 1996, Sears lost 131,000 jobs while Wal-
Mart gained 624,000 jobs. Altogether, more than 17 million workers throughout the economy lost their jobs between 1990 and
1995. But there were never 17 million people unemployed during
this period, nor anything close to that. In fact, unemployment
rates fell to their lowest points in years. Americans were moving
from one job to another, rather than relying on "job security" in
one place.

In Europe, where job security laws and practices are much
stronger than in the United States, jobs have in fact been harder to
come by. During the 1990s, the United States created jobs at triple
the rate of industrial nations in Europe. In the private sector, Europe actually lost jobs, and only increased government employment led to any net gain at all. This should not be surprising. Job
security laws make it more expensive to hire workers. Like anything else that is made more expensive, labor is less in demand at
a higher price than at a lower price. The one exception is govern-

ment employment, where the employers are spending other people's money—the taxpayers' money.

Job security policies save the jobs of existing workers, but at the cost of reducing the flexibility and efficiency of the economy as a whole, thereby inhibiting the creation of new jobs for other workers. Because job security laws make it risky to hire new workers, existing employees may be worked overtime instead or capital may be substituted for labor, such as using huge busses instead of hiring more drivers for regular-sized busses. However it is done, increased substitution of capital for labor leaves other workers unemployed. For the working population as a whole, this is no net increase in job security. It is a concentration of the insecurity on those who happen to be on the outside looking in.

It is much the same story in the academic world, where associate professors and full professors usually have lifetime tenure, while assistant professors, lecturers and instructors work on short-term contracts. The job insecurity of the latter faculty members can be far greater than in other sectors of the economy where there is no tenure. Again, those on the inside looking out benefit at the expense of those on the outside looking in.

Even in the absence of formal laws and policies on job security, there are many efforts to preserve jobs threatened by technological change, foreign imports or other sources of cheaper or better products. Virtually all these efforts likewise ignore the danger that greater security for some given set of workers can come at the expense of lessened job opportunities for other workers, as well as needlessly high prices for consumers.

One of the emotionally powerful arguments heard in politics and the media during the "down-sizing" of many large American corporations during the 1990s was that workers were being laid off in industries where sales and profits were going up and the top executives were getting large and rising pay. For example, the workforce at General Motors was cut by 50,000 in just 5 years, while sales were rising and the price of General Motors stock increased 50 percent. From an economic standpoint, this meant that it was possible to do more business with fewer workers, creating better prospects for profit, which in turn led to rising stock prices.

Should General Motors have kept these workers on, as a humanitarian good deed? The argument for doing this might have been stronger if the workers had nowhere to go and no other means of supporting themselves and their families. But the unusually low rates of unemployment in the economy as a whole during this period of widespread corporate down-sizing suggests that these workers had plenty of places to go.

These workers were classic examples of scarce resources which have alternative uses. If unneeded workers had been retained at General Motors as disguised welfare cases, they would not have added to the output of other parts of the economy where there was much genuine work for them to do. Moreover, consumers would have had to pay needlessly higher price for automobiles to subsidize featherbedding, as well as losing the benefits of all the other goods and services that displaced automobile workers produced in other sectors of the economy to which they were forced to move.

It has sometimes seemed especially galling that corporate executives who got rid of thousands of workers were rewarded by pay increases for themselves. However, it is worth considering the consequences of the situation in government, where executives are likely to be rewarded according to how many people they supervise and how large a budget they administer. These different situations create opposite incentives—to get as much work done with as few people and resources as possible in private industry and with as many people and resources as available in government. This is one reason why it often costs much less for private companies to perform the same tasks as a government agency performs. The public pays the costs, whether as consumers or as taxpayers.

MINIMUM WAGE LAWS

Just as we can better understand the economic role of prices in general when we see what happens when prices are not allowed to function, so we can better understand the economic role of workers' pay by seeing what happens when that pay is not allowed to vary with supply and demand. Historically, authorities set maximum wage levels centuries before they set minimum wage levels. Today, however, only the latter are widespread.

Minimum wage laws make it illegal to pay less than the government-specified price for labor. By the simplest and most basic economics, a price artificially raised tends to cause more to be supplied and less to be demanded than when prices are left to be determined in a free market. The result is a surplus, whether the price that is set artificially high is that of farm produce or labor.

Unemployment

Because the government does not hire surplus labor the way it buys surplus agricultural output, the labor surplus takes the form of unemployment, which tends to be higher under minimum wage laws than in a free market. Because people differ in many ways, those who are unemployed are not likely to be a random sample of the labor force. In country after country around the world, those whose employment prospects are reduced most by minimum wage laws are those who are younger, less experienced, and less skilled. This same pattern has been found in New Zealand, France, Canada, the Netherlands, and the United States, for example.

As in other cases, a "surplus" is a price phenomenon, just as "shortages" are. Unemployed workers are not surplus in the sense of being useless or in the sense that there is no work around that needs doing. Most of these workers are perfectly capable of producing goods and services, even if not to the same extent as more skilled workers. The unemployed are made idle by wage rates artificially set above the level of their productivity. By being idled in their youth, they are of course prevented from acquiring the job skills and experience which could make them more productive and higher earners later on.

Although most modern industrial societies have minimum wage laws, not all do. Switzerland and Hong Kong have been among the exceptions—and both have had very low unemployment rates, that in Hong Kong being as low as 1.5 percent. Minimum wage rates in Europe tend generally to be set higher than in the United States, and European countries tend to have correspondingly higher unemployment rates than the United States—and job growth rates only a fraction of the American rate. A belated recognition of this connection has caused some countries to allow their minimum wage laws to be eroded by inflation, avoiding the political risks of trying explicitly to repeal these laws.

The huge financial, political, emotional, and ideological investment of various groups in issues revolving around minimum wage laws means that dispassionate analysis is not always the norm. Moreover, the statistical complexities of separating out the effect of minimum wages on employment from all the other ever-changing variables that also effect employment means that honest differences are possible. However, when all is said and done, most empirical studies indicate that minimum wage laws reduce employment in general, and especially the employment of younger, less skilled and minority workers. A majority of professional economists surveyed in Britain, Germany, Canada, Switzerland, and the United States agreed that minimum wage laws increase unemployment among low- skilled workers. Economists in France and Austria did not. However, the majority among Canadian economists was 85 percent and among American economists 90 percent.

Those officially responsible for administering minimum wages laws, such as the U. S. Department of Labor and various local agencies, prefer to claim that these laws do not create unemployment. So do labor unions, for whom minimum wage laws serve as tariff barriers against potential competitors for their members' jobs. Even though most studies show unemployment caused by minimum wages, those few studies that seem to indicate otherwise are hailed as having "refuted" this "myth," while the devastating criticisms of the defects of such studies by economists are ignored.

One common problem with research on the employment effects of minimum wage laws is that surveys of employers before and after a minimum wage increase can survey only those businesses which survive in both periods. Given the high rates of business failures in many fields, the results for the survivors may be completely different from the results for the industry as a whole.[1] As Nobel-Prizewinning economist George Stigler once said about such surveys of survivors, using these methods you can prove that no soldier was killed in World War II—a comforting conclusion, but one whose validity is open to considerable doubt.

It would be similarly comforting to believe that the government can simply decree higher pay for low-wage workers, without having to worry about unfortunate repercussions, but the validity of that belief is likewise in considerable doubt. The preponderance of evidence indicates that labor is not exempt from the basic economic principle that artificially high prices cause surpluses. In the case of surplus human beings, that can be a special tragedy when they are already from low-income, unskilled, or minority backgrounds and urgently need to get on the job ladder if they are ever to move up the ladder by acquiring skills and experience.

Informal Minimum Wages

Sometimes a minimum wage is imposed not by law, but by custom, informal government pressures, labor unions or—especially in the case of Third World countries—by international public opinion pressuring multinational companies to pay Third World workers the kinds of wages usually found in more industrially developed countries. Although organized public pressures for higher pay for Third World Workers in Southeast Asia made news in the United States in the late twentieth century, such pres-

---

[1]Imagine that an industry consists of 7 firms, each hiring 1,000 workers before a minimum wage increase, for an industry total of 7,000 employees. If two of these firms go out of business between the first and the second surveys and only one new firm enters the industry, then only the five firms that were in existence both "before" and "after" can be surveyed and their results reported. Both they and the new firm may now have 1,100 employees each, but the industry as a whole will have 6,600 employees—400 fewer than before the minimum wage increase. Yet this study can show a 10 percent increase in employment in the five firms surveyed, rather than the 6 percent decrease for the industry as a whole. Since minimum wages can cause unemployment by (1) reducing employment among all the firms, (2) by pushing a marginal firm into bankruptcy, or (3) discouraging the entry of replacement firms, false reports based on surveying only survivors are a clear danger.

sures were not new. Similar pressures were put on companies operating in colonial West Africa half a century earlier.

Informal minimum wages imposed in these ways have had effects very similar to those of explicit minimum wage laws. An economist studying colonial West Africa in the mid-twentieth century found signs telling job applicants that there were "no vacancies" almost everywhere. Nor was this peculiar to West Africa. The same economist—Professor P. T. Bauer of the London School of Economics—noted that it was "a striking feature of many under-developed countries that money wages are maintained at high levels" while "large numbers are seeking but unable to find work." These are of course not high levels compared to what is earned by workers in more industrialized economies, but high relative to Third World workers' productivity and high relative to their alternative earning opportunities in sectors of the economy not subject to pressures to maintain an artificially inflated level of earnings, such as agriculture, domestic service, or self-employment as street vendors and the like.

The magnitude of the unemployment created by artificially high wages that multinational companies felt pressured to pay in West Africa was indicated by Professor Bauer's first-hand observations:

> I asked the manager of the tobacco factory of the Nigerian Tobacco Company (a subsidiary of the British-American Tobacco Company) in Ibadan whether he could expand his labour force without raising wages if he wished to do so. He replied that his only problem would be to control the mob of applicants. Very much the same opinion was expressed by the Kano district agent of the firm of John Hold and Company in respect of their tannery. In December 1949 a firm of produce buyers in Kano dismissed two clerks and within two days received between fifty and sixty applications for the posts without having publicized the vacancies. The same firm proposed to erect a groundnut crushing plant. By June 1950 machinery had not yet been installed; but without having advertised a vacancy it had already received about seven hundred letters asking for employment . . .
> I learnt that the European-owned brewery and the recently es-

tablished manufacturers of stationery constantly receive shoals of applications for employment.

The misfortunes of eager but frustrated African job applicants are only part of the story. The output that they could have produced, if employed, would have made a particularly important contribution to the economic wellbeing of the consuming public in a very poor region, lacking many things that others take for granted in more prosperous nations. It is not at all clear that workers as a class are benefitted by artificially high wage rates in the Third World. Employed workers—those on the inside looking out—obviously benefit, while those on the outside looking in lose. The only category of clear beneficiaries are people living in richer countries who enjoy the feeling that they are helping people in poorer countries.

Just as a price set below the free market level tends to cause quality deterioration in the product that is being sold, because a shortage means that buyers will be forced to accept things of lower quality than they would have otherwise, so a price set above the free market level tends to cause a rise in average quality, as the surplus allows the buyers to cherry-pick and purchase only the better quality items being sold. What that means in the labor market is that job qualification requirements are likely to rise and that some workers who would ordinarily be hired in a free market may become "unemployable" when there are minimum wage laws. Unemployability, like shortages and surpluses, is not independent of price. In a free market, low-productivity workers are just as employable at a low wage as high-productivity workers are at a high wage.

Differential Impact

Some countries in Europe have lower minimum wages for teenagers than for adults and New Zealand simply exempted teenagers from the coverage of its minimum wage law until 1994. This was tacit recognition of the fact that those workers less in demand were likely to be hardest hit by unemployment created by minimum wage laws.

Another group disproportionately affected by minimum wage laws are members of unpopular racial or ethnic minority groups. Indeed, minimum wage laws were once advocated explicitly because of the likelihood that they would reduce or eliminate the competition of particular minorities, whether they were Japanese in Canada during the 1920s or blacks in the United States and South Africa at about the same time. Such expressions of overt racial discrimination were both legal and socially accepted in all three countries at that time.

Again, it is necessary to note how price is a factor even in racial discrimination. That is, surplus labor resulting from minimum wage laws makes it cheaper to discriminate against minority workers than it would be in a free market, where there is no chronic excess supply of labor. Passing up qualified minority workers in a free market means having to hire other workers to take the jobs they were denied, and that in turn usually means either having to raise the pay to attract the additional workers or lowering the job qualifications at the existing pay level—both of which amount to the same thing, higher labor costs for getting a given amount of work done.

The history of black workers in the United States illustrates the point. The American federal minimum wage law—the Fair Labor Standards Act—was passed in 1938. However, wartime inflation had the effect of repealing this law for all practical economic purposes during the 1940s, since the wages set in the marketplace for even unskilled labor rose well above what the law specified. The real impact of the law began to be felt after 1950, when the first major revision of the Act began a series of escalations of the federal minimum wage.

From the late nineteenth-century on past the middle of the twentieth century, the labor force participation rate of American blacks was slightly higher than that of American whites. In other words, during this long period before the escalation of minimum wage rates, blacks were just as employable at the wages they received as whites were at their very different wages. The minimum wage law changed that and those particularly hard hit by the resulting unemployment have been black teenage males.

Even though 1949—the year before the series of minimum wage escalations began—was a recession year, black male teenage unemployment that year was lower than it was to be at any time during the later boom years of the 1960s. The usual explanations of high unemployment among black teenagers— inexperience, lack of skills, racism—cannot explain their rising unemployment, since all these things were worse during the earlier period when black teenage unemployment was much lower.

Taking the more normal year of 1948 as a basis for comparison, black male teenage unemployment then was less than half of what it would be at any time during the decade of the 1960s and less than one-third of what it would be in the 1970s. Moreover, unemployment among 16 and 17-year-old black males was no higher than among white males of the same age in 1948. It was only after a series of minimum wage escalations began that black male teenage unemployment not only skyrocketed itself but became more than double the unemployment rates among white male teenagers.

COLLECTIVE BARGAINING

So far we have been considering labor markets in which both workers and employers are numerous and compete individually and independently, with supply and demand determining rates of pay and numbers of jobs. These, however, are not the only kinds of markets for labor. Some labor markets are controlled by laws or by collective bargaining agreements, or both. Some workers are members of labor unions which negotiate pay and working conditions with employers, whether employers are acting individually or as members of some employers' association.

Employer Organizations

In earlier centuries, it was the employers who were more likely to be organized and setting pay and working conditions as a group. In medieval guilds, the master craftsmen collectively made the rules determining the conditions under which apprentices and journeymen would be hired and how much customers would be charged for the products. Today, major league baseball owners collectively make the rules as to what is the maximum total salaries any given ball club can pay to its players.

Clearly, pay and working conditions tend to be different when determined collectively than in a labor market where employers compete against one another individually for workers and workers compete against one another individually for jobs. It would obviously not be worth the trouble of organizing employers if they were not able to keep the salaries they pay lower than they would be in a free market.

Much has been said about the fairness or unfairness of the actions of medieval guilds, modern labor unions or other forms of collective bargaining. Here we are studying their economic consequences—and especially their effects on the allocation of scarce resources which have alternative uses.

Almost by definition, all these organizations exist to keep the price of labor from being what it would be otherwise in free and open competition in the market. Just as the tendency of market competition is to base rates of pay on the productivity of the worker, thereby bidding labor away from where it is less productive to where it is more productive, so organized efforts to make wages artificially low or artificially high defeat this process and thereby make the allocation of resources less efficient in the economy as a whole.

For example, if an employers' association keeps wages in the widget industry below the level that workers of similar skills receive elsewhere, fewer of these workers are likely to apply for jobs producing widgets than if the pay rate were higher. If widget manufacturers are paying $10 an hour for labor that would get $15 an hour if they had to compete with each other for workers in a free market, then some workers will go to other industries that pay $12 an hour. From the standpoint of the economy as a whole, this means that people capable of producing $15 an hours' worth of output are instead producing only $12 an hours' worth of output. This is a clear loss to the consumers—that is, to society as a whole.

The fact that it is a more immediate and more visible loss to the workers in the widget industry does not make that the most important fact from an economic standpoint. Losses and gains between employers and employees are social or moral issues, but they do not change the key economic issue, which is how the allocation of resources affects the total wealth available to society as a whole. What makes the total wealth produced by the economy less than it would be in a free market is that wages set below the market level cause workers to work where they are not as productive.

The same is true of wages set above the market level. If a labor union is successful in raising the wage rate for the same workers in the widget industry to $20 an hour, then employers will employ fewer workers at this higher rate than they would at either the $12 an hour they set under employer collusion or the $15 an hour that would have prevailed in free market competition. In fact, the only workers it will pay the employers to hire are workers whose productivity is $20 an hour or more. This higher productivity can be reached in a number of ways, whether by retaining only the most skilled and experienced employees, by adding more capital to enable the labor to turn out more products per hour, or by other means—none of them free.

Those workers displaced from the widget industry must go to their second-best alternative. Those worth $15 an hour producing widgets may end up working in another industry at $12 an hour. Again, this is not simply a loss to those particular workers but a loss to the economy as a whole, because scarce resources are not being allocated where their productivity is highest.

Under these conditions, Widget manufacturers are not only paying more money for labor, they are also paying for additional capital or other complementary resources to raise the productivity of labor above the $20 an hour level. Higher productivity may seem on the surface to be greater "efficiency," but producing fewer widgets at higher cost per widget does not benefit the economy, even though less labor is being used. Other industries receiving more labor than they normally would, because of the workers displaced from the widget industry, can expand their output. But that expanding output is not the most productive use of the additional labor. It is only the artificially-imposed union wage rate which causes the shift from a more productive use to a less productive use.

Note that either artificially low wage rates caused by an employer association or artificially high wage rates caused by a labor union reduces employment in the widget industry. Another way of saying the same thing is that the maximum employment in any industry is achieved under free and open market competition, without organized collusion among either employers or employees. Looked at more generally, the only individual bargains that can be made anywhere in a free market are those whose terms are acceptable to both sides—that is, buyers and sellers of labor, computers, shoes or whatever. Any other terms, whether set higher or lower, and whether set by collective actions of employers or unions or imposed by government decree, favors one side or the other and therefore causes the disfavored side to make fewer transactions.

From the standpoint of the economy as a whole, the real loss is that things that both sides wanted to do now cannot be done because the range of mutually acceptable terms has been artificially narrowed. One side or the other must now go to their second-best alternative—which is also second-best from the standpoint of the economy as a whole, because scarce resources have not been allocated to their most valued uses.

The parties engaged in collective bargaining are of course preoccupied with their own interests, but those judging the process as a whole need to focus on how such a process affects the economic interests of the entire society, rather than the internal division of economic benefits among contending members of the society.

Labor Unions

Labor unions often boast of the pay rate and other benefits they have gotten for their members and of course that is what enables unions to continue to attract members. The wage rate per hour is typically a key indicator of a union's success, but the further ramifications of that wage rate seldom receive as much attention. Legendary labor leader John L. Lewis, head of the United Mine Workers from 1925 to 1960, was enormously successful in winning higher pay for his union's members. However, an economist also called him "the world's greatest oil salesman," because the resulting higher price of coal and the disruptions in its production due to numerous strikes caused many users of coal to switch to using oil instead. This of course reduced employment in the coal industry.

By the 1960s, declining employment in the coal industry left many mining communities economically stricken and some virtual ghost towns. Media stories of their plight seldom connected their current woes with the former glory days of John L. Lewis. In fairness to Lewis, he made a conscious decision that it was better to have fewer miners doing dangerous work underground and more heavy machinery down there, since machinery could not be killed by cave-ins, explosions and the other hazards of mining.

To the public at large, however, these and other trade-offs were largely unknown. Many simply cheered at what Lewis had done to improve the wages of miners and, years later, were compassionate toward the decline of mining communities—but made little or no connection between the two things. Yet what was involved was one of the simplest and most basic principles of economics, that less is demanded at a higher price than at a lower price. That principle applies whether considering the price of coal, of mine workers or anything else.

Very similar trends emerged in the automobile industry, where the danger factor was not what it was in mining. Here the United Automobile Workers' union was also very successful in getting higher pay, more job security and more favorable work rules for its members. In the long run, however, all these additional costs raised the price of automobiles and made American cars less competitive with Japanese and other imports, not only in the United States but around the world.

As of 1950, the United States produced three-quarters of all the cars in the world and Japan produced less than one percent of what Americans produced. Twenty years later, Japan was producing almost as many automobiles as the United States and, five years after that, more automobiles. By 1990, one-third of the cars sold in the United States were made in Japan. In 1996, the Honda Accord and the Toyota Camry each sold more cars in the United States than any car sold by General Motors. All this of course had its effect on employment. During the 1980s, the number of jobs in the American automobile industry declined by more than

100,000. By 1990, the number of jobs in the American automobile industry was 200,000 less than it had been in 1979.

Political pressures on Japan to "voluntarily" limit its export of cars to the U.S. led to the creation of Japanese automobile manufacturing plants in the United States, hiring American workers. By 1990, these transplanted Japanese factories were producing nearly as many cars as were being exported to the United States from Japan. Many of these transplanted Japanese car companies had workforces that were non-union—and which rejected unionization when votes were taken among the employees.

This was part of a more general trend among industrial workers in the United States. The United Steelworkers of America was another large and highly successful union in getting high pay and other benefits for its members. But here too the number of jobs in the industry declined by more than 200,000 in a decade, while the steel companies invested $65 million in machinery that replaced these workers, while the towns where steel production was concentrated were economically devastated.

The once common belief that unions were a blessing and a necessity for workers was now increasingly mixed with skepticism about the unions' role in the economic declines and reduced employment in many industries. Faced with the prospect of seeing some employers going out of business or having to drastically reduce employment, some unions were forced into "give-backs"—that is, relinquishing various wages and benefits they had obtained for their members. Painful as this was, many unions concluded that it was the only way to save members' jobs.

The proportion of the American labor force that was unionized began to decline as skepticism about their economic effects spread among workers who increasingly voted against being represented by unions. Unionized workers were 32 percent of all workers in the middle of the twentieth century, but only 14 percent by the end of the century. Moreover, there was a major change in the composition of unionized workers.

In the first half of the century, the great unions were in mining, automobiles, steel, and trucking. But, as the twentieth century drew to a close, the large and growing unions were those of government employees. The largest union in the country by far was the union of teachers—the National Education Association. The economic pressures of the marketplace, which had created such problems for unionized workers in industry and commerce, did not apply to government workers. Government employees could continue to get pay raises, benefits, and job security without worrying that they would suffer the fate of miners, automobile workers, and other unionized industrial workers. Those who hired government workers were not spending their own money but the taxpayers' money, and so had little reason to resist union demands and faced no competitive forces in the market that could force them to lose business to imports or substitute products.

In private industry, many companies remained non-union by a policy of paying their workers at least as much as unionized workers received. Such a policy implies that the cost to an employer of having a union exceeds the wages and benefits paid to workers. The hidden costs of union rules on seniority and many other details of operations are for some companies worth being rid of, even if that means paying their employees more than they would have to pay to unionized workers.

Chapter 11

An Overview

Employee earnings are the largest category of income in the American economy, constituting about 70 percent of national income for decades on end. Because wages and salaries are so important in the lives of most individuals, there is a tendency to look at income solely from the standpoint of the individuals receiving it. However, this overlooks the important role of the price of labor in allocating resources in ways which determine the standard of living in the society as a whole. Looking at income solely from the standpoint of individual recipients also tends to portray the economy as a zero-sum game, in which what is gained by some is lost by others. But there would obviously never have been the great rises in the general standard of living which have occurred over the years and generations if that were true.

By 1994, for example, most American households *living below the official poverty line* had a microwave oven and a videocassette recorder, things that less than one percent of all American households had in 1971. For the population at large, homes were much bigger, automobiles were much better, and more people were connected to the Internet at the end of the century than were connected to a water supply at the beginning of the century. This was clearly not a zero-sum game, in which what some won was lost by others.

Fights over which individuals and groups get how big a slice of the pie create the kind of emotions and controversy on which the media and politicians thrive. But the economic reality is that the main reason most Americans have prospered is that the pie itself has gotten much bigger, not because this group or that changed a few percentage points in its share. The changing allocation of scarce resources which makes continuing prosperity possible may change these percentages back and forth over time, as changing pay and employment prospects direct individuals to where their productivity would be higher and away from where it is lower. But it is changes in productivity and allocation which are crucial to the economic wellbeing of the population, not the few percentage point changes in relative shares which attract so much media, political, and other attention.

So-called "income distribution" statistics are very misleading when we focus on comparisons between fixed income brackets, such as the top 20 percent or bottom 20 percent, rather than on the actual flesh-and-blood people who are constantly moving from one bracket to another in the American economy. Well over 90 percent of the people who were in the bottom 20 percent of the American income earners in 1975 had a higher standard of living by 1991. In fact, more than half of those at the bottom in 1975 had a higher standard of living in 1991 than the average American had in 1975. Even in relative terms, more of those who were in the bottom 20 percent in 1975 were in the top 20 percent by 1991 than remained in the bottom 20 percent. Indeed, an absolute majority of those who were in the bottom 20 percent in 1975 had reached the top 20 percent at some point during those 16 years.

Media and even academic preoccupation with instant snapshot statistics create major distortions of economic reality. "The rich" and "the poor" have become staples of income discussions, even though most of the people in the top and bottom income categories are the same people at different stages of their lives, rather than fixed classes of people who remain at the top and bottom throughout their lives. Even a couple of economists who should have known better used analogies that treated people in various income brackets as if they were permanently in those brackets. Lower income people were likened to "dwarfs" less than three feet tall, while people in the top brackets were likened to "giants" 20 feet tall. A much more apt analogy would be between children and adults, since children grow up to become adults, while dwarfs and giants remain dwarfs and giants throughout their lives.

Even among millionaires, studies show that four-fifths of them did not inherit their fortune but earned it during their own lifetimes. The great historic American fortunes—Carnegie, Ford,

Vanderbilt, etc.—were often created by people who began in modest or even humble circumstances. Richard Warren Sears, Aaron Montgomery Ward, and James Cash Penney all began working to support themselves in lowly jobs as teenagers, too young to be allowed to work under today's child labor laws, though each eventually rose to become fabulously wealthy as creators of the retail store chains which bear their respective names.

Similar stories could be told of teenage Henry Ford, who became fed up with farm work and walked eight miles to Detroit to look for a job. David Sarnoff, who went on in later life to create the NBC broadcasting network, also began working to support himself as a teenager. So did an immigrant lumberyard worker named Frederick Weyerhauser, who went on to establish a wood products empire. A middle-aged salesman making $12,000 a year went on to create the McDonald's fast-food empire of nearly 25,000 restaurants that literally circles the globe. The list goes on and on.

While the great American fortunes may come to mind when speaking of "the rich," most people in the top 10 or 20 percent of the income or wealth distribution have no such fortunes. Even people in the top one percent in wealth bear little resemblance to "the idle rich" conjured up in popular legend or ideological rhetoric. As of 1998, a household income of $75,000 a year was enough to put the people in that household in the top 20 percent. A couple making $38,000 each hardly seems like "the rich." Even the top 5 percent of households could be reached with a combined income of $133,000—comfortable, but hardly in the same category as millionaires and billionaires.

As in so many other aspects of economics, the basic principles involved in work and pay are not terribly complicated, nor the facts particularly obscure. What gets complicated is disentangling a fairly straightforward story from a jungle of preconceptions and emotion-laden myths. Political movements and even whole nations have been seized by a vision of the idle rich exploiting the toiling masses, of people mired in grinding poverty from birth to death, and of labor unions or socialist or communist movements as the only forlorn hope for those otherwise economically doomed. Plain facts have no such dramatic impact nor generate such excitement on television, or in politics, or around a seminar table.

Even when considering the top and bottom one percent of income earners, we are not talking about the idle exploiters and the toiling masses. Our social visions and our rhetoric are about "the rich" and "the poor," as if we were talking about people who are born, live, and die in poverty or luxury, while the reality is that most Americans do not stay in the same income quintile for as long as a decade.

However important payments to individuals are from the standpoint of their own material wellbeing, these payments are also a means of allocating the work of those individuals in ways which affect the efficiency of the economy and therefore the standard of living in the society as a whole. In an ever-changing economy with new and more productive technologies emerging and more efficient methods of organization being devised, to keep workers employed where they are already is to force society to forego the economic benefits of such new developments.

Unless workers are to be ordered to move from one industry, region, or occupation to another, as under totalitarianism, economic incentives and constraints must accomplish these transfers in a market economy. Higher pay may attract workers to the newer and more productive sectors or unemployment may force them out of sectors whose products or technologies are becoming obsolete. Simple and obvious as this may seem, it is often misunderstood by those who are shocked to see some sectors of the economy prospering at the same time when others are being "left behind" or are even suffering losses of business and jobs. Too often there is no sense that these are all part of the same process, rather than separate happenstances that are good for some and bad for others.

There were, for example, many laments in the nineteenth century for the plight of the handloom weavers, increasingly displaced by power looms that made more clothing more affordable to millions. Today, in an affluent age, when physically adequate clothing is so widely available that only issues of style and brand name concern most Americans, it is difficult to imagine the hardships endured by many people unable to afford enough clothing to provide adequate protection against the elements—or what a blessing it was to them to have the prices of clothes brought down to a level where they could finally afford them, because of advances in the mechanization of production. Their good fortune and the misfortunes of the handloom weavers were inseparably part of the same process.

In our own time as well, "saving jobs"—whether from displacement by technological advances at home or from imports from other countries—means forcing other people to have a lower standard of living than what is available with the existing resources and technology. However one might wish to resolve this trade-off, it must first be recognized as a trade-off, not as some strange or sinister "unfairness" arbitrarily imposed on victims.

Pay differentials are likewise typically reflections of productivity differences and are part of the process of allocating scarce labor resources which have alternative uses. Again, a fairly obvious economic fact can become very confused when intertwined with very different moral questions about whether one group of people merit so much more than others. Productivity and merit are wholly different things. Someone born and raised in highly favorable circumstances may find it easier to become a brain surgeon than someone born and raised in highly unfavorable circumstances may find it to become a skilled carpenter. But that is very different from saying that brain surgeons are paid "too much" or carpenters "too little."

In policy terms, making it easier for people born in less fortunate circumstances to acquire the knowledge and skills to become brain surgeons is very different from simply decreeing that pay differentials between brain surgeons and carpenters be reduced or eliminated. The latter policy affects the allocation of resources, affecting not only how hard existing brain surgeons will work or how early they will retire, but also how many replacements they will have, as young people decide whether or not it is worth all the years and effort it takes to become a brain surgeon.

Those who have the biggest stake in all this are people suffering from medical conditions that require brain surgery. Despite a tendency in some quarters see economic choices as a zero-sum game involving a trade-off between the interests of competing groups, very often the third parties who are ignored are affected most of all. Moreover, seeing economic issues as simply issues about how to divide up money ignores the larger role of financial incentives in allocating resources. From the standpoint of society as a whole, money is just an artifact used to get real things done.

How well those real things are done is what determines the material wellbeing of the people in that society.

PART IV:
TIME AND RISK

Chapter 12

Investment and Speculation

> *A tourist in New York's Greenwich Village decided to have his portrait sketched by a sidewalk artist. He received a very fine sketch, for which he was charged $100.*
>
> *"That's expensive," he said to the artist, "but I'll pay it, because it is a great sketch. But, really, it took you only five minutes."*
>
> *"Twenty years and five minutes," the artist said.*

Artistic talent is only one of many things which are accumulated over time for use later on. If the earlier sacrifices and risks are ignored, the reward for what was done within the present time period may often seen exorbitant. Oil wells can repay their costs many times over—but they must also cover the costs of all the dry holes that were drilled in the ground while searching in vain for petroleum deposits before finally striking a gusher.

Add to this the cost of keeping people alive while waiting for their artistic talent to develop, their oil exploration to finally pay off, or their academic credits to finally add up to enough to earn their degree, and there may be a considerable investment to be repaid. The repaying of the investment is not a matter of morality, but of economics. If the return on the investment is not enough to make it worthwhile, fewer people will make that particular investment in the future, and consumers will therefore be denied the use of the goods and services that would otherwise have been produced. No one is under any obligation to make all investments pay off, but how many need to pay off, and to what extent, is determined by how many consumers value the benefits of other people's investments.

Where the consumers do not like what is being produced, the investment should *not* pay off. When people insist on specializing in a field for which there is little demand, their investment has been a waste of scarce resources that could have produced something that others wanted. The low pay and sparse employment opportunities in that field are a compelling signal to them—and to others coming after them—to stop making such investments.

The same principle is involved in activities that do not pass through the marketplace, and are not normally thought of as economic. Putting things away after you use them is an investment of time in the present to reduce the time required to find them in the future. Explaining yourself to others can be a time-consuming, and even unpleasant, activity but it is engaged in as an investment to prevent greater unhappiness in the future from misunderstandings.

Economic activities, like other activities, take place over varying spans of time and with varying risks. Time alone is a cost—"hope deferred maketh the heart sick"—but often other things must be sacrificed as well. Both as individuals and as a society, we deny ourselves tangible benefits that are within our grasp today in order to save for other benefits in the future. These other benefits may not even exist at present. Sometimes we don't even know what these non-existent benefits are when they are paid for. If you are paying for health insurance, for example, then you are giving up some of the goods you could be enjoying today, in order that you may in the future have the benefit of bandages, penicillin, blood transfusions, or whatever medical resources you might turn out to need. You don't know which of these things it will be, and you would just as soon never need any of them. But you know that you might, which is why you are willing to pay—that is, to *invest* for future benefits, just as people invest on Wall Street.

Like other things, investment has a price —namely the interest, dividends or other future returns on the investment. Because these returns are in the future, risk is an inherent part of investment and the return must be higher when the risks are higher, or else people will refuse to part with their money. Moreover, these risks are constantly changing, as is our knowledge of particular risks. That is why the stock market is constantly fluctuating, as investors acquire more information (including misinformation) about the condition of the companies they have invested in, or the condition of other companies or industries which look like a better place to put their money.

Saving is usually thought of as putting things away for the future, and especially putting money away for the future. But, however important money is for the individual, what matters most for the society as a whole are the real things which this money represents. The government could easily print twice as much money, but the country would not be twice as rich, because the same amount of goods would then simply end up with larger numbers on their price tags. For the economy as a whole, it is these real goods and services that matter—and many of these goods and services cannot be saved for very long. Food spoils, paper eventually turns yellow and brittle, machinery rusts and corrodes. Therefore the economy as a whole saves, not necessarily by putting things in inventory for years, but by creating today the productive capacity needed to produce those things in the future, whether that means building a hydroelectric dam, an automobile factory or a computer software company.

What is being saved and invested in the present are not the goods and services that will be used in the future, but the *capacity* to produce those things in the future. That capacity may consist of machine tools that will produce an automobile five years from now or accumulating experience that will allow an artist to make a sketch worth $100 twenty years from now. The society saves and invests for the future by devoting resources to these productive capacities, instead of using those resources to produce consumer goods directly for use during the current year. This is true whether that society is primitive or high-tech. Farmers have known for centuries that they could either eat a potato or save it to plant in the ground to grow more potatoes next year. It is the same potato either way, so consumer goods and investment goods need not differ physically, but only in the uses to which they are put.

When economic actions taken at one time bear fruit at a later time, risk is introduced or increased. Knowledge is never perfect, and the longer the time between a decision and its consequences, the wider the gray area of uncertainty. One of the ways of dealing with this uncertainty is to prepare alternative courses of action. These may be in the form of contingency plans or in the form of material goods stored to cover a variety of possibilities.

In short, *inventory* is a substitute for knowledge. If a soldier going into battle knew that he would fire exactly 36 bullets in combat, he would not need to weigh himself down with more bullets than that or with a variety of first aid and other items that he would never use. Only his lack of knowledge makes it prudent for him to carry such an inventory.

Speculation is another way of dealing with risks and uncertainties.

SPECULATION

When an American wheat farmer in Idaho or Nebraska is getting ready to plant his crop, he has no way of knowing what the price of wheat will be when the crop is harvested. That depends on innumerable other wheat farmers, not only in the United States but as far away as Russia or Argentina. If the wheat crop fails in Russia or Argentina, the world price of wheat will shoot up, causing American wheat farmers to get very high prices for their crop. But if there are bumper crops of wheat in Russia or Argentina, there may be more wheat on the world market than anybody can use, with the excess having to go into expensive storage facilities. That will cause the world price of wheat to plummet, so that the American farmer may have nothing to show for all his work and be lucky to avoid taking a loss on the year. Meanwhile, he and his family will have to live on their savings or borrow from whatever sources will lend to them.

This is one of innumerable risky economic activities which give rise to the kind of specialized activity known as speculation. A professional speculator makes contracts to buy or sell at prices fixed today for goods to be delivered at some future date. This shifts the risk of the activity from the person engaging in it—such as the wheat farmer, in this case—to someone who is, in effect, betting that he can guess the future prices better than the other person and has the financial resources to ride out the inevitable wrong bets to make a profit on the bets that work out as predicted.

Speculation is often misunderstood as being the same as gambling, when in fact it is the opposite of gambling. What gambling involves, whether in games of chance or in actions like playing Russian roulette, is creating a risk that would otherwise not exist, in order either to profit or to exhibit one's skill or lack of fear. What economic speculation involves is coping with an *inherent* risk in such a way as to minimize it and to leave it to be borne by whoever is best equipped to bear it.

When a commodity speculator offers to buy wheat that has not yet been planted, that makes it easier for a farmer to plant wheat, without having to wonder what the market price will be like later, at harvest time. A futures contract guarantees the seller a specified price in advance, regardless of what the market price may turn out to be at the time of delivery. This separates farming from economic speculation, allowing each to be done by different people, in each case by the person best able to do it. The speculator uses his knowledge of the market, and of economic and statistical analysis, to try to arrive at a better guess than the farmer may be able to make, and thus is able to offer a price that the farmer will consider an attractive alternative to waiting to sell at whatever price happens to prevail in the market at harvest time.

Although speculators seldom make a profit on every transaction, they must come out ahead in the long run, in order to stay in business. Their profit depends on paying the farmer a price that is lower on average than the price which actually emerges at harvest time. The farmer also knows this, of course. In effect, the farmer is paying the speculator for carrying the risk. As with other goods and services, the question may be raised as to whether the service rendered is worth the price charged. At the individual level, each farmer can decide for himself whether the deal is worth it. Each speculator must of course bid against other speculators, as each farmer must compete with other farmers, whether in making futures contracts or in selling at harvest time. From the standpoint of the economy as a whole, competition determines what the price will be and therefore what the speculator's profit will be. If that profit exceeds what it takes to entice investors to risk their money in this volatile field, more investments will flow into this segment of the market until competition drives profits down to a level that just compensates the expenses, efforts, and risks.

Competition is visibly frantic among speculators who shout their offers and bids in commodity exchanges. Prices fluctuate from moment to moment and a five-minute delay in making a deal can mean the difference between profits and losses. Even a modest-sized firm engaging in commodity speculation can gain or lose hundreds of thousands of dollars in a day, and huge corporations can gain or lose millions in a few hours.

One of the most dramatic examples of what can happen with commodity speculation involved the rise and fall of silver prices in 1980. Silver was selling at $6.00 an ounce in early 1979 but skyrocketed to a high of $50.05 an ounce in early 1980. However, this price began a decline that reached $21.62 on March 26th. Then, in just one day, that price was cut in half to $10.80. In the process, the billionaire Hunt brothers, who were speculating heavily in silver, lost more than a billion dollars *within a few weeks*. Speculation is perhaps the most extreme example of a price system at work in allocating resources.

Speculation may be engaged in by people who are not normally thought of as speculators. As far back as 1880, the H. J. Heinz food-processing company signed contracts to buy cucumbers from farmers at pre-arranged prices, regardless of what the market prices might be when the cucumbers were harvested. Then as now, those farmers who did *not* sign futures contracts with anyone were necessarily engaging in speculation about prices at harvest time, whether or not they thought of themselves as speculators.

Because risk is the whole reason for speculation in the first place, being wrong is a common experience, though being wrong too often means facing financial extinction. Predictions, even by very knowledgeable people, can be wrong by vast amounts. The distinguished British magazine *The Economist* predicted in March 1999 that the price of oil would fall to $5 a barrel, but in fact the price of oil *rose* to $25 a barrel by December. Anyone speculating in oil on the basis of *The Economist*'s prediction could have been ruined financially.

Futures contracts are made for delivery of gold, oil, soybeans, foreign currencies and many other things at some price fixed in advance for delivery on a future date. When the speculator offers delivery at a price below the price prevailing when the contract is signed, he is said to be "selling short"—that is, betting that the price is going to go down so much in the meantime that he will still make a profit at the lower price. When he goes "long" that means his contract charges more than the current price. That in turn means that the other party expects the price to rise to a level even higher than the amount in the contract. All these contracts depend on different people having different estimates and the speculator's survival depends on his being right more often than the other party.

Commodity speculation is only one kind of speculation. One can also speculate in real estate, corporate stocks, or other things. For example, the stock of the Internet bookseller Amazon.com rose sharply for years before the company made a cent of profit. Why were buyers bidding up the price of this stock, which had yet to pay a dividend, from a company which as yet had no profits from which dividends might be paid if they wanted to? One reason was the belief that Amazon.com would eventually become profitable. Another reason was that the price of the stock was expected to continue to rise, so that the initial buyers could make a profit by selling to subsequent buyers, regardless of whether Amazon.com made a profit or not. This second reason was pure speculation.

The full cost of risk is not only the amount of money involved, it is also the worry that hangs over the individual while waiting to see what happens. A farmer may expect to get $100 a ton for his crop but also knows that it could turn out to be $50 a ton or $150. If a speculator offers to guarantee to buy his crop at $90 a ton, that price may look good if it spares the farmer months of sleepless nights wondering how he is going to support his family if the harvest price leaves him nothing to cover his costs. Not only may the speculator be better equipped financially to deal with being wrong, he may be better equipped psychologically, since the kind of people who worry a lot do not usually go into commodity speculation. A commodity speculator I know had one year when his business was operating at a loss going into December, but things changed so much in December that he still ended up with a profit for the year—to his surprise, as much as anyone else's. This is not an occupation for the faint of heart.

Economic speculation is another way of allocating scarce resources—in this case, knowledge. Neither the speculator nor the farmer knows what the prices will be when the crop is harvested. But the speculator happens to have more knowledge of markets and of economic and statistical analysis than the farmer, just as the farmer has more knowledge of how to grow the crop. My commodity speculator friend admitted that he had never actually seen a soybean and had no idea what they looked like, although he had probably bought and sold millions of dollars worth of them over the years. He simply transferred ownership of his soybeans on paper to soybean buyers at harvest time, without ever taking physical possession of them from the farmer. He was not really in the soybean business, he was in the risk management business.

Speculation means that complementary knowledge is thus coordinated, creating greater efficiency in the production of products which have inherent risks associated with their production. These risks can never be eliminated, but they can be minimized by having them borne by those best able to bear them, both from the standpoint of specialized knowledge and skills and from the standpoint of having sufficient financial accumulations to ride out losing speculations while waiting for them to be offset by winning speculations in the long run.

INVENTORIES

Inherent risks must be dealt with by the economy not only through economic speculation but also by maintaining inventories.

Put differently, *inventory is a substitute for knowledge*. No food would ever be thrown out after a meal, if the cook knew beforehand exactly how much each person would eat and could therefore cook just that amount. Since inventory costs money, a business enterprise must try to limit how much inventory it has on hand, while covering the possibility that its best guess as to how much it will need may be inadequate.

Clearly, those businesses which come closest to the optimal size of inventory will have their profit prospects enhanced. More important, the total resources of the economy will be allocated more efficiently, not only because each enterprise has an incentive to be efficient, but also because those firms which turn out to be right more often are more likely to survive and continue making such decisions, while those who repeatedly carry far too large an inventory, or far too small, are likely to disappear from the market through bankruptcy.

Some of the same economic principles involving risk apply to activities far removed from the marketplace. A soldier going into battle does not take just the number of bullets he will fire or just the amount of first aid supplies he will need if wounded in a particular way, because neither he nor anyone else has the kind of foresight required to do that. The soldier carries an inventory of both ammunition and medical supplies to cover various contingencies. At the same time, he cannot go into battle loaded down with huge amounts of everything that he might possibly need. This would slow him down and reduce his maneuverability, making him an easier target for the enemy. In other words, beyond some point, attempts to increase his safety can make his situation more dangerous.

RETURN ON INVESTMENT

Delayed rewards for costs incurred earlier are a return on investment, whether these rewards take the form of dividends paid on corporate stock or increases in incomes resulting from having gone to college or medical school. One of the largest investments in many people's lives consists of the time and energy expended over a period of years in raising their children. At one time, the return on that investment included having the children take care of the parents in old age, but today the return on this investment often consists only of the parents' satisfaction in seeing their children's well-being and progress. From the standpoint of society as a whole, each generation that makes this investment in its offspring is repaying the investment that was made by the previous generation in raising those who are parents today.

There are also investments made outside the family that transfer wealth back and forth across the generations. As noted in Chapter 9, income varies greatly with age. People in their forties and fifties tend to have much higher incomes than people in their twenties. People in the older generation often put their money into banks and other financial institutions, which in turn lend it to young people buying homes or getting an education. What this means is that the amount of income that older and higher-income people are entitled to spend is not in fact all spent by them. A significant amount of their money is spent by younger people who borrow through banks, for example, and use their elders' money to pay for mortgages, tuition, and the like. Later, when people in the older generation retire, they begin to consume more than they are currently producing by using money now being repaid to banks and other financial institutions, which share with them the interest and principal they are receiving from the younger generation, whose incomes have usually been rising over the years.

Looking beyond money to the actual goods and services exchanged over the years, the younger generation acquires more cars, houses, education and furniture than they can afford at the moment and the older generation is paid back later in golf carts, cruises, medical care, and retirement homes.

Although making investments and receiving the delayed return on those investments takes many forms and has been going on all over the world throughout the history of the human race, misunderstandings of this process have also been widespread. Sometimes these delayed benefits are called "unearned" income, simply because they do not represent rewards for contributions made during the current time period. Investments that build a factory may not be repaid until years later, after workers and managers have been hired and products manufactured and sold. During the particular year when dividends finally begin to be paid, investors may not have done anything, but this does not mean that the reward they receive is "unearned," simply because it was not earned that particular year. Yet elaborate ideologies and mass movements have been based on the notion that only the workers really create wealth, while others merely skim off profits, without having contributed anything to producing the wealth in which they unjustly share.

Similar misconceptions have had fateful consequences for money-lenders around the world. For many centuries, money-lenders have been widely condemned in many cultures for receiving back more money than they lent—that is, for getting an "unearned" income for waiting. Often the social stigma attached to money lending has been so great that only minorities who lived outside the existing social system anyway have been willing to take on such stigmatized activities. Thus, for centuries, the Jews predominated in such occupations in Europe, as the Chinese did in Southeast Asia, the Chettiars and Marwaris in India, and other minority groups in other parts of the world. At various times and places, the hostility to such groups has reached the point where these minorities have been expelled by governments or have been forced to flee from mob violence. Although often depicted as useless parasites, the contribution of money-lending minorities has been demonstrated after their departure by shortages of credit and general economic declines in the countries that forced them out.

Just as prices in general affect the allocation of resources from one place to another at a given time, so returns on investment affect the allocation of resources from one time period to another. A high rate of return provides incentives for people to save and invest more than they would at a lower rate of return. To say the same thing differently, a higher rate of return encourages people to consume less in the present, in order to consume more in the future. It allocates resources over time. The individual saver need not invest directly. Money saved in a bank, for example, can be lent out to someone else and invested in establishing or enlarging a business.

Investment plays another very important role in the economy. When teenage Henry Ford walked from the farm where he worked all the way into Detroit, in order to look for a job, he clearly did not have the kind of money needed to manufacture millions of automobiles. Where did he get that money, then? Obviously, someone thought enough of his ideas and abilities to risk some money backing him to get started. As he proved himself at one step after another, more and more people were willing to put their money behind him, in order to cash in on the product and the mass-production industry that he was creating. Investment is a way of transferring resources to where they have alternative uses that are more valuable than where they are.

Numerous other entrepreneurs, starting with little more than an idea and determination, have found investors willing to take a chance on them, just as investors take chances on oil wells or soybean futures. Although willing to take risks, these investors cannot be reckless or they will end up with nothing to invest. In this way, entrepreneurial talent gets a chance to prove itself in the marketplace, even if that talent originates in someone with no money of his own and utterly unknown to the general public or to the political powers that be. It is yet another way in which a free market system taps knowledge and abilities that have no avenues to emerge in more restrictive societies.

Present Value

Whether a home, business, or farm is maintained, repaired or improved today determines how long it will last and how well it will operate, and therefore what it will be worth in the future. However, the owner does not have to wait to see the effects on the property's value. These future returns are immediately reflected in the property's *present value*. The "present value" of an asset is in fact nothing more than its anticipated future returns, added up and discounted for the fact that they are delayed.

Conversely, if the city announces that it is going to begin building a sewage treatment plant next year, on a piece of land next to your home, the value of your home will decline *immediately*, before the adjoining land has been touched. The present value of an asset reflects its future benefits or detriments, so that anything which is expected to enhance or reduce those benefits or detriments will immediately affect the price at which the asset can be sold today.

Present value links the future to the present. It makes sense for a ninety-year-old man to begin planting trees that will take 20 years before they reach their maturity because his land will *immediately* be worth more because of those trees. He can sell the land six months later and go live in the Bahamas if he wishes, because he will be receiving additional value from the fruit that is expected to grow on those trees, years after he is no longer alive. Part of the value of his wealth today consists of the value of food that has not yet been grown—and which will be eaten by children who have not yet been born.

Any series of future payments can be reduced to a present value that can be paid immediately in a lump sum. Winners of lotteries who are paid in installments over a period of years can sell those payments to a financial institution that will give them a fixed sum immediately. So can accident victims who have been awarded installment payments from insurance companies. Because the present value of a series of payments due over a period of decades may be considerably less than the sum total of all those payments, the lump sums paid may be less than half of those totals, causing some people who sold to relieve immediate financial problems to later resent the deal they made. Others, however, are pleased and return to make similar deals in the future.

Natural Resources

Present value profoundly affects the discovery and use of natural resources. There may be enough oil underground to last for centuries, but its present value determines how much it pays anyone to discover—and that may be no more than enough to last for a dozen or so years. A failure to understand this basic economic reality has led to numerous false predictions that we were "running out" of petroleum, coal, or some other natural resource.

In 1960, for example, a best-selling book said that the United States had only a 13-year supply of domestic petroleum at the existing rate of usage. At that time, the known petroleum reserves of the United States were not quite 32 billion barrels. At the end of the 13 years, the known petroleum reserves of the United States were more than 36 billion barrels. Yet the original statistics and the arithmetic based on them were accurate. Why then did we not run out of oil in 13 years? Was it just dumb luck that more oil was discovered—or were there more fundamental economic reasons?

Just as shortages and surpluses are not simply a matter of how much physical stuff there is, either absolutely or relative to the population, so known reserves of natural resources are not simply a matter of how much physical stuff there is underground. For natural resources as well, prices are crucial. So are present values.

How much of any natural resource is known to exist depends on how much it costs to know. Oil exploration, for example, is very costly. This includes not only the costs of geological exploration but also the costs of repeatedly drilling expensive dry holes before finally striking oil. As these costs mount up while more and more oil is being discovered, the growing abundance of known supplies of oil reduces its price through supply and demand. Eventually the point is reached where the cost per barrel of finding more oil exceeds the present value per barrel of the oil you are likely to find. At that point, it no longer pays to keep exploring. Depending on a number of circumstances, the total amount of oil discovered at that point may be no more than the 13 years' supply which led to dire predictions that we were running out.

As one example of the kinds of costs that can be involved, a major oil exploration venture in the Gulf of Mexico spent $80 million on the initial exploration and leases, and another $120 million for exploratory drilling, just to see if it looked like there was enough oil to justify continuing further. Then there were $530 million spent for building drilling platforms, pipelines and infrastructure, and—finally—$370 million for drilling for oil where there were proven reserves. This adds up to a total of $1.1 billion.

Imagine if the interest rate had been twice as high on this much money borrowed from banks or investors, making the total cost of exploration even higher. Or imagine that the oil companies had this much money of their own and could put it in a bank to earn twice the usual interest in safety. Would they have sunk as much as they did into looking for oil? Would you? Probably not. A higher interest rate would probably have meant less oil exploration and therefore smaller amounts of known reserves of petroleum. But that would not mean that we were any closer to running out of oil than if the interst rate were lower and the known reserves were correspondingly higher.[1]

As more and more of the known reserves of oil get used up, the present value of the remaining oil begins to rise and once more exploration for additional oil becomes profitable. But, as of any given time, it never pays to discover all the oil that exists in the ground or under the sea—or more than a minute fraction of that oil. What does pay is for people to write hysterical predictions that we are running out of natural resources. It pays not only in book sales and television ratings, but also in political power and in personal notoriety.

Even the huge usages of energy resources in the twentieth century have not reduced the known reserves of some of these resources. It has been estimated that more energy was consumed in the first two decades of the twentieth century than in all the previously recorded history of the human race. Moreover, energy usage has continued to escalate since then. Yet known petroleum reserves have risen. The known reserves of petroleum in the world were more than twice as large in 1999 as they were in 1969.

The economic considerations which apply to petroleum apply to other natural resources as well. No matter how much iron ore there is in the ground, it will never pay to discover more of it when its present value per ton is less than the cost of exploration and processing per ton. Yet, despite the fact that the twentieth century has seen vast expansions in the use of iron and steel, the proven reserves of iron ore in 1980 were nearly five times what they were in 1950. Copper, aluminum, and lead reserves were also several times as great in 1980 as in 1950.

The difference between the economic approach and the hysterical approach to natural resource usage was shown by a bet between economist Julian Simon and environmentalist Paul

---

[1]Although an extreme example was used to dramatize a point, even a very modest rise in the interest rate—say just one percentage point—would mean increased costs of more than a million dollars a year on a venture with $1.1 billion invested. And since it would be a number of years before the oil being sought actually comes out of a pump at a gas station to be sold to a paying customer, the million-plus dollars a year in additional interest charges would amount to several million dollars more in costs before the money spent could begin to be repaid.

Ehrlich. Professor Simon offered to bet anyone that any set of five natural resources they chose would not have risen in real cost over any time period they chose. A group led by Professor Ehrlich chose five natural resources and chose ten years as the period for measuring how their real costs changed. At the end of that period, not only had the real cost of that set of five resources declined, so had the cost of every individual resource they had expected to rise in cost! Obviously, if we had been anywhere close to running out of these resources, their costs would have risen because the present value of these potentially more scarce resources would have risen.

In some ultimate sense, the total quantity of resources must of course be declining. However, a resource that is going to run out a thousand years after it becomes obsolete, or a century after the sun grows cold, is not a serious practical problem. If it is going to run out within some time period that is a matter of practical relevance, then the rising present value of the resource whose exhaustion looms ahead will automatically force conservation, without either public hysteria or political exhortation.

Just as prices cause us to share scarce resources and their products with others at a given time, present value causes us to share those resources over time with future generations—without even being aware that we are sharing. It is of course also possible to share politically, by having the government assume control of natural resources, as it can assume control of other assets, or in fact of the whole economy.

The efficiency of political control versus impersonal control by prices in the marketplace depends in part on which method conveys the underlying realities more accurately. As already noted, the price controls and direct allocation of resources by political institutions requires far more explicit knowledge by a relatively small number of planners than is required for a market economy to be coordinated by prices to which millions respond according to their own first-hand knowledge of their own individual circumstances and preferences. Moreover, planners can easily make false projections, either from ignorance or from various political motives, such as seeking more power, re-election, or other goals. During the 1970s, a government scientist was asked to estimate the size of the American reserves of natural gas and how long it would last. His estimate was that the United States had enough natural gas to last for 4,000 years! While some might consider this good news, politically it was bad news at a time when the President of the United States was trying to get public support for more government programs to deal with the energy "crisis." This estimate was repudiated by the Carter administration and a new study begun, which reached more politically acceptable results.

Sometimes the known reserves of a natural resource seem especially small because the amount available at currently feasible costs is in fact nearing exhaustion. There may be vast amounts available at a slightly higher cost of extraction, but these additional amounts will of course not be touched until the amount available at a lower cost is exhausted. For example, so long as there were coal deposits available on top of the ground, no one was going to the expense of digging even a few feet into the earth to get more, because the higher-cost coal underground could not compete in the marketplace with the cheaper coal on the surface. During the interim, someone could sound an alarm that we are "running out" of coal that is "economically feasible" to use, coal that can be gotten without "prohibitive costs." But again, the whole purpose of prices is to be prohibitive. In this case, that prohibition prevented more costly resources from being used needlessly, so long as there were less costly sources of the same resource available. This is just one of the ways in which prices contribute to economic efficiency.

If technology never improved, then all resources would become more costly over time, as the most easily obtained deposits were used up first and the less accessible, or less rich, or more difficult to process deposits were then resorted to. However, with improving technology, it can actually cost less to acquire future resources when their time comes, as happened with the resources that Julian Simon and Paul Ehrlich bet on.

Although the reserves of natural resources in a nation are often discussed in terms of physical quantities, economic concepts of cost, prices, and present values must be considered if practical conclusions are to be reached. Sweeping statements that some poor country has so many billions worth of "natural wealth" in the form of iron ore or bauxite deposits mean very little without considering how much it would cost to extract and process those resources. A country with $10 billion worth of some natural resource might as well not have it if the costs of exploration, extraction and processing add up to $11 billion.

Chapter 13

Risks and Insurance

Whenever a home, a business, or any other asset increases in value over time, that increase is called a "capital gain." While it is another form of income, it differs from wages and salaries in not being paid right after it is earned, but usually only after an interval of some years. A thirty-year bond, for example, can be cashed in only after thirty years.

If you never sell your home, then whatever increase in value it has will be called an "unrealized capital gain." The same is true for someone who opens a grocery store that grows more valuable as its location becomes known throughout the neighborhood and as it develops a set of customers who get into the habit of shopping at that particular store. Perhaps after the owner dies, his widow or children may decide to sell the store—and only then will the capital gain be realized.

Sometimes a capital gain comes from a purely financial transaction, where you simply pay someone a certain amount of money today in order to get back a somewhat larger amount of money later on. This happens when you put money into a savings account that pays interest, or when a pawnbroker lends money, or when you buy a $10,000 U. S. Treasury bond for somewhat less than $10,000.

However it is done, this is a trade-off of money today for money in the future. The fact that interest is paid implies that money today is worth more than the same amount of money in the future. How much more depends on many things, and varies from time to time, as well as from country to country at the same time.

In the heyday of 19th-century British industrialization, railroad companies could raise the huge sums of money required to build miles of tracks and buy trains, by selling bonds that paid about 3 percent per year. This was possible only because the public had great confidence in both the railroads and the stability of the money. If inflation had been 4 percent a year, those who bought the bonds would have lost real value instead of gaining it. But the value of the British pound sterling was very stable and reliable during that era. Since those times, inflation has become more common, so the interest rate would now have to cover whatever level of inflation was expected and still leave a prospect of a real gain.

Leaving inflation aside, however, how much would a $10,000 bond that matures a year from now be worth to you today? Clearly it would not be worth $10,000, because future money is not as valuable as the same amount of present money. Even if you felt certain that you would still be alive a year from now, and even if there were no inflation expected, you would still prefer to have the same amount of money right now rather than later. If nothing else, money that you have today can be put in a bank and earn a year's interest on it. For the same reason, if you had a choice between buying a bond that matures a year from now and another bond of the same face value that matures ten years from now, you would not be willing to bid as much for the one that matures a decade later. What this says is that the same nominal amount of money has different values. depending on how long you must wait to get a return on it.

At a sufficiently high interest rate, you might be willing to wait a long time to get your money back. On the other hand, at a sufficiently low interest rate, you would not be willing to wait any time at all to get your money back. Somewhere in between is an interest rate at which you would be indifferent between lending money or keeping it. At that interest rate, the present value of a given amount of future money is equal to some smaller amount of present money. For example if you are indifferent at 4 percent, then a hundred dollars today is worth $104 a year from now to you. Any business or government agency that wants to get $100 from you today with a promise to pay you back a year from now will have to make that repayment at least $104. If everyone else has the same preferences that you do, then the interest rate in the economy as a whole will be 4 percent.

What if everyone does not have the same preferences that you do? Suppose that others will lend only when they get back 5 percent more at the end of the year? In that case, the interest rate in the economy as a whole will be 5 percent, simply because businesses and government cannot borrow the money they need for any less and they do not have to offer any more. Faced with a national interest rate of 5 percent, you would have no reason to accept less, even though you would take 4 percent if you had to. In this situation, let us return to the question of how much you would be willing to bid for a $10,000 bond that matures a year from now.

With an interest rate of 5 percent being available in the economy as a whole, it would not pay you to bid more than $9,523.81 for a $10,000 bond that matures a year from now. By investing that same amount of money somewhere else today at 5 percent, you could get back $10,000 in a year. Therefore, there is no reason for you to bid more than $9,523.81 for the $10,000 bond.

What if the interest rate in the economy as a whole had been 12 percent, rather than 5 percent? Then it would not pay you to bid more than $8,928.57 for a $10,000 bond that matures a year from now. What people will bid for bonds depends on how much they could get for the same money by putting it somewhere else. That is why bond prices go down when the interest rate goes up, and vice-versa.

What this also says is that, when the interest rate is 5 percent, $9,523.81 in the year 2000 is the same as $10,000 in the year 2001. This raises questions about the taxation of capital gains. If someone buys a bond for the former price and sells it a year later for the latter price, the government will of course want to tax the $476.19 difference. But is that really the same as an increase in value, if the two sums of money are just equivalent to one another? What if there has been a one percent inflation, so that the $10,000 received back would not have been enough to compensate for waiting, if the investor had expected inflation to reduce the real value of the bond?

What if there had been a 5 percent inflation, so that the amount received back was worth no more than the amount originally lent, with no reward at all for waiting? Clearly, the investor would be worse off than if he or she had never bought the bond. How then can this "capital gain" really be said to be a gain?

These are just some of the reasons why the taxation of capital gains is more complicated than the taxation of such other forms of income as wages and salaries. Some foreign governments do not tax capital gains at all, while the rate at which such gains are taxed in the United States remains a matter of political controversy.

VARIABLE RETURNS VERSUS FIXED RETURNS

Bonds differ from stocks because bonds are legal commitments to pay fixed amounts of money on a fixed date. Stocks are simply shares of the business that issues them, and there is no guarantee that the business will make a profit in the first place. Bond-holders have a legal right to be paid what they were promised, whether the business is making money or losing money. In that respect, they are like the business' employees, to whom fixed commitments have been made as to how much they would be paid per hour or per week or month. They are legally entitled to those amounts, regardless of whether the business is profitable or unprofitable. The owners of a business—whether that is a single individual or millions of stockholders—are not legally entitled to anything, except whatever happens to be left over after a business has paid its employees, bond-holders and other creditors.

Considering the fact that most new businesses fail within a few years, what is left over can just as easily be negative as positive. In other words, people who set up businesses may not only fail to make a profit but may even lose part or all of what they originally invested. In short, stocks and bonds have different amounts of risk. Moreover, the mixture of stocks and bonds sold by different businesses may reflect the inherent risks of those businesses themselves.

Imagine that someone is raising money to go into a business where (1) the chances are 50–50 that he will go bankrupt and (2) if he does survive financially, his initial investment will increase ten-fold. Perhaps he is drilling for oil or speculating in foreign currencies. What if he wants you to contribute $5,000 to this venture? If you can afford the risk, would you be better off buying $5,000 worth of stock in this enterprise or $5,000 worth of this company's bonds?

If you buy bonds, your chances are only 50–50 of getting your money back at all. And if this enterprise prospers, you are only entitled to whatever rate of return was specified in the bond at the outset, no matter how many millions of dollars the entrepreneur makes with your money. Buying bonds in such a venture does not seem like a good deal. Buying stocks, on the other hand, might make sense. If the business goes bankrupt, your stock could be worthless, while a bond would have some value, based on whatever assets might remain to be sold, even if that only pays the bondholders and other creditors pennies on the dollar. On the other hand, if the business succeeds and its assets increase ten-fold, then the value of your stock increases ten-fold.

If you are a venture capitalist with $50,000 to invest in similar ventures, then you can buy $5,000 worth of stock in ten such enterprises. If the odds are 50–50 on each, then you should expect five of the ten to pay off ten-fold, while you lose $25,000 on the others that go bankrupt. Subtracting that $25,000 from the $250,000 you get from your stock in five that succeed, you still have a phenomenal return of $225,000 on an investment of $50,000. Even if you are unlucky and only two of the ten pay off, you still come out ahead, with $40,000 in losses on the eight that fail and $100,000 on the two that succeed. You get back $60,000 from the $50,000 you invested. That is a 20 percent return on your investment if you get your money back in a year and, of course, correspondingly less if it takes several years for the ventures to pay off.

Now look at the same transaction from the standpoint of the entrepreneur who is trying to raise money for his venture. Knowing that bonds would be unattractive to investors and that a bank would be reluctant to lend to him for the same reasons, he would almost certainly try to raise money by selling stocks instead. At the other end of the risk spectrum, consider a public utility that supplies something the public always needs, such as water or electricity. There is very little risk involved in putting money into such an enterprise, so the utility can issue and sell bonds, without having to pay the higher amounts that investors would earn on stocks.

In short, risks vary among businesses and their financial arrangements vary accordingly. At one extreme, a commodity speculator can go from profits to losses and back again, not only from year to year but even from hour to hour on a given day. That is why there are television pictures of frantic shouting and waving in commodity exchanges, where prices are changing so rapidly that the difference between making a deal right now and making it five minutes from now can be many thousands of dollars.

A more common pattern among those businesses that succeed is one of low income or no income at the beginning, followed by higher earnings after the enterprise becomes established. For example, a dentist first starting out in his profession after graduating from dental school and buying the costly equipment needed, may have little or no income the first year, before becoming widely-enough known in the community to attract a large clientele. During that interim, the dentist's secretary may be making more money than the dentist. Later on, of course, the situation will reverse and some observers may then think if unfair that the dentist makes several times the income of the secretary.

Even when variable sums of money add up to the same total as fixed sums of money, they are unlikely to be equally attractive. Would you be equally as likely to enter two occupations with the same average income—say, $50,000 a year—over the next decade if one occupation paid $50,000 every year while the income in the other occupation might vary from $10,000 one year to $90,000 the next year? Chances are you would require a somewhat higher average income in the occupation with variable pay, to make it equally attractive with the occupation with fixed pay. Accordingly, stocks usually yield a higher average rate of return than bonds, since stocks have a variable rate of return (including, sometimes, no return at all), while bonds have a guaranteed fixed rate of return. This does not happen because of some moral principle. It happens because people will not take the risk of buying stocks unless they can expect a higher average rate of return than they get from bonds.

The degree of risk varies not only with the kind of investment but also with the period of time. For a period of a year, bonds are likely to be much safer than stocks. For a period of 20 or 30 years, however, the risk of inflation threatens the value of bonds or other assets with fixed-dollar amounts, such as bank accounts, while stock prices tend to rise with inflation like real estate, factories, or other real assets. Being shares of real assets, stocks share in the rising price of real assets during inflation. Moreover, even in the absence of inflation, stock prices can generally be relied on to rise over a period of decades, while bond prices and the prices of other fixed-dollar assets do not. Therefore the relative safety of the two kinds of assets can be quite different in the long run than in the short run.

Someone planning for retirement many years in the future may find a suitable mixture of stocks a much safer investment than someone who will need the money in a year or two. "Like money in the bank" is a popular phrase used to indicate something that is a very safe bet, but money in the bank is not particularly safe over a period of decades, when inflation can steal much of its value. The same is true of bonds. Eventually, after reaching an age when the remaining life expectancy is no longer decades, it may be prudent to begin transferring money out of stocks and into bonds, bank accounts, and other assets with grater short-run safety.

The main point here is that safety and risk depend on the time period involved, as well as on the kind of asset. To take an extreme example, while a dollar invested in bonds in 1801 would be worth nearly a thousand dollars by 1998, a dollar invested in stocks that same year would be worth more than half a million dollars. All this is in real terms, taking inflation into account. Meanwhile, a dollar invested in gold in 1801 would by 1998 be worth just 78 cents. The phrase "as good as gold" can be as misleading as the phrase "money in the bank," when talking about the long run. There have been many short-run periods when bonds and gold held their value while stock prices plummeted. The relative safety of these different kinds of investments varies greatly with how long a time period you have in mind.

The relative safety and profitability of various kinds of investments also depends on your own knowledge. An experienced expert in financial transactions may grow rich speculating in gold, while people of more modest knowledge may be losing big.

However, with gold you are unlikely to be completely wiped out, since gold always has a value for jewelry and industrial uses, while any given stock can end up not worth the paper it is printed on. Nor is it only novices who lose money in the stock market. Harvard's $13 billion endowment fell by 10 percent in less than three months. In the past, colleges and universities kept their endowments in safe investments like government bonds but, during the stock market boom of the 1990s, many went for higher rates of return in the financial markets. As *The Wall Street Journal* put it, these academic institutions "are re-learning the lesson that high returns often are achieved by taking high risks."

The various degrees and varieties of risk can be dealt with by having a variety of investments—a "portfolio," as they say—so that when one kind of investment is not doing well, other kinds may be flourishing, thereby reducing the over-all risk to your total assets. For example, bonds may not be doing well during a period when stock are very profitable, and vice versa. A portfolio that includes a combination of both stocks and bonds may be much less risky than investing exclusively in either.

These economic principles have long been understood by those investing their own money. In centuries past shipowners often found it more prudent to own 10 percent of ten different ships, rather than to own one ship outright. The dangers of a ship sinking were much greater in the days of wooden ships and sails than in the modern era of metal, mechanically powered ships. Owning 10 percent shares in ten different ships increased the danger of a loss through sinking but greatly reduced how catastrophic that loss would be.

These are just some of the ways in which risks can be spread, thereby reducing the total risk. Insurance is another example.

INSURANCE

Like commodity speculators, insurance companies deal with inherent and inescapable risks. Insurance both transfers and reduces those risks. In exchange for the premium paid by its policyholder, the insurance company assumes the risk of compensating for losses caused by automobile accidents, houses catching fire, and numerous other misfortunes which befall human beings. There are more than 6,000 insurance companies in the United States and their total assets exceed 2 trillion dollars.

In addition to transferring risks, an insurance company seeks to reduce them. For example, it charges lower prices to safe drivers and refuses to insure some homes until brush and other flammable materials near a house are removed. In a variety of ways, it segments the population and charges different prices to people with different risks. That way it reduces its own over-all risks and, in the process, sends a signal to people engaging in dangerous behavior or living in dangerous neighborhoods, conveying to them the costs created by their chosen behavior or location.

The most common kind of insurance—life insurance—compensates for a misfortune that cannot be prevented. Everyone must die but the risk involved is in the time of death. If everyone were known in advance to die at age 70, there would be no point in life insurance, because there would be no risk involved. Each individual's financial affairs could be arranged in advance to take that predictable death into account. Paying premiums to an insurance company would make no sense, because the total amount to which those premiums grew over the years would have to add up to an amount no less than the compensation to be received by one's surviving beneficiaries. The insurance company would, in effect, become an issuer of bonds redeemable on fixed dates. Buying life insurance at age 30 would be the same as buying a 40-year bond and buying life insurance at age 40 would be the same as buying a 30-year bond.

What makes life insurance different from a bond is that neither the individual insured nor the insurance company knows when that particular individual will die. The financial risks to others that accompany the death of a family breadwinner or business partner are transferred to the insurance company for a price. Those risks are also reduced because the average death rate among millions of policy-holders is far more predictable than the death of any given individual. As with other forms of insurance, risks are not simply transferred from one party to another, but reduced. Where a given party has a large enough sample of risks, there may be no benefit from buying an insurance policy. Hertz car rental agency, for example, has so many automobiles of its own that its risks are sufficiently spread that it need not pay an insurance company to assume those risks. It can use the same statistical methods used by insurance companies to determine the financial costs of its risk and incorporate that cost into what it charges people who rent cars. There is no point transferring a risk that is not reduced in the process, because the insurer must charge as much as the risk would cost the insured—plus enough more to pay the administrative costs of doing business and still leave a profit to the insurer. Self-insurance is therefore a viable option for those with a large enough sample of risks.

Insurance companies do not simply save the premiums they receive and later pay them out when the time comes. They invest these premiums, so that they will have more money available than if they had let the money gather dust in a vault. Obviously, this money has to be put into relatively safe investments—building housing developments, rather than commodity speculation, for example.

Because insurance companies compete with one another for customers, the price of premiums is reduced by these investments, since the premiums paid in do not have to add up to the total amount that will be paid out to the policy-holders. The fact that the money taken in over the years grows because of the returns on the investments financed by insurance companies means that there can be more money at the end than was paid in by the policy-holders over the years.

While it might seem that the insurance company could keep the profit from these investments for itself, in reality competition forces the price of insurance down, as it forces other prices down, to a level that will cover costs and provide a rate of return sufficient to compensate investors without attracting additional competition. In an economy where investors are always on the lookout for higher profits, an inflated rate of profit in the insurance industry would tend to cause new insurance companies to be created, in order to share in this bonanza. This can be prevented when there is a state regulatory agency that controls who can and cannot be allowed to sell insurance, so that higher profits are possible when such an agency protects the existing firms from competition.

The politics of insurance regulation is far more complicated than the basic economics of insurance. The very process by which insurance companies reduce risk is often under political attack. It may be considered "unfair," for example, that a driver with an unblemished record must pay a higher premium because of the neighborhood in which he or she happens to live. The fact that the risk to the car comes not only from its driver but also from other drivers, as well as from car thieves and vandals, is easily lost sight of during emotional political appeals, though it can never be lost sight of by an insurance company whose own money is at stake.

Similar arguments are often made—and laws passed accordingly—that it is "unfair" that a safe young driver is charged a higher premium because other young drivers have higher accident rates, or that young male drivers are charged more than female drivers the same age for similar reasons. Running through such political arguments is the notion that it is wrong for people to be penalized for things that are not their fault. This implicitly changes the subject from risk to morality—and insurance companies exist because of risk. Forcing them to charge the same premiums to groups of people with different risks means that premiums must rise over all, with safer groups subsidizing more dangerous groups. In the case of automobile insurance, it also means that more unsafe drivers can afford to be on the road, so that their victims pay the highest and most unnecessary price of all in injuries and deaths.

Government programs that deal with risk are often analogized to insurance, or may even be officially called "insurance" without in fact being insurance. Federal disaster relief helps victims of floods, hurricanes and other natural disasters to recover and rebuild but, unlike insurance, it does not reduce the over-all risk. Often people rebuild homes and businesses in the well-known paths of hurricanes and floods, often to the applause of the media for their "courage." But the financial risks created are not paid by those who create them, as with insurance, but are instead paid by the taxpayers.

In short, there is now more risk than if there were no disaster relief available and more risk than if private insurance companies were charging these people premiums which cover the full cost of their risky behavior. Sometimes the government subsidizes insurance for earthquakes or other disasters for which private insurance would be "prohibitively expensive." What that means is that the government makes it less expensive for people to live in risky places—and more costly to the society as a whole, when people distribute themselves in more risky ways than they would do if they had to bear the costs themselves, either in high insurance premiums or in financial losses and anxieties.

There is an almost politically irresistible inclination to help people struck by earthquakes, wildfires, tornadoes and other natural disasters. The tragic pictures on television over-ride any consideration of what the situation was when they decided to live where they did. But government-subsidized insurance is, in effect, disaster relief provided for them beforehand, and is therefore a factor in people's choices of where to live and what risks to take with other people's money.

Competition among insurance companies involves not only price but service. When flood, hurricanes or other disasters strike an area, insurance company *A* cannot afford to be slower than insurance company *B* in getting money to their policy-holders. Imagine a policy-holder whose home has been destroyed by a flood or hurricane, and who is still waiting for his insurance agent to show up, while his neighbor's insurance agent arrives on the scene within hours to advance a few thousand dollars immediately, so that the family can afford to go find shelter somewhere. Not only will the customer of the tardy insurance company be likely to change companies afterward, so will people all across the country, if word gets out as to who provides prompt service and who drags their feet. For the tardy insurance company, that can translate into losing billions of dollars worth of business. The lengths to which some insurance companies go to avoid being later than the competing insurance companies was indicated by a *New York Times* story:

> Prepared for the worst, some insurers had cars equipped with global positioning systems to help navigate neighborhoods with

downed street signs and missing landmarks, and many claims adjusters carried computer-produced maps identifying the precise location of every customer.

The kind of market competition which forces such extraordinary efforts is of course lacking in government emergency programs, which have no competitors. They may be analogized to insurance but do not have the same incentives.

Social Security

Another form of government program that has been analogized to insurance, and is in fact called insurance in the "Federal Insurance Contributions Act," is Social Security. The "F.I.C.A." premiums deducted from paychecks for Social Security are immediately spent upon their arrival in Washington—either to pay pensions to existing Social Security retirees or to pay for any of the many other government activities, from fighting wars to paying the travel expenses of members of Congress on junkets.

The reason for the crisis atmosphere surrounding many discussions of how to "save" Social Security comes from the fact that F.I.C.A. premiums are not invested, like insurance premiums, but are spent. Therefore, future pensions for those currently paying F.I.C.A. premiums will not be paid out of those premiums, but out of *future* F.I.C.A. premiums paid by people who are working in the future—and from future general taxes, if and when future F.I.C.A. premiums are insufficient.

That is why there is such worry in Washington about the size of the next generation that will have to pay the pensions of the current generation. So long as each successive generation was larger than the previous one, Social Security operated successfully like a pyramid scheme in its early phases, where enough new people are joining that their payments in can provide a good return on the investment made by earlier members. In particular, when the relatively small generation born during the 1930s was being paid retirement pensions from the premiums received from the larger postwar "baby boom" generation, they received back far more than they paid in. However, with the prospect of the large baby boom generation themselves retiring in the twenty-first century, there are no longer as high a ratio of working people paying into the system, in proportion to the retirees to whom money must be paid out. Although this problem is often de-scribed as being due to changing demographics, the only reason changing demographics are a problem is because Social Security was never insurance in the first place, even though it was politi-cally expedient to describe it that way.

In a genuine insurance, the premiums paid by the current gen-eration are invested and the returns used to pay either annuities to that very same generation or to pay death benefits to their sur-vivors. That is why insurance companies do not have to worry about how big the next generation is going to be, but politicians do. Politicians do not invest the Social Security premiums but spend the money as fast as they get their hands on it.

The illusion of investment is maintained by giving the Social Security trust fund government bonds in exchange for the money that is taken from it and spent on current government programs. But these bonds represent no tangible assets. They are simply promises to pay money collected from future taxpayers. The country as a whole is not one dime richer because these bonds were printed, so there is no analogy with private investments which create apartment complexes, clothing factories, or automo-bile plants, whose productions and sales will provide the real in-come needed by a retired generation whose premiums built these things.

Chapter 14

An Overview

Time adds a new dimension to economics, as it does to other aspects of life. Future money is not the same as present money, even if there has been no inflation to reduce its purchasing power. A bond worth $105 a year from now is not worth buying for $100 today if the current interest rate is 6 percent.

Interest is the price of time and it affects not only financial transactions, but even such apparently unrelated things as the amount of a country's known reserves of natural resources. If the interest rate doubles, then the rising cost of exploring for oil and other natural resources will reduce the amount of exploration, which in turn means that the explorers will probably find less. To those who do not understand the role of interest rates in all this, it may appear that we are going to run out of these resources even sooner than they thought before. But that is precisely why it is necessary to take interest rates into account, so as not to be so easily stampeded by the media, politicians, and others with a vested interest in creating excitement or alarming the public.

With time comes risk. This *inherent* risk must be sharply distinguished from the kinds of risk that are created by such activities as gambling, mountain climbing, or playing Russian roulette. Economic activities for dealing with inescapable risks seek both to minimize those risks and shift them to those best able to carry them. A commodity speculator can reduce risks overall by engaging in a wider variety of risky activities than a farmer, for example. A wheat farmer can be wiped out if bumper crops of wheat around the world force the price far below what was expected when the crop was planted. But a similar disaster would be unlikely to strike wheat, gold, cattle, and foreign currencies simultaneously, so that someone who speculated in all these things would be in less danger than someone who speculated in any one of them.

Whatever statistical or other expertise the speculator has further reduces the risks below what they would be for the farmer or other producer. More fundamentally, from the standpoint of the efficient use of scarce resources, speculation reduces the costs associated with risks for the economy as a whole. One of the important consequences, in addition to more people being able to sleep well at night because of having a guaranteed market for their output, is that more people find it worthwhile to produce things under risky conditions than would have found it worthwhile if they had to bear those risks personally. In other words, the economy can produce more soybeans because of soybean speculators, even if the speculators themselves know nothing about soybeans.

It is especially important to understand the interlocking mutual interests of different economic groups—the farmer and the speculator being just one example—and, above all, the effects on the economy as a whole, because these are things often neglected in the zest of the media for emphasizing conflicts that sell newspapers and get larger audiences for television news programs. Political demagogues likewise benefit from portraying different groups as enemies of one another and themselves as the saviors of the group they claim to represent.

When wheat prices soar, for example, nothing is easier for a demagogue than to cry out against the injustice of a situation where speculators sitting comfortably in their air-conditioned offices grow rich on the sweat of farmers toiling in the fields for months under a hot sun. The years when the speculators took a financial beating, while the farmers lived comfortably on the guaranteed wheat prices paid by speculators, are of course forgotten.

Similarly, when an impending or expected shortage drives up prices, much indignation is often expressed in politics and the media about the higher retail prices being charged for things that the sellers bought when prices were lower. What things cost under earlier conditions is history; what the supply and demand are today is economics. During the 1991 Persian Gulf War, for example, oil prices rose sharply around the world, in anticipation of a disruption of Middle East oil exports because of military action. A speculator then rented an oil tanker and filled it with oil purchased in Venezuela to be shipped to the United States. But, before the tanker arrived, the Gulf War was over sooner than anyone expected and oil prices fell, leaving the speculator unable to sell his oil for enough to recover his costs. Here too, what he paid in the past was history and what he could get now was economics.

From the standpoint of the economy as a whole, oil purchased at different times, under different sets of expectations, are the same when they enter the market today. There is no reason why they should be priced differently, if the goal is to allocate scarce resources in the most efficient way.

Politics and economics differ radically in the way they deal with time. For example, when it becomes clear that the fares being charged on municipal buses is too low to permit these buses to be replaced as they wear out, the logical economic conclusion for the long run is to raise the fares. Politically, however, a candidate who opposes the fare increase as "unjustified" may gain the votes of bus riders at the next election. Moreover, since all the buses are not going to wear out immediately, the consequences of holding down the fare will not appear all at once but will be spread out over time. It may be some years before enough buses start breaking down and wearing out, without adequate replacements, for the bus riders to notice that there now seem to be longer waits between buses and they do not arrive on schedule as often as they used to.

By the time municipal transit system gets so bad that many people begin moving out of the city, taking the taxes they pay with them, so much time may have elapsed since the political fare controversy that few people see any connection. Meanwhile, the politician who won a municipal election by assuming the role of champion of the bus riders may now have moved on up to statewide office or even national office on the basis of his popularity. As a declining tax base causes deteriorating city services and neglected infrastructure, the erstwhile hero of the bus riders may even be able to boast that things were never this bad when he was a city official, and blame the current problems on the failings of his successors.

In economics, however, future consequences are anticipated in the concept of "present value." If, instead of fares being regulated by municipal government, these fare were set by a private bus company operating in a free market, any neglect of financial provisions for replacing buses as they wear out would begin immediately to reduce the value of the bus company's stock. In other words, the present value of the bus company would decline as a result of the long-run consequences that were anticipated by investors concerned about the safety and profitability of their own money.

If a private bus company's management decided to keep fares too low to maintain and replace its buses as they wore out, or decided to pay themselves higher executive salaries instead of setting aside funds for the maintenance of their bus fleet, 99 percent of the public might still be unaware of this or its long-run consequences. But among the other one percent who would be far more likely to be aware would be financial institutions that owned stock in the bus company, or were considering buying that stock or lending money to the bus company. For these investors, potential investors, or lenders examining financial records, the company's present value would be seen as reduced, long before the first bus wore out.

As in other situations, a market economy allows accurate knowledge to be effective in influencing decision-making, even if 99 percent of the population does not have that knowledge. In politics, however, the 99 percent who do not understand can create immediate political success for officials and policies that will turn out in the end to be harmful to society as a whole. It would of course be unreasonable to expect the general public to become financial experts or any other kind of experts. What may be more reasonable is to expect enough of them to see the dangers in letting economic decisions be made through political processes.

Time makes foresight a crucial variable in economics, even if the political time horizon is bounded by the next election. Many policies are made as if the citizens subject to them are like pieces on a chessboard, to be moved here and there as the policy-makers wish. For example, when tax rates are raised 10 percent, it may be assumed that tax revenues will also rise by 10 percent. But in fact more people may move out of the heavily taxed jurisdiction, or buy less of the heavily taxed commodity, so that the revenues received may be disappointingly far below what was estimated.

When traffic fines were raised steeply in California in 1992, the state estimated that there would be an increase of more $500 million in revenues, but the actual increase was less than half of that. After the new and heftier fines went into effect, more motorists began challenging their tickets in court, some chose to go to jail instead, and others simply failed to pay. In San Francisco, a two-week wait to get a date in traffic court in 1991 became a two-month wait in 1992. In short, people do not passively accept whatever government does, as too many officials and others assume.

In Third World countries where confiscation of land for redistribution to the poor is contemplated, the long time which can elapse between the political campaign for redistribution of land and the time when it is actually done can be years, during which existing landlords neglect to maintain the property as well as they did when they expected to reap the long-terms benefits of weeding, draining, fencing and otherwise caring for the land. By the time the land actually reaches the poor, it may be much poorer land. As one development economist put it, land reform can be "a bad joke on those who can least afford to laugh."

The point here is not the wisdom or lack of wisdom of particular tax, traffic, or land redistribution policies. The point is that people have foresight, whether they are landlords, welfare mothers, drivers, taxpayers or whatever. A government which proceeds as if the planned effect of its policies is the only effect often finds itself surprised or shocked because those subject to the policies react in ways that benefit or protect themselves, often with the side effect of causing the polices to produce very different results from what was planned.

Time produces both calculable risks and incalculable uncertainties. It is a calculable risk that playing Russian roulette will lead to death about one time out of six but there is simply uncertainty as to what the stock market will do next. These risks and uncertainties that are inseparable from life must be distinguished from gambling, which is creating a risk that would otherwise not exist.

Investors carry their own risks, in hopes of profits or dividends, while speculators and insurance companies carry other people's risks—for a price. Like other enduring features of a market economy, speculation and insurance are not zero-sum games, in which what is gained by some comes from what is lost by others. The total risk is reduced, along with the inventories of money or resources that must be kept idle in case there are losses to cover. An insurance company does not need to have as large a contingency fund to cover losses as the total of the contingency funds that all its policy-holder would need if they were uninsured.

That is because large numbers make risks more calculable and the pooling of risks produces the large numbers necessary for invoking the law of averages. However, when one individual or organization has sufficiently large numbers itself—such as the number of cars owned by Hertz—there is no benefit in buying insurance from someone else, since the same statistical principles can be applied directly and the costs that are calculated can then be included in the price of what is being sold or rented.

Understanding the basic economic functions of investment, speculation, and insurance in a market economy is not overly complicated. However, it is necessary to stop and think about it, if only because so many unthinking people in many countries and periods of history have regarded these functions are not "really" contributing anything to the economy and the people who engage in such activities as mere parasites.

This was especially so at a time when most people engaged in hard physical labor in agriculture and were both suspicious and resentful of people who simply sat around handling paper and money, while producing nothing that could be seen or felt. Centuries-old hostilities have been felt—and acted upon—against groups who played such roles, whether they were Jews in Europe, overseas Chinese minorities in Southeast Asia, or Chettiars in their native India or in Burma, East Africa, or Fiji. Often such groups have been expelled or harassed into leaving because of popular beliefs that they were just parasites. Those with such misconceptions have then been surprised to discover economic activity and the standard of living declining in the wake of their departure.

An understanding basic economics could have prevented many human tragedies, as well as many economic inefficiencies.

PART V:
THE NATIONAL
ECONOMY

Chapter 15

NATIONAL OUTPUT

In the three years following the great stock market crash of 1929, the money supply in the United States declined by a staggering one-third. This meant that it was now impossible to continue to sell as many goods and hire as many people *at the old price levels*, including the old wage levels.

If prices and wage rates had also declined immediately by one-third, then of course the reduced money supply could still have bought as much as before, and the same real output and employment could have continued. There would have been the same amount of real things produced, just with smaller numbers on their price tags, so that paychecks with smaller numbers on them could have bought just as much as before. In reality, however, a complex national economy can never adjust that fast or that perfectly, so there was a massive decline in total sales, with corresponding declines in production and employment.

Thus began the Great Depression of the 1930s, during which as many as one-fourth of all workers were unemployed and American corporations as a whole operated at a loss for two years in a row. General Motors stock, which peaked at $72 3/4$ in 1929, hit bottom at $7 5/8$ in 1932. U. S. Steel stock went from $261 3/4$ to $21 1/4$ and General Electric fell from $396 1/4$ to $70 1/4$. For the entire decade of the 1930s, unemployment averaged more than 18 percent. It was the greatest economic catastrophe in the history of the United States. The fears, policies and institutions it generated were still evident more than half a century later.

What this enormous and deadly reaction to a declining money supply illustrates is that there are economic principles which apply to the national economy as a whole, as well as to particular industries, markets, and occupations. However, in thinking about the national economy, the most fundamental challenge is to avoid what philosophers call "the fallacy of composition"—the mistaken assumption that what applies to a part applies to the whole.

For example, the 1990s were dominated by stories about massive reductions in employment in particular firms and industries—tens of thousands being laid off by some large companies and hundreds of thousands in some industries—and yet the rate of unemployment in the American economy as a whole was the lowest in years during the 1990s and the number of jobs nationwide rose to record high levels. What was true of the various sectors of the economy that made news in the media was not true of the economy as a whole.

The fallacy of composition threatens confusion in many aspects of the study of the national economy as a whole, because what is true of an individual or even an industry is not necessarily true for the economy. For example, any given individual who doubles the amount of money he has will be richer, but a nation cannot be made richer by printing twice as much money. That is because the price level will rise in the economy if there is twice as much money in circulation and the same amount of goods. For any given individual, more money may be earned from other individuals, who have correspondingly less, leaving the price level unaffected.

The fallacy of composition is not peculiar to economics. In a sports stadium, any given individual can see the game better by standing up but, if everybody stands up, everybody will not see better. In a burning building, any given individual can get out faster by running than by walking. But, if everybody runs, the stampede is likely to create bottlenecks at doors, preventing escapes by people struggling against one another to get out, causing some of these people to lose their lives needlessly. That is why there are fire drills, so that people will get in the habit of leaving in an emergency in an orderly way, so that more lives can be saved.

What is at the heart of the fallacy of composition is that it ignores *interactions* among individuals, which can prevent what is true for one of them from being true of them all.

Among the common economic examples of the fallacy of composition are attempts to "save jobs" in some industry threatened with higher unemployment for one reason or another. Any given firm or industry can always be saved by a sufficiently large government intervention, whether in the form of subsidies, purchases of the firm's or industry's products by government agencies, or by other such means. The interaction that is ignored by those advocating such policies is that everything the government spends is taken from somebody else. The 10,000 jobs saved in the widget industry may be at the expense of 15,000 jobs lost elsewhere in the economy by the government's taxing away the resources needed to keep these other people employed.

We need only imagine what would have happened if the government had decided to "save jobs" in the typewriter industry when personal computers first appeared on the scene and began to take away customers from the typewriter manufacturers. If laws had been passed restricting the number of computers that could be sold, this would undoubtedly have saved the jobs of many people who manufactured typewriters or who produced typewriter ribbons, carbon paper, and other accessories. But there would have been fewer jobs created in the computer-manufacturing industry and in the many branches of the software industry. The fallacy is not in believing that jobs can be saved in given industries or given sectors of the economy. The fallacy is in believing that these are *net* savings of jobs for the economy as a whole.

When dealing with the national economy, we encounter terms like Gross National Product and the national debt, as well as institutions like the Federal Reserve System. We also encounter a great deal of confusion spread by politicians and media commentators with no training in economics. As in many other areas, the facts are relatively straightforward and not difficult to understand. What gets complicated are the misconceptions that have to be unravelled.

One of the most basic things to understand about the national economy is how much its total output adds up to. We also need to understand the important role of money in the national economy, which was so painfully demonstrated in the Great Depression of the 1930s. The government is almost always another major factor in the national economy, even though it may not be in particular industries.

MEASURING NATIONAL OUTPUT

A country's total wealth includes everything it has left from the past plus everything currently being produced. National output, however, is what is produced during a given year. Both are important for indicating how much is available to a nation's people, for maintaining or improving their personal standard of living, or to business, government and other institutions for carrying out their various functions.

National output during a year can be measured in a number of ways. The most common measure today is the Gross Domestic Product (GDP), which is the sum total of everything produced within a nation's borders. An older and related measure, the Gross National Product (GNP) is the sum total of all the goods and services produced by the country's people, wherever they or their resources may be located. These two measures of national output are sufficiently similar that people who are not economists need not bother about the differences. For the United States, the difference between GDP and GNP is less than one percent.

The real distinction that must be made is between both these measures of national output during a given year—a *flow* of real income—versus the accumulated *stock* of wealth as of a given time. For example, at any given time, a country can live beyond its current production by using up part of its accumulated stock of wealth from the past. During World War II, for example, American production of automobiles stopped, so that factories which normally produced cars could instead produce tanks, planes and other military equipment. This meant that existing cars simply deteriorated, as did most refrigerators, apartment buildings and other parts of the national stock of wealth. Wartime government posters said:

> Use it up,
> Wear it out,
> Make it do,
> Or do without.

After the war was over, there was a tremendous increase in the production of cars, refrigerators, housing, and other parts of the nation's accumulated stock of wealth which had been allowed to wear down or wear out while production was being devoted to urgent wartime purposes.

Just as national income does not refer to money or other paper assets, so national wealth does not consist of these pieces of paper either, but of the real goods and services that such things can buy. Otherwise, any country could get rich immediately just by printing more money. Sometimes national output or national wealth is added up by using the money prices of the moment, but most serious long-run studies measure output and wealth in real terms, taking into account price changes over time.

THE COMPOSITION OF OUTPUT

Prices are not the only things that change over time. The real goods and services which make up the national output also change. The cars of 1950 are not the same as the cars of the year 2000. The older cars did not have air-conditioning, seat belts, anti-lock brakes, or many other features that have been added over the years. So when we try to measure how much the production of automobiles has increased in real terms, a mere count of how many cars there were in both time periods misses a huge qualitative difference in what we are defining as being the same thing—cars. The same is true of housing as well. The average house at the end of the twentieth century was much larger, had more bathrooms, and was far more likely to have air conditioning and other amenities than houses that existed in the middle of that century. Just counting how many more houses there were at both times does not tell us how much the production of housing had increased.

While these are problems which can be left for professional economists and statisticians to try to wrestle with, it is important for others to at least be aware of these problems, so as not to be misled by politicians or media pundits who throw statistics around for one purpose or another.

Over a period of generations, the goods and services which constitute national output change so much that statistical comparisons become practically meaningless, because they are comparing apples and oranges. At the beginning of the twentieth century, the national output did not include any airplanes, television sets, computers or nuclear power plants. At the end of the century, national output did not include many typewriters, slide rules (once essential for engineers), or a host of equipment and supplies once widely used in connection with horses that formerly provided the basic transportation of the country.

What then, does it mean to say that the Gross National Product was X percent larger in the year 2000 than in 1900, when it consisted of very different things? It may mean something to say that output was 5 percent higher or 3 percent lower than it was the previous year because it consisted of much the same things in both years. But the longer the time span involved, the more such statistics approach meaninglessness.

The same problems which apply when comparing a given country's output over time can also apply when comparing the output of two very different countries at the same time. If some Caribbean nation's output consists largely of bananas and other tropical crops, while some Scandinavian country's output consists more of industrial products and crops more typical of cold climates, how is it possible to compare totals made up of such differing items?

One way is to compare the total money value of their respective outputs. However, this gets us into other complications created by official exchange rates between their respective currencies which may or may not reflect the actual purchasing power of those currencies. Governments may set their official exchange rates anywhere they want, but that does not mean that the actual purchasing power of the money will be whatever they say it is. Country A may have more output per capita than Country B if we measure by official exchange rates, while it may be just the reverse if we measure by the purchasing power of the money. Surely we would say that Country B has the larger total value of output if it could purchase everything produced in country A and still have something left over.

As in other cases, the problem is not with understanding the basic economics involved. The problem is with confusion spread by politicians, the media and others trying to prove some point with statistics. For example, some have claimed that Japan has a higher per capita income than the United States, using statistics based on official exchange rates of the dollar and the Yen. But, in fact, the United States has significantly higher per capita income than Japan when measured by the purchasing power of the two countries' national outputs.

The average American's annual income could buy everything the average Japanese annual income buys and still have thousands of dollars left over. Therefore the average American has a higher standard of living than the average Japanese. Yet statistics based on official exchange rates show the average Japanese earning thousands of dollars more than the average American, leaving the false impression that the Japanese are more prosperous than Americans.

Another complication in comparisons of output between nations is that more of one nation's output may have been sold through the marketplace, while more of the other nation's output may have been produced by government and either given away or sold at less than its cost of production.

When too many automobiles have been produced in a market economy, the excess cars have to be sold for whatever they will bring, even if that is less than they cost to produce. When the value of national output is added up, these cars are counted according to what they sold for. But, in an economy where the government provides many free or subsidized goods, these goods are valued at what it cost the government to produce them. These ways of counting exaggerate the value of government-provided goods and services, many of which are provided by government precisely because they would never cover their costs of production if sold in a free market economy.

Both capitalism and socialism can produce more of particular things than people want, but a capitalist economy reduces the value of the surplus goods and services, while a socialist economy counts them according to what they cost, whether or not those costs could be recovered from the consuming public. Given this tendency to overvalue the output of socialist economies relative to capitalist economies when adding up their respective Gross National Products, it is all the more striking that capitalist economies still show higher per capita output.

TRENDS OVER TIME

One of the problems with comparisons of national output over time is the arbitrary choice of the year to use as the beginning of the time span. For example, one of the big political campaign issues of 1960 was the rate of growth of the American economy under the existing administration. Presidential candidate John F. Kennedy promised to "get American moving again" economically if he were elected, implying that the national economic growth rate had stagnated under the party of his opponent. The validity of this charge depended entirely on which year you chose as the year from which to begin counting.

The long-term average annual rate of growth of the Gross National Product of the United States had been about 3 percent per year. As of 1960, this growth rate was as low as 1.9 percent (since 1945) or as high as 4.4 percent (since 1958). Whatever the influence of the existing administration on any of this, whether it was doing a wonderful job or a terrible job depended entirely on the base year arbitrarily selected.

Many "trends" reported in the media or proclaimed in politics depend entirely on which year has been chosen as the beginning of the trend. Crime has been going up if you measure from 1960 to the present, but down if you measure from 1990 to the present. It has been claimed that automobile fatality rates have declined since the federal government began imposing various safety regulations. This is true—but it is also true that automobile fatality rates were declining continuously for decades before the federal government imposed any safety regulations. Is the continuation of a trend that existed before a given policy was begun proof of the effectiveness of that policy?

National output data, like many other statistics, fluctuate over time. That makes it possible to say that the trends are going up or down, depending on which point in these fluctuations you choose as the base year from which to begin counting. As in many other aspects of economics, the concept is relatively simple but it can be made complicated and confused by people with axes to grind.

Chapter 16

Money and
the Banking System

Money is one of those things that are so common and so taken for granted that we seldom bother to ask why we want it and what it can do. We all know that money can do very important things in our own personal lives, but the more important question is: What does it do in the national economy as a whole? We need to know not only how it functions but also how it can malfunction, for the malfunctions of money have created economic disasters and even destroyed nations and empires.

THE ROLE OF MONEY

Everyone seems to want money, but there have been particular times in particular countries when no one wanted money, because they considered it worthless. In reality, it was the fact that no one would accept money that made it worthless. When you can't buy anything with money, it becomes just useless pieces of paper or useless metal disks. In France during the 1790s, a desperate government passed a law prescribing the death penalty for anyone who refused to sell in exchange for money. What all this suggests is that the mere fact that the government prints money does not mean that it will in fact function as money. We therefore need to understand how money functions, if only to avoid reaching the point where it malfunctions.

Many economies in the distant past have functioned without money, just by having people barter their products and labor with one another. But these have usually been small, simple economies, with relatively few things to trade, because most people provided themselves with food, shelter and clothing, while trading with others for a limited range of amenities or luxuries.

Barter is awkward. If you produce chairs and want some apples, you certainly are not likely to trade one chair for one apple, and you may not want enough apples to add up to the value of a chair. But if chairs and apples can both be exchanged for something that can be subdivided into very small amounts, then more trades can take place, benefitting both chair-makers and apple-growers, as well as everyone else. All that people have to do is to agree on what will be used as an intermediary means of exchange and that means of exchange becomes money.

Some societies have used sea shells as money, others have used gold or silver, and still others have used special pieces of paper printed by their government. What makes all of them money is that people will accept them in payment for the goods and services that actually constitute real wealth. Money is equivalent to wealth for an individual only because other individuals will supply him with the real goods and services that he wants in exchange for his money. But, from the standpoint of the national economy as a whole, money is not wealth. It is just a way to transfer wealth or to give people incentives to produce wealth.

INFLATION

As we have already noted, doubling a nation's money supply will not double its wealth but will more likely lead to higher prices for everything. Prices in general rise for the same reason that prices of particular goods and services rise—namely, that there is more demanded than supplied at a given price. When people have more money, they tend to spend more. Without a corresponding increase in the volume of output, the prices of existing output simply rises because the quantity demanded exceeds the quantity supplied.

Whatever the money consists of—whether sea shells, gold, or paper—more of it in the national economy means higher prices. This relationship between the total amount of money and the general price level has been seen for centuries. When Alexander the

Great began spending the captured treasures of the Persians, prices rose in Greece. Similarly, when the Spaniards removed vast amounts of gold from their colonies in the Western Hemisphere, price levels rose not only in Spain, but across Europe. The Spaniards used much of their wealth to buy imports from other European countries, sending their gold to those countries to pay for these purchases, thereby adding to the total money supply across the continent.

None of this is hard to understand. Complications and confusion come in when we start thinking about such things as the "intrinsic value" of money or believe that gold somehow "backs up" our money or in some mysterious way gives it value.

For much of history, gold has been used as money by many countries. Sometimes the gold was used directly in coins or (for large purchases) in nuggets, gold bars or other forms. Even more convenient for carrying around were pieces of paper money printed by the government that were redeemable in gold whenever you wanted it. It was not only more convenient to carry around paper money, it was also safer than carrying large sums of money as metal that jingled in your pockets or was conspicuous in bags, attracting the attention of criminals.

The big problem with money created by the government is that those who run the government always face the temptation to create more money and spend it. Whether among ancient kings or modern politicians, this has happened again and again over the centuries, leading to inflation and many economic and social problems that flow from inflation. For this reason, many countries have preferred using gold, silver, or some other material that is inherently limited in supply, as money. It is a way of depriving governments of the power to expand the money supply to inflationary levels.

Gold has long been considered ideal for this purpose, since there is a limited supply of gold in the world. When paper money is convertible into gold whenever the individual chooses to do so, then the money is said to be "backed up" by gold. This expression is misleading only if we imagine that the value of the gold is somehow transferred to the paper money, when in fact the gold simply limits the amount of paper money that can be issued.

The American dollar was once redeemable in gold on demand, but that was ended back in 1933. Since then, we have simply had paper money, limited in supply only by what officials thought they could or could not get away with politically. To give some idea of the cumulative effects of inflation, a one-hundred-dollar bill in 1998 would buy less than a twenty-dollar bill bought in the 1960s. Among other things, this means that people who saved money in the 1960s had four-fifths of its value silently stolen from them over the next three decades.

Sobering as such inflation may be in the United States, it pales alongside levels of inflation reached in some other countries. "Double-digit inflation" during a given year in the United States creates political alarms, but various countries in Latin America and Eastern Europe have had periods when the annual rate of inflation was in four digits.

Since money is whatever we accept as money in payment for real goods and services, there are a variety of other things that function in a way very similar to money. Credit cards and checks are obvious examples. Mere promises may also function as money, when the person who makes the promises is highly trusted. IOUs from reliable merchants were once passed from hand to hand as money. Some banks used to issue their own currency, which had no legal standing, but which was nevertheless widely accepted in payment when the particular bank was regarded as sufficiently reliable and willing to redeem their currency in gold. In those times and places where bankers had more credibility than government officials, bank notes might be preferred to the official money printed by the government. Sometimes money issued by some other country is preferred to money issued by one's own. Beginning in the late tenth century, Chinese money was preferred to Japanese money in Japan. In twentieth century Bolivia, most of the savings accounts were in dollars in 1985, during a period of runaway inflation of the Bolivian peso.

Gold continues to be preferred to many national currencies, even though gold earns no interest, while money in the bank does. The fluctuating price of gold reflects not only the changing demands for it for making jewelry or in some industrial uses but also, and more fundamentally, the degree of worry about the possibility of inflation that could erode the value of official currencies.

That is why a major political or military crisis can send the price of gold shooting up, as people dump their holdings of the currencies that might be affected and begin bidding against each other to buy gold, as a more reliable way to hold their existing wealth, even if it does not earn any interest or dividends.

Conversely, long periods of prosperity with price stability are likely to see the price of gold falling, as people are willing to move their wealth out of gold and into other financial assets that can increase their wealth. The great unspoken fear behind this and many other transactions in the financial markets is the fear of inflation. Nor is this fear irrational, given how often governments of all types have resorted to inflation, as a means of getting more wealth without having to directly confront the public with higher taxes.

Raising tax rate has always created political dangers to those who hold political power, whether in a modern democracy or in an ancient monarchy. Political careers can be destroyed when the voting public turns against those who raised their tax rates. In undemocratic societies, public reaction can range up to armed revolts, such as those that led to the American war of independence from Britain or to the overthrow of other government at other times and places.

In addition to adverse political reactions to higher taxes, there can be adverse economic reactions. As tax rates reach higher levels, particular economic activities may be abandoned by those who do not find the net rate of return on these activities, after taxes, to be enough to justify their efforts. Thus many people abandoned agriculture and moved to the cities during the declining era of the Roman Empire, adding to the number of people needing to be taken care of by the government, at the very time when the food supply was declining because of those who had stopped farming.

In order to avoid the political dangers that raising tax rates can create, governments around the world have for thousands of years resorted to inflation instead. If fighting a major war requires half the country's annual output, then rather than raise tax rates to 50 percent of everyone's earnings in order to pay for it, the government may choose instead to create more money for itself and spend that money buying war materiel. With half the country's resources being used to produce military equipment

and supplies, civilian goods will become more scarce just as
money becomes more plentiful. This changed ratio of money to
civilian goods will lead to inflation as more money is bid for
fewer goods and prices rise as a result.

Not all inflation is caused by war, though inflation has often
accompanied military conflicts. Even in peacetime, governments
have found many things to spend money on, including luxurious
living by kings or dictators and numerous showy projects that
have been common with both democratic and undemocratic governments. To pay for such things, using the government's power
to create more money has often been considered easier than raising tax rates. Put differently, inflation is in effect a hidden tax. The
money that people have saved is robbed of part of its purchasing
power, which is quietly transferred to the government that issues
new money.

In the modern era of paper money, increasing the money supply is a relatively simple matter of turning on the printing presses.
However, long before there were printing presses, governments
were able to create more money by the simple process of reducing
the amount of gold or silver in coins of a given denomination.
Thus a French franc or a British pound might begin by containing
a certain amount of precious metal, but coins later issued by the
French or British government would contain less and less of those
metals, enabling these governments to issue more money from a
given supply of gold and silver. Since the new coins had the same
legal value as the old, the purchasing power of them all declined
as coins became more abundant.

More sophisticated methods of increasing the quantity of
money have been used in countries with government-controlled
central banks, but the net result is still the same: An increase in the
amount of money, without a corresponding increase in the supply
of real goods, means that prices rise—which is to say, inflation.
(Conversely, when output increased during Britain's industrial
revolution in the nineteenth century, its prices declined because
its money supply did not increase correspondingly.)

Doubling the money supply while the amount of goods remains the same may more than double the price level, as the
speed with which the money circulates increases when people

lose confidence in its retaining its value. During the drastic decline in the value of the Russian ruble in 1998, a Moscow correspondent reported: "Many are hurrying to spend their shrinking rubles as fast as possible while the currency still has some value."

Something very similar happened in Russia during the First World War and in the years after the revolutions of 1917. By 1921, the amount of currency issued by the government was hundreds of times greater than the currency in circulation on the eve of the war in 1913—and the price level rose to *thousands* of times higher than in 1913. When the money circulates faster, the effect on prices is the same as if there were more money in circulation. When both things happen on a large scale simultaneously, the result is runaway inflation.

Perhaps the most famous inflation of the twentieth century occurred in Germany during the 1920s, when 40 marks were worth one dollar in July 1920 but it took more than 4 trillion marks to be worth one dollar by November 1923. People discovered that their life savings were not enough to buy a pack of cigarettes. The German government had, in effect, stolen virtually everything they owned by the simple process of keeping more than 1,700 printing presses running day and night, printing money.

Here too, the circulation of money speeded up, causing the inflation to increase even more than the increase in the money supply. During the worst of the inflation, In October 1923, prices rose 41 percent *per day*. Workers were paid twice a day and some were allowed time off in the middle of the day to enable them to rush off to the stores to buy things before the prices rose yet again. In other cases, wives showed up at work at lunchtime to take their husband's pay and rush off to spend it before it lost too much value. Some have blamed the economic chaos of this era for setting the stage for the rise of Adolf Hitler and the Nazis.

DEFLATION

While inflation has been a problem that is centuries old, at particular times and places deflation has also been devastating.

As noted at the beginning of chapter 15, the money supply in the United States declined by one-third from 1929 to 1932, making it impossible for Americans to buy as many goods and services as before *at the old prices*. Prices did come down — the Sears catalog for 1931 had many prices lower than they had been a decade earlier —but some prices could not change because there were legal contracts involved.

Mortgages on homes, farms, stores, and office buildings all specified monthly mortgage payments in money terms. These terms might have been quite reasonable and easy to meet when the total amount of money in the economy was substantially larger, but now it was the same as if these payments had been arbitrarily raised—as in fact they were raised in real purchasing power terms. Many home-owners, farmers and businesses simply could not pay after the national money supply contracted—and therefore lost the places that housed them. People with leases faced very similar problems, as it became increasingly difficult to come up with the money to pay the rent. The vast amounts of goods and service purchased on credit by businesses and individuals alike produced debts that were now harder to pay off than when the credit was extended in an economy with a larger money supply.

Those whose wages and salaries were specified in contracts— whether unionized workers or baseball players—were now legally entitled to more real purchasing power than when these contracts were originally signed. So were government employees whose salary scales were fixed by law. But, while deflation benefitted these particular groups *if they kept their jobs*, the difficulty of paying them meant that many would lose their jobs. Similarly, banks that owned the mortgages which many people were struggling to pay were benefitted by receiving mortgage payments worth more purchasing power than expected—*if they received the payments at all*. But so many people were unable to pay their debts that many banks began to fail—more than 900 in 1930 alone. Other creditors likewise lost money when debtors simply could not pay them.

Theoretically, the government could have increased the money supply to bring the price levels back up to where they had been before. However, what a government can do theoretically is not necessarily the same as what it is likely to do politically or what it understands intellectually. Both liberal and conservative economists looking back on this period have seen the Federal Reserve System's monetary policies as confused or incompetent. In addition, both Republican President Herbert Hoover and his Democratic successor, Franklin D. Roosevelt, thought that wage rates should not be reduced, so this way of adjusting to deflation was discouraged by the federal government—for both humanitarian and political reasons, with the best of intentions, but with the worst consequences nevertheless.

The net effect of keeping wage rates from adjusting as far downward as the reduced money supply required was that workers were entitled to more real purchasing power than ever, but in fact had trouble keeping or finding jobs. In that sense, workers were in a position similar to that of banks and other creditors, who were legally entitled to far more money than they could actually collect.

One painfully revealing sign of the thinking of the times was that, after the election of 1932 and before FDR took office in 1933, President Hoover wrote to the president-elect, asking him to announce publicly "that there will be no tampering or inflation of the currency" and that the budget would be balanced, even if that required higher taxes. While FDR made no such pledge, his own thinking at the time was very similar to Hoover's, however mistaken both of them may have been in the eyes of economists.

Monetary policy is just one of many areas in which it is not enough that the government could do things to make a situation better. What matters is what government is in fact likely to do, which can in many cases make the situation worse.

THE BANKING SYSTEM

We have already noted in Chapter 12, one of the most important roles of a bank—serving as intermediaries to transfer savings from some people to others who need to borrow. Not only does this happen across generations, as discussed there, it happens also when money is lent to individuals and organizations of all sorts. A student just emerging from dental school seldom has enough cash on hand to buy all the equipment and supplies needed to get started as a dentist.

Even opening a small grocery store means buying an inventory to stock the shelves, as well as renting space, paying for utilities, and perhaps hiring employees. Few people have enough money of their own on hand to do all that, so they use other people's money—whether loans from relatives and friends or from a bank, or some combination. Almost no one has enough cash on hand to buy a house and many must buy a car with instalment payments. Typically, the seller of a home or an automobile receives the full price immediately, not from the buyer, but from some financial intermediary whom the buyer must repay in installments.

Modern banks, however, do more than simply transfer cash. Each individual bank may do that but the banking system as a whole does something more. It creates credits which, in effect add to the money supply through what is called "fractional reserve banking." A brief history of how this practice arose may make the process clearer.

Goldsmiths have for centuries had to have some safe place to store the precious metal that they used to make jewelry and other items. Once they had established a vault or other secure storage place, other people often stored their own gold with the goldsmith, rather than take on the cost of creating their own secure storage facilities. In other words, there were economies of scale in storing gold in a vault or other stronghold, so goldsmiths ended up storing other people's gold, as well as their own.

Naturally, the goldsmiths gave out receipts entitling the owners to reclaim their gold whenever they wished to. Since these receipts were redeemable in gold, they were in effect "as good as gold" and circulated as if they were money, buying goods and services as they were passed on from one person to another.

From experience, goldsmiths learned that they seldom had to redeem all the gold that was stored with them at any given time. If a goldsmith felt confident that he would never have to redeem more than one-third of the gold that he held for other people at any given time, then he could lend out the other two-thirds and earn interest on it. Since the receipts for gold and two-thirds of the gold itself were both in circulation at the same time, the gold-smiths were, in effect, adding to the total money supply.

In this way, there arose two of the major features of modern banking—(1) holding only a fraction of the reserves needed to cover deposits and (2) adding to the total money supply. Since all the depositors are not going to want their money at one time, the bank lends most of it to other people, in order to earn interest on those loans. Some of this interest they share with the depositors by paying interest on their bank accounts. Again, with the depositors writing checks on their accounts while part of the money in those accounts is also circulating as loans to other people, the banking system is in effect adding to the national money supply, over and above the money printed by the government.

One of the reasons this system worked has worked is that the whole banking system has never been called upon to actually supply cash to cover all the checks written by depositors. Instead, if the Acme Bank receives a million dollars worth of checks written by depositors whose accounts are with the Zebra Bank, it does not ask the Zebra Bank for the million dollars, but balances that off against whatever checks were written by Acme Bank depositors and ended up in the hands of the Zebra Bank.

For example, if its own depositors had written $1,200,000 worth of check to people who then deposited those checks in the Zebra Bank, then Acme Bank would just pay the difference, using $200,000 to settle more than $2 millions worth of checks that had been written on accounts in the two banks. Both banks could keep just a fraction of their deposits in cash because all depositors would not want their money at the same time and because all the checks written on all the banks required just a fraction of the amounts on those checks to settle the differences between banks, rather than paying the full amounts on all the checks.

This system, called "fractional reserve banking," worked fine in normal times. But it was very vulnerable in times when many depositors wanted hard cash at once. While most depositors are not going to ask for their money at the same time under normal conditions, there are situations where more depositors will ask for their money than the bank can supply. Usually, this would be when the depositors fear that they will not be able to get their money back. At one time, a bank robbery would cause depositors to fear that the bank would have to close and therefore they would all run to the bank at the same time, trying to withdraw their money before the bank collapsed. If the bank had only one-third as much money available as the total depositors were entitled to and one-half of the depositors asked for their money, then the bank ran out of money and collapsed, with the remaining depositors losing everything.

Under this system of fractional reserve banking, anything that could set off a run on the banks could cause these banks to collapse. Not only would many depositors lose their savings, the nation's total money supply could suddenly decline, if this happened to enough banks at the same time. After all, part of the money supply consisted of credits created by the banking system during the process of lending out money. When that credit disappeared, there was no longer enough money to buy everything that was being produced—at least not at the prices that had been set when the money supply was larger. This is what happened in the Great Depression of the 1930s, when literally hundreds of banks in the United States collapsed in one year and the total money supply of the country contracted by one-third.

In order to prevent a repetition of this catastrophe, the Federal Deposit Insurance Corporation was created, guaranteeing that the government would reimburse depositors whose money was in an insured bank when it collapsed. Now there was no longer a reason for depositors to start a run on a bank, so very few banks collapsed, and there was less likelihood of a sudden and disastrous reduction of the nation's total money supply.

While the Federal Deposit Insurance Corporation is a sort of firewall to prevent bank failures from spreading throughout the system, a more fine-tuned way of trying to control the national supply of money and credit is through the Federal Reserve System. The Federal Reserve is a central bank run by the government to control all the private banks. It has the power to tell the banks what fraction of their deposits must be kept in reserve, with only the remainder being allowed to be lent out. It also lends money to the banks, which the banks can then re-lend to the general public.

By setting the interest rate on the money that it lends to the banks, the Federal Reserve System indirectly controls the interest rate that the banks will charge the general public. All of this has the net effect of allowing the Federal Reserve to control the total amount of money and credit in the economy as a whole, to one degree or another.

Because of the powerful leverage of the Federal Reserve System, public statements by the chairman of the Federal Reserve Board are scrutinized by bankers and investors for clues as to whether "the Fed" is likely to tighten the money supply or ease up. An unguarded statement by the chairman of the Federal Reserve Board, or a statement that is misconstrued by financiers, can set off a panic in Wall Street that causes stock prices to plummet. Or, if the Federal Reserve Board chairman sounds upbeat, stock prices may soar. Given such drastic repercussions, which can affect financial markets around the world, Federal Reserve Board chairmen over the years have learned to speak in highly guarded and Delphic terms that leave listeners puzzled as to what they really mean.

In assessing the role of the Federal Reserve, as well as any other organs of government, a sharp distinction must be made between their stated goals and their actual performance or effect. The Federal Reserve System was established in 1914 as a result of fears of such economic consequences as deflation and bank failures. Yet the worst deflation and the worst bank failures in the country's history occurred after the Federal Reserve was established.

Chapter 17

The Role of Government

*... it is not enough to show that a situation is bad;
it is also necessary to be reasonably certain that the
problem has been properly described, fairly certain
that the proposed remedy will improve it, and virtually certain that it will not make it worse.*

- Robert Conquest

A modern market economy cannot exist in a vacuum. Market
transactions take place within a framework of rules and require someone with the authority to enforce those rules. Government not only enforces its own rules but also enforces contracts
and other agreements among the numerous parties in the economy. Sometimes government also sets standards, defining what
is a pound, a mile, or a bushel. And to support itself, governments must also collect taxes, which in turn affect economic
decision-making.

Beyond these basic functions, which virtually everyone can
agree on, governments can play more expansive roles, all the way
up to directly owning and operating all the farms and industries
in the nation. Controversies have raged around the world,
throughout the twentieth century, on the role that the government should play in the economy. For much of that century, those
who favored a larger role for government were clearly in the ascendancy. Russia, China, and others in the Communist bloc of nations were at one extreme, but democratic countries like Britain,
India, and France also took over ownership of various industries
and tightly controlled the decisions made in other industries that
were allowed to remain privately owned.

During the 1980s, however, the tide began to turn toward reducing the role of government, first in Britain and the United

States and then such trends spread rapidly through the democratic countries and were climaxed by the collapse of communism in the Soviet bloc. As a 1998 study put it:

> All around the globe, socialists are embracing capitalism, governments are selling off companies they had previously nationalized, and countries are seeking to entice back multinational corporations that they had expelled just two decades earlier.

Experience—often bitter experience—had more to do with such changes than any new theory or analysis. However, in order to understand basic economics, it is not necessary to enter into these controversies. Here we can examine the basic functions of government that virtually everyone can agree on and explain why these functions are important for the allocation of scarce resources which have alternative uses.

The most basic function of government is to provide a framework of law and order, within which the people are free to engage in whatever economic and other activities they choose. There are also certain activities which generate significant costs and benefits which extend beyond those people who engage in these activities. Here government can take account of these costs and benefits when the marketplace cannot.

Finally, the individuals who work for government in various capacities tend to respond to the incentives facing them, just as people do in corporations, in families, and in other human institutions and activities. Government is neither a monolith nor simply the public interest personified. To understand what it does, its incentives and constraints must be taken into account, just as the incentives and constraints of the marketplace must be for those who engage in market transactions.

LAW AND ORDER

Where government restricts its economic role to that of an enforcer of laws and contracts, some people say that such a policy means "doing nothing." However, what is called nothing has often taken centuries to achieve—namely, a reliable framework of laws, within which economic activity can flourish, and without which even vast riches in natural resources may go unused and the people remain much poorer than they need to be. For example, oil deposits worth an estimated $4 trillion remained largely untapped under the Caspian Sea because the laws and policies of the adjoining nations of Azerbaijan and Georgia, and the political uncertainties of the region, made the venture too risky to attract that vast amount of capital investment needed to extract the oil and establish pipelines to take it from these landlocked countries to seaports serving world markets.

Because human beings have foresight, the mere prospect of government economic intervention in the future can cause an immediate reduction in current investment. In 1999, for example, a military coup in Venezuela put in control a general whose sweeping powers and sweeping rhetoric made foreign investors leery of putting their money there, despite the economic assets of this oil-rich country and despite assurances issued by the general that he would respect foreign investments. So long as he held autocratic powers, there would be no way to hold him to his word, as there would be in a country with reliable laws and independent courts to enforce these laws.

The Framework of Laws

For fostering economic activities and the prosperity resulting from them, laws must be reliable, above all. If the law varies with the whims of kings or dictators, with changes in democratically elected governments, or with the caprices or corruption of appointed officials, then the risks surrounding investment rise, and consequently the amount of investing is likely to be less than purely economic considerations would produce in a market economy under a reliable framework of laws.

One of the important advantages that enabled nineteenth-century Britain to become the first industrialized nation was the dependability of its laws. Not only could Britons feel confident in investing in their country's economy, without fear that their earnings would be confiscated or the contracts they made voided for political reasons, so could foreigners doing business or making investments in Britain. For centuries, the reputation of British law for dependability and impartiality attracted merchants and investments from continental Europe, as well as skilled immigrants and refugees. In short, both the physical capital and the human capital of foreigners contributed to the development of the British economy from one of the more backward economies of Western Europe to one of the most advanced, setting the stage for Britain's industrial revolution that led the world into the industrial age.

In other parts of the world as well, a framework of dependable laws encouraged both domestic and foreign investment, as well as attracting immigrants with skills lacking locally. In Southeast Asia, for example, the imposition of European laws under the colonial regimes of the eighteenth and nineteenth centuries replaced the powers of local rulers and tribes. Under these new frameworks of laws—often uniform across wider geographical areas, as well as being more dependable at any given place—a massive immigration from China and a smaller immigration from India brought in people whose skills and entrepreneurship created whole industries and transformed the economies of the countries throughout the region.

European investors also sent capital to Southeast Asia, financing many of the giant ventures in mining and shipping that were often beyond the resources of the Chinese and Indian immigrants. In colonial Malaya, for example, the tin mines and rubber plantations which provided much of the country's export earnings were financed by European capital and worked by laborers from China and India, while most local commerce and industry were in the hands of the Chinese, leaving the indigenous Malays largely spectators at the modern development of their own economy.

While impartiality is also a desirable quality in laws, even discriminatory laws can promote economic development, if the nature of the discrimination is spelled out in advance, rather than taking the form of biased, unpredictable, and corrupt decisions by judges, juries, and officials. The Chinese and Indians who settled in the European colonial empires of Southeast Asia never had the same rights as Europeans there, nor the same rights as the indigenous population. Yet whatever rights they did have could be relied upon and therefore served as a basis for the creation of Chinese and Indian businesses in the region.

Similarly in the Ottoman Empire, Christians and Jews never had the same rights as Moslems. Yet, during the flourishing centuries of that empire, the rights that Christians and Jews did have were sufficiently dependable to enable them to prosper in commerce, industry, and banking to a greater extent than the Moslem majority. Moreover, their economic activities contributed to the prosperity of the Ottoman Empire as a whole. Similar stories could be told of the Lebanese minority in colonial West Africa, Indians in colonial Fiji, German immigrants in Brazil, and other minority groups in other countries who prospered under laws that were dependable, if not impartial.

Dependability is not simply a matter of the government's own treatment of people. It must also prevent some people from interfering with other people, so that criminals and mobs do not make economic life risky and thereby stifle the economic development required for prosperity. Governments differ in the effectiveness with which they can enforce their laws in general, and even a given government may be able to enforce its laws more effectively in some places than in others. For centuries, the borderlands between English and Scottish kingdoms were not effectively controlled by either country and remained lawless and economically backward. Mountainous regions have often been difficult to police, whether in the Balkans, the Appalachian region of the United States, or elsewhere. Such places have likewise tended to lag in economic development and to attract few outsiders and little outside capital. Today, high-crime neighborhoods and neighborhoods subject to higher than normal rates of vandalism or riots similarly suffer economically from a lack of law and order.

Property Rights

One of the most misunderstood aspects of law and order are property rights. While these rights are cherished as personal benefits by those fortunate enough to own substantial property, what matters from the standpoint of economics is how they affect the allocation of scarce resources which have alternative uses.

There are all sorts of social and economic arrangements possible, with and without property rights, or with property rights reduced by various laws and policies to varying degrees, including to an extent that virtually abolishes these rights or makes them worthless. Under rent control, for example, property rights can be reduced to worthlessness or even become negative. That is why owners of many apartment buildings in New York City have simply abandoned their buildings and fled the scene, when the costs of the legally mandated services that they are required to provide exceed the rents that they are allowed to collect. Since abandonment of buildings is illegal, these owners go underground when the value of their property right becomes negative. Under these conditions, selling the building is out of the question, since it has become an economic liability, rather than an asset, and finding a buyer may be impossible.

Resources can be allocated without property rights and have been in various societies. The economic consequences of having or not having property rights is what matters, as far as the prosperity of the population as a whole is concerned, as distinct from what matters to the usually relatively small number of people who own extraordinary amounts of property.

A house or a hammer is the same, whether it is owned or not owned, or owned by the government in the name of the people, as distinct from being owned by individuals in their own respective names. But, while physical things are the same, whether they are owned or not owned, property rights matter economically because of the incentives they create and the consequences of those incentives for people's behavior.

What is different with and without property rights? One small but telling example was the experience of a delegation of American farmers who visited the Soviet Union. They were appalled at the way various agricultural produce was shipped, carelessly packed and with spoiled fruit or vegetables left to spread the spoilage to other fruits and vegetables in the same sacks or boxes. Coming from a country where individuals owned agricultural produce as their private property, American farmers had no experience with such gross carelessness and waste, which would have caused somebody to lose much money needlessly in the United States. In the Soviet Union, the loss was even more painful, since the country often had trouble feeding itself, but there were no property rights to convey those losses directly to the produce handlers and shippers who caused it.

In a country without property rights, or with the food being owned "by the people," there was no given individual with sufficient incentives to ensure that this food did not spoil needlessly before it reached the consumers. Those who handled the food in transit were paid a salary, which was fixed independently of how well they did or did not safeguard the food.

In theory at least, closer monitoring of produce handlers could have reduced the spoilage. But monitoring is not free. It is itself one of the scarce resources which have alternative uses. Moreover, monitoring raises the further question: Who will monitor the monitor? The Soviets tried to deal with this problem by having Communist Party members honeycombed throughout the society to report on derelictions of duty and violations of law. However, the widespread corruption and inefficiency found even under Stalinist totalitarianism suggests the limitations of official monitoring, as compared to automatic self-monitoring by property owners.

No one has to stand over an American farmer and tell him to take the rotten peaches out of a basket before they spoil the others, because these peaches are his private property and he is not about to lose money if he doesn't have to. Property rights create self-monitoring, which tends to be both more effective and less costly than third-party monitoring.

The only animals threatened with extinction are animals not owned by anybody. Colonel Sanders is not about to let chickens become extinct. Nor will McDonald's stand idly by and let cows become extinct. It is things not owned by anybody (air and water, for example) which are polluted. In centuries past, sheep were allowed to graze on unowned land —"the commons," as it was called—with the net result that land on the commons was so heavily grazed that it had little left but patchy ground and the shepherds had hungry and scrawny sheep. But privately owned land adjacent to the common was usually in far better condition.

Legally speaking, property rights are essentially rights to exclude other people from the use of resources or the goods and services produced by those resources. Expressed in this negative way, property rights seem rather unattractive. But, while the people who own Yankee Stadium have a legal right to lock the place up and keep everybody else out, they are very unlikely to do so in a market economy. On the contrary, their incentives are to charge admission and to try to induce as many people as possible to come in and pack the place full.

Property rights are a legal mechanism for the use of free market prices to allocate resources. As such, these rights need to be assessed in terms of their economic effects on the prosperity of the population at large, not how they affect the wellbeing of those people who own Yankee Stadium, peaches, houses or hammers.

Shifting the focus to the fortunate few who own great amounts of property enables phrase-makers to speak of "property rights versus human rights" or otherwise depict the issue as being one of the wellbeing of the many versus the wellbeing of the few. But it is precisely the empirical question of how the existence or non-existence of property rights affects the economic wellbeing of society as a whole which provides the strongest evidence for the social benefits of property rights. Most Americans do not own any agricultural land or agricultural crops, but they have more and better food available at lower prices than in countries where there are no property rights in agricultural land or its produce.

While strict adherence to property rights would allow landlords to evict tenants at will, the economic incentives are for them to do just the opposite—to try to keep their apartments as fully rented and as continuously occupied as possible, so long as the tenants pay their rent and behave themselves. Only when rent control or other restrictions on their property rights are enacted are they likely to do otherwise. Under rent control and tenants rights laws, landlords have been known to try to harass tenants into leaving, whether in New York or in Hong Kong.

Under stringent rent control and tenants rights laws in Hong Kong, landlords were known to sneak into their own buildings late at night to vandalize the premises, in order to make them less attractive or even unlivable, so that tenants would move out and the empty building could then be torn down legally, to be replaced by something more lucrative as commercial or industrial property.

This of course was by no means the purpose or intention of those who had passed such laws in Hong Kong. But it illustrates again the importance of making a distinction between intentions and effects—and not just as regards property rights laws. In short, incentives matter and property rights need to be assessed economically in terms of the incentives created by their existence, their modifications, or their elimination.

The powerful incentives created by a profit-and-loss economy depend on the profits being private property. When government-owned enterprises in the Soviet Union made profits, those profits were not their private property but belonged to "the people"—or, in more mundane terms, could be taken by the government for whatever purposes higher officials chose to spend them on. Soviet economists Schmelev and Popov pointed out and lamented the adverse effects of this on incentives:

> But what justifies confiscating the larger part—sometimes 90–95 percent—of enterprises' profits, as is being done in many sectors of the economy today? What political or economic right—ultimately what human right—do ministries have to do that? Once again we are taking away from those who work well in order to keep afloat those who do nothing. How can we possibly talk about independence, initiative, rewards for efficiency, quality, and technical progress?

Of course, the country's leaders could continue to *talk* about such things, but destroying the incentives which exist under property rights meant that there was a reduced chance of achieving these goals.

While government officials in the United States cannot arbitrary confiscate profits as directly as Soviet officials could, American legislators can pass laws imposing costs on private enterprises, thereby causing profits to be reduced—and incentives to be changed. In California, for example, the state legislature passed a law requiring landlords to give elderly tenants a year's notice before evicting them and to pay up to $3,000 to each tenant evicted, to help with relocation costs. This legislation was intended to deal with the danger of mass evictions by landlords who were losing money under rent control and who wanted to stop renting.

Since this legislation went into effect on January 2, 2000, owners of cheap hotels evicted many elderly tenants during December 1999, in order to escape these impending costs of shutting down their hotels. Laws are often proposed or passed because of the *goals* they seek to achieve—and without regard to the *incentives* actually created—which, in this case, caused many poor and elderly single men to be thrown out on the streets during the Christmas season. Far more anger and indignation were directed at the hotel owners than at those who had passed such legislation. Yet, in the absence of attempts to confiscate profits through both rent control laws and laws on evictions, the ordinary incentives of property rights and a free market would have caused the hotel owners to want to keep all the tenants they could.

Social Order

Order extends beyond laws. The honesty and reliability of the people themselves, and their sense of responsibility and cooperation also influence their economic prospects. These things can vary greatly between one country and another. As one knowledgeable observer put it: "While it is unimaginable to do business in China without paying bribes, to offer one in Japan is the greatest faux pas."

During czarist Russia's industrialization in the late nineteenth and early twentieth centuries, one of its biggest handicaps was the widespread corruption within the general population, in addition to the corruption that was rampart within the Russian government. Foreign firms which hired Russian workers and even Russian executives made it a point *not* to hire Russian accountants. This corruption continued under the Communists and has become an international scandal in the post-Communist era.

By contrast, some minority groups have such strong internal standards and social controls that they are able to transact business among themselves on the basis of relying on each other's verbal agreements, without recourse to contracts or to the legal system of the larger society. Hasidic Jews in New York's jewelry business, for example, often give consignments of jewels to one another and share the sales proceeds on the basis of verbal agreements among themselves. The extreme social isolation of the Hasidic community from the larger society, and even from other Jews, makes it very costly for anyone who grows up in that community to disgrace his family and lose his own standing, as well as his own economic and social relationships, by cheating on an agreement with a fellow Hasidim.

It is much the same story halfway around the world, where the overseas Chinese in various southeast Asian countries make verbal agreements among themselves, without the sanction of the local legal system. Given the unreliability and corruption of some of these post-colonial legal systems, the ability of the Chinese minority to rely on their own social and economic standards gives them an economic advantage over their indigenous competitors who lack an equally reliable way of making transactions. The costs of doing business are thus less for the Chinese than for Malay, Indonesian or other businesses in the region, giving the Chinese competitive advantages.

Honesty is more than a moral issue. It is a large economic influence as well. While government can do little to create honesty, in various ways it can either support or undermine the traditions on which honest conduct is based. This it can do by what it teaches in its schools, by the examples set by public officials, or by the laws that it passes. These laws can create incentives toward either moral or immoral conduct. Advocates of rent control, for example, often point to examples of villainy among landlords to demonstrate the need for both the rent control itself and for related tenants' rights legislation. However, rent control can itself widen the difference between the value of a given apartment building to honest owners and dishonest owners.

Where the cost of legally mandated services is high enough to equal or exceed the amount of rent permitted under the law, the value of a building to an honest landlord can be zero or even negative. Yet, to a landlord willing to violate the law and save money by neglecting required services, or being willing to accept bribes from prospective tenants, the building may still have value.

Where something has different values to different people, it tends to move through the marketplace to its most valued use, which is where the bids will be highest. In this case, dishonest landlords can easily bid apartment buildings away from honest landlords, some of whom may be happy to escape the bind that rent control puts them in. Landlords willing to resort to arson may find the building most valuable of all, if they can sell the site for commercial or industrial use after burning the building down, thereby getting rid of both tenants and rent control.

As one study of housing deterioration in New York found: "Buildings that have no or little or declining asset value are destined and often programmed for abandonment (and, hence, ultimate destruction) from the moment they are acquired." Shrewd and unscrupulous landlords have made virtually a science out of milking a rent-controlled building by neglecting maintenance and repairs, defaulting on mortgage payments, falling behind in the payment of taxes, and then finally letting the building become the property of the city, while they move on to repeat the same destructive process with other rent-controlled buildings.

None of this has been peculiar to New York. A similar pattern of deliberate destruction of rent-controlled buildings by their owners was found halfway around the world in Hong Kong. Similar incentives tend to produce similar results, even in very different societies.

Without rent control, the incentives facing landlords are directly the opposite—that is, to maintain the quality of the property, in order to attract tenants, and to safeguard it against fire and other sources of dangers to the survival of the building. In short, complaints against landlords' behavior by rent control advocates can be valid, even though few of these advocates see any connection between rent control and a declining moral quality in people who become landlords. When honest landlords stand to lose money under rent control, while dishonest landlords can still make a profit, it is virtually inevitable that the property will pass from the former to the latter.

KNOWLEDGE

In some respects, governments are able to assemble vast amounts of knowledge, but the kind of knowledge involved is often in the form of statistical generalities or verbal generalities known as "expertise," while many economic decisions depend crucially on highly specific knowledge of particular things.

Agriculture is especially difficult to plan because of the amount of highly specific knowledge required. The qualities of the soil can vary significantly on a single acre, much less on a whole farm or on all the farms spread out across a nation. Someone sitting in a distant capital city cannot know where on a given farm it would be better to grow carrots and where wheat would better suit the soil itself or the way the land slopes and water runs off it after a rain. Without having such a minutely detailed map of the country—which would itself probably cover several square miles—they would have little chance of deciding which farms would have land best suited for which crops.

Moreover, the products of agriculture are more perishable than the products of industry. Central planners may be able to look at official documents that tell them how many tons of what kind of steel exist in which warehouses, but strawberries would have spoiled before any such national data could be collected on all of them. Specific knowledge is one of the scarcest of all resources, regardless of how many people there may be who can talk in glib generalities.

The net result of all this is that even countries which have long been food exporters often begin to have difficulty feeding themselves after the government takes control of agriculture. This has happened over the centuries and in many countries, among people of every race, and under governments ranging from democracies to totalitarian dictatorships. Even the centrally planned economies of the Soviet Union and the Soviet bloc in Eastern Europe ended up having to allow a larger role for individual farming decisions, made by farmers guided by prices and sales, than they would permit in industry. Nevertheless, they did not permit a fully free market in agriculture and so ended up repeatedly being forced to import large amounts of food to feed their populations. Ironically, many of these countries in the Soviet bloc, including Russia and the Ukraine, had been large exporters of food for centuries before the Communists took power and took control of agriculture. In the last peacetime year of the Czarist regime, 1913, Russia exported more than 9 million tons of grain.

Nothing illustrates the role of prices in a free market more dramatically than the consequences of their absence—or the dramatic increases in agricultural output when markets and prices are again permitted to operate freely, as in China under Deng Xiao Peng. Nor are such economic consequences confined to Communist countries. The output of cocoa in Ghana likewise increased after the government there loosened its price controls on cocoa.

One of the classic disasters of government planning involved the British government's attempts to grow peanuts in colonial Rhodesia after World War II. Although this scheme turned out to be a costly failure, ordinary farmers around the world had been deciding for generations where and how to grow peanuts, each on his own particular land, whose individual characteristics were known directly from personal experience. Why was this government plan to grow peanuts such an economic disaster, when poorly educated or even illiterate farmers have been able to do what highly educated experts were not able to do? The farmers had highly specific knowledge, which is often far more important than general "expertise."

While central planning has an unimpressive record in industry as well, the fact that its agricultural failures are usually far worse, and more often catastrophic, suggests the crucial role of knowledge. Industrial products and industrial production processes have a far greater degree of uniformity than is found in agriculture. Orders from Moscow on how to make steel in Vladivostok have more chances of achieving their goal than orders from Moscow on how to grow carrots or strawberries in Vladivostok.

One of the most dangerous powers of any government, democratic or despotic, is the power to foreclose knowledge from affecting decisions. Given that most specific knowledge is widely scattered in fragments among vast numbers of human beings, decisions made by any manageably small number of government planners is likely to be based on far less knowledge than is available in the society as a whole. Yet, once the government's decisions have been turned into laws and policies, it no longer matters whether the beliefs on which they were based are true or false. Power trumps truth. The economic history of the Soviet Union is a monument to counterproductive policies behind widespread poverty in one of the most richly endowed countries on the face of the earth.

For example, the richness of the soil in vast regions of the European portion of the Soviet Union was so widely known that Hitler had plans to have trainloads of that soil transported to Germany for the benefit of German agriculture, after he conquered the U.S.S.R. But his own foreclosure of knowledge from his military officers in the field on the Russian front prevented the victory that might have permitted that scheme to be tried. However, the fact that a country with soil of such renowned quality as that in the Soviet Union should have had to import food to feed its own people is one measure of the importance of economic efficiency and inefficiency in the allocation of scarce resources.

EXTERNAL COSTS AND BENEFITS

Economic decisions made through the marketplace are not always better than decisions that governments can make. Much depends on whether those market transactions accurately reflect both the costs and the benefits which result. Under some conditions, they do not.

When someone buys a table or a tractor, the question as to whether it is worth what it cost is answered by the actions of the purchaser who made the decision to buy it. However, when an electric utility company buys coal to burn to generate electricity, a significant part of the costs of this operation is paid by people who breathe the smoke that results from the burning of the coal and whose homes and cars are dirtied by the soot. Cleaning, repainting and medical costs paid by these people are not taken into account in the marketplace, because these people do not participate in the transactions between the coal producer and the

utility company. Their costs are called "external costs" by economists because such costs fall outside the parties to the transaction
which creates the costs. External costs are therefore not taken into
account in the marketplace, even when these are very substantial
costs, which extend beyond monetary losses to include bad health
and premature death.

While there are many decisions that can be made more efficiently through the marketplace than by government, this is one of
those decisions that can be made more efficiently by government
than by the marketplace. Clean air laws can reduce harmful emis-
sions by legislation and regulations. Clean water laws and laws
against disposing of toxic wastes can likewise force decisions to be
made in ways that take into account the external costs that would
otherwise be ignored by those transacting in the marketplace.

By the same token, there may be transactions that would be *beneficial* to people who are not party to the decision-making, and
whose interests are therefore not taken into account. The benefits of
mud flaps on cars and trucks may be apparent to anyone who has
ever driven in a rainstorm behind a car or truck that was throwing
so much water or mud on his windshield as to dangerously obscure vision. Even if everyone agrees that the benefits of mud flaps
greatly exceed their costs, there is no feasible way of buying those
benefits in a free market, since you receive no benefits from the
mud flaps that you buy and put on your own car, but only from
mud flaps that other people buy and put on their cars and trucks.

These are "external benefits." Here again, it is possible to obtain
collectively through government what cannot be obtained individually through the marketplace, simply by having laws passed requiring all cars and trucks to have mud flaps on them.

Some benefits are indivisible. Either everybody gets these benefits or nobody gets them. Military defense is one example. If military defense had to be purchased individually through the
marketplace, then those who felt threatened by foreign powers
could pay for guns, troops, cannon and all the other means of military deterrence and self-defense, while those who saw no dangers
could refuse to spend their money on such things. However, the
level of military security would be the same for both, since support-

ers and non-supporters of military forces are intermixed in the same society and exposed to the same dangers from enemy action.

Given the indivisibility of the benefits, even some citizens who fully appreciate the military dangers, and who consider the costs of meeting it to be fully justified by the benefits, would still have no reason to spend their own money for military purposes, since their individual contribution would have no serious effect on their own individual security, which would depend primarily on how much others contributed. In such a situation, it is entirely possible to end up with inadequate miliary defense, even if everyone understands the cost of effective defense and considers the benefits worth it.

By collectivizing this decision and having it made by government, an end result can be achieved that is more in keeping with what most people want than if those people were allowed to decide individually what to do. Even the strongest defenders of the free market do not suggest that each individual should buy military defense in the marketplace. In short, there are things that government can do more efficiently than individuals because external costs or external benefits make individual decisions, based on individual interests, a less effective way of weighing costs and benefits to the whole society.

Setting standards is another government function which falls into this category. For centuries governments have set standards of measurement or prescribed certain measurements, such as the width of rails on railroads. The inch, the yard, and the mile are all government-prescribed units of measurement, as are pints, quarts, and gallons. If individuals had each set up their own units of measurement, transactions and contracts would be a nightmare of complications, as would the legal enforcement process. When railroads first began, each company was free to decide for itself how wide apart its rails would be set. The net result was that rail widths differed from one railroad to another, which meant that the space between train wheels also differed, so that trains from one rail line could not run on another. To tie a country together with railroads would be vastly more costly if a train from San Francisco could reach Chicago only if there happened to be rails of the same width covering that entire distance. To do this when rails were of different widths would have required far more railroads to be built, many with tracks running parallel to tracks of different widths, to reach the same places. Governmentally-imposed standards for the distance between rails eliminated this vastly expensive problem.

INCENTIVES AND CONSTRAINTS

Government is of course inseparable from politics, especially in a democratic country, so a distinction must made and kept in mind between what a government *can* do to make things better than they would be in a free market and what it is in fact *likely* to do under the influence of political incentives and constraints. The distinction between what the government can do and what it is likely to do can be lost when we think of the government as simply an agent of society or even as one integral performer. In reality, the many individuals and agencies within a national government have their own separate interests and incentives, to which they may respond far more often than they respond to either the public interest or to the policies set by political leaders.

In the Soviet Union, for example, industrial enterprises in different ministries avoided relying on each other for equipment or resources, if at all possible. Thus an enterprise located in Vladivostok might order equipment or natural resources that it needed from another enterprise under the same ministry in Minsk, thousands of miles away, rather than depend on getting what they needed from another enterprise located nearby in Vladivostok that was under the control of a different ministry. Thus materials might be shipped thousands of miles eastward on the overburdened Soviet railroads while the same kinds of materials were also being shipped westward on the same railroads by another enterprise in another ministry.

Such economically needless cross-hauling was one of many inefficient allocations of scarce resources due to the political reality that government is not a monolith, even in a totalitarian society. In democratic societies, where innumerable interest groups are free to organize and influence different branches and agencies of government, there is even less reason to expect that the government will follow one coherent policy, much less a policy that would be followed by an ideal government representing the public interest.

Under popularly elected government, the political incentives are to do what is popular, even if the consequence are worse than the consequences of doing nothing, or doing something that is less popular. As an example of what virtually everyone now agrees was a mistaken policy, the Nixon administration in 1971 created the first peacetime wage controls and price controls in the history of the United States. Among those at the meeting where this fateful decision was made was internationally renowned economist Arthur F. Burns, who argued strenuously against the policy being considered—and was over-ruled. Nor were the other people present economically illiterate. The president himself was a conservative who had long resisted the idea of wage and price controls. Indeed, he had publicly rejected the idea just eleven days before doing an about-face and accepting it. But inflation had created mounting pressures from the public and the media to "do something."

With a presidential election due the following year, the government could not afford to be seen as doing nothing while inflation raged out of control. However, even aside from such political concerns, the participants in this meeting were "exhilarated by all the great decisions they had made" that day, according to those who were present. Looking back, they later recalled "that more time was spent discussing the timing of the president's speech than how the economic program would work." There was particular concern that, if his speech were broadcast in prime time, it would cause cancellation of the very popular television program *Bonanza*, leading to public resentments. Here is what happened:

> Nixon's speech—despite the preemption of *Bonanza*—was a great hit. The public felt that the government was coming to its defense against the price gougers . . . During the next evening's newscasts, 90 percent of the coverage was devoted to Nixon's new policy. The coverage was favorable. And the Dow Jones In-

dustrial Average registered a 32.9 point gain—the largest one-day increase up to then.

In short, the controls were a complete success politically. As for their economic consequences:

> Ranchers stopped shipping their cattle to the market, farmers drowned their chickens, and consumers emptied the shelves of supermarkets.

Price controls produced essentially the same results under the Nixon administration as they had produced in the Roman Empire under Diocletian, in the Soviet Union under the Communists, in Ghana under Nkhrumah, and in numerous other times and places where such policies had been tried before. Nor was this particular policy unique politically in how it was conceived and carried out. Veteran economic adviser Herbert Stein observed, 25 years after the Nixon administration meeting at which he had been present, "failure to look ahead is extremely common in government policy making." Another way of saying the same thing is that political time horizons tend to be much shorter than economic time horizons. Before the full economic consequences of the wage and price control policies became widely apparent, Nixon had been re-elected with a landslide victory at the polls.

The constraints within which government policy-making operates are as important as the incentives. Important and beneficial as a framework of rules of law may be, what that also means is that many matters must be dealt with categorically, rather than incrementally. A Protestant president cannot stop people from going to Catholic churches or vice versa. No one can be executed without being convicted of a crime. The application of such categorical laws prevents the enormous powers of government from being applied at the discretion or whim or officials. However, there are many things which require discretionary incremental adjustments, as noted in Chapter 4, and for these things categorical laws can be difficult to apply or can produce counterproductive results.

For example, while prevention of air pollution and water pollution are widely recognized as legitimate functions of government, which can achieve more economically efficient results than those of the free market, doing so through categorical laws can create major problems. Despite the political appeal of categorical phrases like "clean water" and "clean air," there are in fact no such things, never have been, and perhaps never will be. Moreover, there are diminishing returns in removing impurities from water or air. Reducing truly dangerous amounts of impurities from water or air can be done at costs that most people would agree were quite reasonable. But, as higher and higher standards of purity are prescribed by government, in order to eliminate ever more minute traces of ever more remote or more questionable dangers, the costs escalate out of proportion. But the appeal of categorical phrases like "clean water" may be as politically potent when the water is already 99.99 percent pure as when it was dangerously polluted.

Depending on what the particular impurity is, minute traces may or may not pose a serious danger. But there are controversies raging over the presence of some impurities in water that is already 99.999999 percent pure. These controversies are unlikely to be settled at the scientific level when political passions can be whipped up in the name of non-existent "clean water." No matter how pure the water becomes, someone can always demand the removal of more impurities. And, unless the public understands the logical and economic implications of what is being said, that demand can become politically irresistible, since no public official wants to be known as being opposed to clean water.

The same principle applies in many other contexts, where minute traces of impurities can produce major political and legal battles—and consume millions of tax dollars with little or no net effect on the health or safety of the public. One legal battle raged for a decade over the impurities in a New Hampshire toxic waste site, where these wastes were so diluted that children could have eaten some of the dirt there for 70 days a year without any significant harm—if there had been any children playing there, which there were not. As a result of spending more than $9 million, the level of impurities was reduced to the point where children could have eaten the dirt there 245 days a year. Moreover, without anything being done at all, both parties to the litigation agreed that

more than half the volatile impurities would have evaporated by
the year 2000. Yet hypothetical dangers to hypothetical children
kept the issue going.

With environmental safety, as with other kinds of safety, some
forms of safety in one respect creates dangers in other respects.
California, for example, required a certain additive to be put into
all gasoline sold in that state, in order to reduce the air pollution
from automobile exhaust fumes. However, this new additive
tended to leak from filling station storage tanks and automobile
gas tanks, polluting the ground water in the first case and leading
to more automobile fires in the second. Similarly, government-
mandated air bags in automobiles, introduced to save lives in car
crashes, have themselves killed small children.

These are all matters of incremental trade-offs to find an optimal amount and kind of safety, in a world where being categorically safe is as impossible as achieving 100 percent clean air or
clean water. Incremental trade-offs are made all the time in individual market transactions, but it can be politically suicidal to op-
pose demands for more clean air, clean water or automobile
safety. Therefore saying that the government *can* improve over the
results of individual transactions in a free market is not the same
as saying that it *will* in fact do so. Among the greatest external
costs imposed in a society can be those imposed politically by legislators and officials who pay no costs whatever, while imposing
billions of dollars in costs on others, in order to respond to political pressures from advocates of particular interests or ideologies.

By the same token, while external costs are not automatically
taken into account in the marketplace, this is not to say that there
may not be some imaginative ways in which they can be. In
Britain, for example, ponds or lakes are often privately owned,
and these owners have every incentive to keep them from becoming polluted, since a clean body of water is more attractive to fish-
ermen or boaters who pay for its use. Similarly with shopping
malls: Although maintaining clean, attractive malls with benches,
restrooms and security personnel costs money that the mall owners do not collect from the shoppers, a mall with such things at-
tracts more customers, and so the rents charged the individual

storeowners can be higher because a location in such malls is more valuable than in a mall without such amenities.

In short, while externalities are a serious consideration in determining the role of government, they do not simply provide a magic word which automatically allows economics to be ignored and politically attractive goals to be pursued without further ado. Both the incentives of the market and the incentives of politics must be weighed when choosing between them on any particular issue.

Just as we must keep in mind a sharp distinction between the goals of a particular policy and the actual consequences of that policy, so we must keep in mind a sharp distinction between the purpose for which a particular power is created and the purposes for which that power can be used. President Franklin D. Roosevelt took the United States off the gold standard in 1933 under presidential powers created during the First World War to prevent trading with enemy nations. Though that war had been over for more than a dozen years and we no longer had any enemy nations, the power was still there to be used for wholly different purposes.

Chapter 18

An Overview

One of the most dangerous ways of reasoning about the national economy is by analogy to the circumstances of individuals or by anecdotal observations about what happens in individual situations. That way lies the fallacy of composition. Yet politicians, the media and others who seek to over-simplify often use such analogies, whether innocently or in order to sway others in their direction.

The fallacy in the fallacy of composition comes from ignoring the *interactions* which prevent what is true of a part from being true of the whole. Because a national economy involves many complex interactions among millions of individuals, businesses and other organizations, what is true for some of them need not be true for the economy as a whole. For example, saving jobs in the steel industry by restricting imports of steel from other countries does not mean that the economy as a whole will have more jobs. When American-made steel becomes more expensive than imported steel, that additional cost translates into more expensive American-made automobiles, refrigerators and other products made with steel—all of which have to compete with imported products made with less expensive steel overseas. Even aside from international competition, more expensive steel products mean fewer sales of these products than there would have been at lower prices, and that in turn means lower production and employment in all those industries. The jobs lost in these other industries can easily exceed the jobs saved in the steel industry, quite aside from needlessly lowering the purchasing power of American consumers because of artificially higher prices for products made with steel.

Although the fallacy of composition shows up in many aspects of economics—and of life—it is especially likely to show up in questions involving the national economy as a whole. Politicians love to come to the rescue of particular industries, professions, classes, or racial or ethnic groups—and to represent the benefits to these groups as net benefits to the country. Media journalists likewise love to feature the fortunes or misfortunes of particular individuals, groups, organizations, or regions of the country. They too tend to present these stories as if they were typical or indicative of what is happening over all.

Not only may the fates of particular parts of the economy differ from the fate of the economy as a whole, to some extent it is inevitable that parts of the economy suffer from the progress of the whole. Where are the new technologies, the new industries, and the new ways of distributing products to get the resources they need, except by taking capital, labor and other resources away from other parts of the economy? Automobiles, trucks, and tractors necessarily displaced horses from their historically large role in transportation and farming, thereby freeing up all the resources required to feed and maintain vast numbers of horses. Workers were also displaced from agriculture as farming methods became more efficient. One of the key factors in the growth of industrial output has been the ever-growing availability of workers displaced from agriculture. How else could American industries have gotten all the millions of workers needed to fill their factories, except by taking them from the farms?

Those who lament the passing of the family farm often see no connection between that and the greater outpouring of goods and services from industry that created a rising standard of living for millions of Americans. Nothing is easier for the media or for politicians than to present "human interest" stories about someone whose family has been farming for generations and who has now been forced out of the kind of life they knew and loved by the impersonal economic forces of the marketplace. What is forgotten is that these impersonal forces represent benefits to consumers who are just as much persons as the producers who have been arbitrarily selected as the focus of the discussion. The temptation is always there to try to "solve" the problem of those whose plight has been singled out for attention, without regard for the effects elsewhere.

Because the national economy is so large and complex, it is often described in gross statistics which may or may not reflect economic realities. We have noted how an arbitrary choice of a base year for beginning to follow trends over time can be completely misleading as regards economic growth. It can also be misleading in many other ways. For example, real wage rates and real salaries were often at unprecedented highs at the depth of the Great Depression of the 1930s, because the reduced money supply increased the purchasing power of any given income. Millions of people were unemployed or employed part-time, or only sporadically employed, but the statistics on real pay per unit of time for those employed nevertheless represented unusually high purchasing power.

In later years, many representatives of salaried government employees, such as civil servants or school teachers, used some year during the Great Depression as their base period from which to measure how their pay had failed to keep up with inflation or had lagged behind the pay of people in other occupations—all obviously intended as arguments for raising their incomes. Whether or not their pay should have been raised on other grounds, this particular statistical exercise compares apples and oranges.

People who kept their jobs—as most teachers and civil servants did during the Great Depression—were of course better off when their fixed money incomes could buy more goods and services during a deflationary period. And of course a return to full employment meant that others who had suffered much more economically during the Great Depression were now improving their economic position relative to that of teachers and civil servants during that unusual period of deflation and depression. There is no need to freeze the economic relationship of these different groups to one another where they were in 1932—or any other year.

The tragic bungling of economic policy by presidents of both political parties, as well as by officials of the Federal Reserve System, during the Great Depression of the 1930s has sobering implications for those who regard government as a force to save the economy from the imperfections of the marketplace. Markets are indeed imperfect, as everything human is imperfect. But "market failure" is not a magic phrase that automatically justifies government intervention, because the government can also fail—or even make things worse.

When a home run slugger strikes out (as most of them do with some frequency), he is not automatically taken out of the game and a pinch hitter sent in. After all, pinch-hitters can also strike out, and they may not be as likely to hit a home run. Although it was fashionable at one time to represent the Roosevelt administration as having rescued the country from the Great Depression, all previous depressions had come and gone without significant government action—and prosperity had returned much more quickly in earlier times. Presidents Hoover and Roosevelt both tried to use the powers of the federal government to restore the economy. However good their intentions, economists and other scholars who have studied that era in depth have increasingly concluded that they made matters worse.

Because a national economy includes such a huge mixture of ever-changing goods and services, merely measuring the rate of inflation is much more chancy than confident discussions of statistics on the subject might indicate. As already noted, cars and houses have changed dramatically over the years. If the average car today costs X percent more than it used to, does that mean that there has been X percent inflation or that most of that change has represented higher prices paid for higher quality? No one calls it inflation when someone who has been buying Chevrolets begins to buy Cadillacs and pays more money. Why then call it inflation when a Chevrolet begins to have features that were once reserved for Cadillacs and its costs rise to levels once charged for Cadillacs?

Another source of inaccuracy in measuring inflation is in the things that are included and not included in the statistics used to create an index of inflation, such as the Consumer Price Index. Everything cannot be included in an index, both because of the enormous time and money this would require and because "everything" itself changes over time with the creation of new products and the disappearance of old ones. Instead, the prices of a collection of commonly purchased items are followed over the years, measuring how much those particular prices rise or fall.

The problem with this is that what is commonly used depends on prices. Within living memory, television sets were so expensive that only rich people could afford them. So were air-conditioned cars and portable computers. At that time, no one would have dreamed of including such rare luxuries in a price index to measure the cost of living of the average American. Only after their prices fell to a fraction of what they once were did such items become commonplace possessions. What this means is that the price indexes missed all the *falling* prices of such things in the years before they became widely used, while counting all the *rising* prices of other things that were already widely used. In short, these indexes were biased upward in their estimates of inflation.

Because government policies and private contracts were often based on the cost of living, as measured by these indexes, huge sums of money changed hands across the country, as a result of exaggerated estimates of inflation. Social Security recipients, for example, received billions of dollars in cost-of-living increases in their pension checks because of an inflation that was in part a statistical artifact, rather than a real increase in the prices of buying what they had always bought. This was a factor in creating an official panel of distinguished scholars to revise the indexes. But, no matter how distinguished the individuals, or how conscientiously they worked, the task they were attempting could never achieve precision, even if it could be made more realistic than it was.

The national economy is such a large and complex subject that it cannot be covered comprehensively here. This section is not meant to answer all questions. It has succeeded to the extent that you know what kinds of questions to ask when people start throwing statistics around and claiming to have "proved" this or that.

PART VI:
THE
INTERNATIONAL
ECONOMY

Chapter 19

International Trade

When the historic North American Free Trade Agreement of 1993 (NAFTA) was approaching its controversial passage in Congress, the *New York Times* said:

> Abundant evidence is emerging that jobs are shifting across borders too rapidly to declare the United States a job winner or a job loser from the trade agreement.

Posing the issue in these terms committed the central fallacy in many discussions of international trade—assuming that one country must be a "loser" if the other country is a "winner." International trade is not a zero-sum game. Otherwise, nations would not continuously engage in it. Both must gain or it would make no sense.

As for jobs, there were dire predictions of "a giant sucking sound" as jobs would be sucked out of the United States to Mexico and other countries with lower wage rates after the free-trade agreement went into effect. In reality, the number of American jobs *increased* after the agreement and the unemployment rate in the United States fell to the lowest levels seen in decades. Before NAFTA was passed, Congressman David Bonior of Michigan warned: "If the agreement with Mexico receives congressional approval, Michigan's auto industry will eventually vanish." But what actually happened was that employment in the automobile industry increased by more than 100,000 jobs over the next six years.

Such results clearly surprised many people. But it should not have surprised anyone who understood economics.

Let's go back to square one. What happens when a given country, in isolation, becomes more prosperous? It tends to buy more because it has more to buy with. And what happens when it buys more? There are more jobs created making the additional goods and services that are now in greater demand.

Make that two countries and the principle remains the same. There is no *fixed* number of jobs that the two countries must fight over. If they both become more prosperous, they are both likely to create more jobs. The only question is whether international trade tends to make both countries more prosperous.

As with any other exchange, the only reason international trade takes place in the first place is because both parties expect to benefit. If either side discovers that it is worse off, then it stops trading.

The facts about international trade are not difficult to understand. What is difficult to untangle are all the misconceptions and jargon which so often clutter up the discussion.

THE BASIS FOR INTERNATIONAL TRADE

While international trade takes place for the same reason that other trades take place—because both sides gain—it is necessary to understand just why both countries gain, especially since there are so many politicians and journalists who muddy the waters with claims to the contrary.

The reasons why countries gain from international trade are usually grouped together by economists under three labels: absolute advantage, comparative advantage, and economies of scale.

Absolute Advantage

It is obvious why Americans buy bananas grown in the Caribbean. It is much cheaper to grow bananas in the tropics than in places where greenhouses and other artificial means of maintaining warmth would be necessary. In tropical countries, nature provides free the warmth that people have to provide by costly means in cooler climates.

This is just one example of what economists call "absolute advantage"—one country, for any of a number of reasons, can produce some things cheaper than another. These reasons may be due to climate, geography, or the mixture of skills in their respective populations. Whatever the reason may be in each particular case, one country can simply produce a given product more cheaply than another.

There is another more subtle, but at least equally important, reason for international trade. This is what economists call "comparative advantage."

Comparative Advantage

To illustrate what is meant by comparative advantage, suppose that one country is so efficient that it is capable of producing *anything* more cheaply than another country. Should the two countries trade?

Yes.

Why? Because, even in an extreme case where one country can produce anything more cheaply than another country, it may do so to varying degrees. For example, it may be twice as efficient at producing chairs but ten times as efficient at producing television sets. In this case, the total number of chairs and television sets produced in the two countries combined would be greater if one country produced all the chairs and the other produced all the television sets. Then they could trade with one another and each end up with more chairs and more television sets than if they each produced both products for themselves.

As economists would say, country A has an "absolute advantage" in producing both products but country B has a "comparative advantage" in producing chairs while A has a "comparative advantage" in producing television sets.

Let's look at this on a small, human scale. Imagine that you are an eye surgeon and that you paid your way through college by washing cars. Now that you have a car of your own, should you wash it yourself or should you hire someone else to wash it—even if your previous experience allows you to do the job more efficiently than the person you hire?

Obviously, it makes no sense to you financially, or to society in terms of over-all wellbeing, for you to be spending time sudsing down a car instead of being in an operating room saving someone's eyesight. In other words, even though you have an "absolute advantage" in both activities, your comparative advantage in treating eye diseases is far greater.

The key to understanding both individual examples and examples from international trade is the basic economic reality of scarcity. The surgeon has only 24 hours in the day, like everyone else. Time that he is spending doing one thing cannot be spent doing something else. The same is true of countries, which do not have an unlimited amount of labor, time, or other resources, and so must do one thing at the cost of not doing something else.

Although country A may be capable, in the abstract, of producing *anything* more cheaply than country B, it cannot in reality produce *everything* more cheaply because the time it spends producing one thing comes at the expense of the time that could have been spent producing other things. As we saw in Chapter 2, the real cost of producing anything is the loss of other things that could have been produced with the same time, effort, and resources. If country B is very inexperienced in producing television sets, it will take an inordinate amount of time to make one—time that could have been better spent producing chairs and trading them to Country A to get television sets.

Conversely, while Country A can produce either product more efficiently, the time it spends producing chairs would pay off much bigger in producing television sets, some of which it can trade for chairs from Country B, ending up with more of both products than if it produced both for itself.

Each country's economic well-being—and the world's economic well-being—will be greatest if it devotes its scarce resources to producing those things in which it has the greater "comparative advantage" and trades with another country to get the rest of what it wants.

A numerical example may make the point clearer. The numbers in the table below illustrate what is meant by "comparative advantage."

Imagine that the United States and Canada both produce shirts and shoes and that the United States produces both products with less labor and other resources than is required in

Canada. For the sake of simplicity, let us let labor stand for all the resources used. Assume for the sake of argument that the United States can produce 75 shirts per man-hour, while Canada produces only 30 and that the United States produces 25 shoes per man-hour, while Canada produces only 20. Here is the situation if they each produce both products:

PRODUCTS	AMERICAN MAN-HOURS	AMERICAN OUTPUT	CANADIAN MAN-HOURS	CANADIAN OUTPUT
Shirts	300	22,500	300	9,000
Shoes	200	5,000	200	4,000

With both countries producing both products, their combined output would come to a grand total of 31,500 shirts and 9,000 shoes from a grand total of 1,000 man-hours of work.

In this hypothetical example, the United States has an "absolute advantage" in producing both products but Canada has a "comparative advantage" in producing shoes. Even with such one-sided differences as those assumed and shown on this table, it would still pay for the United States to produce only shirts and to buy its shoes from Canada. Similarly, it would pay Canada to produce only shoes and buy its shirts from the United States. With the very same output per man-hour in both countries, they could produce a larger grand total of the two products.

If they engage in international trade, with each country specializing in producing the product in which it has a comparative advantage, the table below illustrates the output under these conditions and with the same individual productivity as before:

PRODUCTS	AMERICAN MAN-HOURS	AMERICAN OUTPUT	CANADIAN MAN-HOURS	CANADIAN OUTPUT
Shirts	500	37,500	0	0
Shoes	0	0	500	10,000

Even though output per man-hour remains the same in each country as before, now their combined total of 1,000 man-hours produces 37,500 shirts and 10,000 shoes, instead of 31,500 shirts and 9,000 shoes as before. By utilizing their comparative advantages, the two countries can produce 6,000 more shirts and 1,000 more shoes than before, with no more resources than before and with no technological change. That gain comes from each country concentrating on producing those things for which it has a comparative advantage. In other words, Americans can get more shoes by producing shirts and trading them with Canadians for shirts, instead of by producing their own shirts at the expense of labor and other resources that could have gone into producing something where their advantage is not as great. Conversely, Canadians can get more shirts by producing shoes and trading them for American-made shirts.

Only if the United States produced everything more efficiently than Canada *by the same percentage for each product* would there be no gain from trade because there would then be no comparative advantage. This is virtually impossible to find in the real world. Comparative advantage is very important not only in theory but in practice. It has been more than a century since Great Britain produced enough food to feed itself. Britons have been able to eat only because the country has concentrated its efforts on producing those things in which it has had a comparative advantage, such as manufacturing, shipping, and financial services— and using the proceeds to buy food from other countries.

British consumers end up better fed and with more manufactured goods than if the country grew enough of its own food to feed itself. Since the real cost of anything that is produced are the other things that could have been produced with the same efforts, it would cost the British too much industry to put enough efforts into agriculture to become self-sufficient in food. They are better off getting food from some other country whose comparative advantage is in agriculture, even if that other country's farmers are not as efficient as British farmers.

Economies of Scale

While absolute advantage and comparative advantage are the key reasons for benefits from international trade, they are not the only reasons. Sometimes a particular product requires such huge investment in machinery and in developing a skilled labor force that the resulting output can be sold at a low enough price to be competitive only when some enormous amount of output is produced, because of what economists call "economies of scale."

If General Motors produced only a hundred Chevrolets, the cost per car would be astronomical, since all the expensive machinery and all the engineering research and development that went into creating the automobile would have to be recovered from the sale of just 100 vehicles. However, by spreading these fixed overhead costs over hundreds of thousands of Chevrolets, the cost per car shrinks to a fraction of what it would be otherwise, and thus it can be sold at a price that enables it to compete in the marketplace. It has been estimated that the minimum output of automobiles needed to achieve an efficient cost per car is somewhere between 200,000 to 400,000 automobiles per year.

Producing in such huge quantities is not a serious problem in a country of the size and wealth of the United States. But, in a country with a much smaller population—Australia, for example—there is no way to sell enough cars within the country to be able to develop and produce automobiles from scratch to sell at prices that would compete with automobiles produced in much larger quantities overseas. The largest number of cars of a given make sold in Australia in 1996 was 112,000 Fords, well below the quantities needed to reap all the cost benefits of economies of scale.

The Australian government's program to gradually reduce tariffs on imported cars has been bitterly opposed by the domestic automobile manufacturers, who would have to compete with automobiles produced more cheaply overseas. Such competition has been estimated to cost thousands of jobs in Australia and some analysts say that it would probably force all four Australian automobile producers out of business. Even the cars that have been manufactured in Australia have been developed in other countries—Ford and General Motors cars from the United States and Toyotas and Mitsubishis from Japan. They are essentially Australian-built American and Japanese cars, but they lack the economies of scale that are possible in the much larger markets in the United States and Japan.

Exports enable some countries to achieve economies of scale that would not be possible from domestic sales alone. Some companies make most of their sales outside their respective countries' borders. For example, the Dutch retailer Royal Ahold has more than two-thirds of its sales outside of the Netherlands and the Swedish retailer Hennes & Mauritz has more than four-fifths of its sales outside of Sweden. While the American retailer Wal-Mart has larger overseas sales than either of these two companies, more than four-fifths of Wal-Mart's sales are in the huge American market, where it can realize great economies of scale domestically. But small countries like South Korea and Taiwan depend on international trade to be able to produce on a scale far exceeding what can be sold domestically.

In short, international trade is necessary for many countries to achieve economies of scale that will enable them to sell at competitive prices. For some products requiring huge investments in machinery and research, only a very few large and prosperous countries could reach the levels of output needed to repay all these costs from domestic sales alone. International trade creates greater efficiency by allowing more economies of scale, as well as by taking advantage of each country's absolute or comparative advantages.

Over time, even the comparative advantages change, causing international production centers to shift from country to country. For example, when the computer was a new and exotic product, much of its early development and production took place in the United States. But, after much of the technological work was done that turned it into a widely used product that many people knew how to produce, the United States retained its comparative advantage in the development of computer technology and software design, but the machines themselves could now easily be assembled in poorer countries overseas—and were.

Those who think of American production moving overseas as a loss of jobs in the United States have been proved wrong by the facts, as the number of American jobs increased and unemployment rates fell while all these jobs were being "lost." But the opaque facts are not enough. What also needs to be understood is *why* things happened this way, when so many politicians and journalists painted an entirely different picture when making their dire predictions.

Labor is one of innumerable scarce resources which have alternative uses. The computer software industry in the United States could not have expanded so much and so successfully if all American computer engineers were tied down with the production of machines that could have been just as easily produced in some other country. Since the same American labor cannot be in two places at one time, it can move to where its comparative advantage is greatest only if the country "loses jobs" where it has no comparative advantage. That is why the United States could have unprecedented levels of prosperity and rapidly growing employment at the very times when media headlines were regularly announcing lay-offs by the tens of thousands in some industries and by the hundreds of thousands in others.

Desperate attempts to salvage their wrong predictions have led some to assert that the new jobs were only low-wage jobs "flipping hamburgers" and the like. But if Americans in general were losing higher-paid jobs and being forced to take lower-paid jobs, how then could the American standard of living have continued to rise, as all data show? In reality, when the shifting of low-skill jobs to other countries enables an American company to become more profitable, it can then afford to hire Americans for higher-skill jobs. It is not a zero-sum game when there are more total resources available after the shift.

While it is undoubtedly true that some particular individuals, or even many employees of some particular firms or industries, may have lost ground during the transition, we cannot commit "the fallacy of composition" and assume that what is true for some is true in general. The rise in the general level of real income in the United States means that the gains have clearly outstripped the losses. But, where those who lose jobs are organized, their complaints carry more political weight.

When the number of jobs in the American steel industry was cut from 340,000 to 125,000 during the decade of the 1980s, that had a devastating impact and was big economic and political news. It also led to a variety of laws and regulations designed to reduce the amount of steel imported into the country to compete with domestically produced steel. Of course, this reduction in supply led to higher steel prices within the United States and therefore higher costs for all American industries producing objects made of steel, ranging from automobiles to oil rigs. With American manufacturers paying more than a hundred dollars more per ton of steel, and having to recover such increased costs from increased prices charged the consumers, all these products were at a disadvantage in competing with similar foreign-made products, both within the United States and in international markets.

The steel products manufacturers' choices were to lose sales or to shift production of their products overseas—with, of course, a loss of jobs in the United States. It has been estimated that the gain in domestic American steel production due to import restrictions led to a net loss in the production of domestic American steel products as a whole. In other words, American industry as a whole was worse off, on net balance, as a result of the import restrictions. While such steel import restrictions made no sense economically, it made sense politically to those in Washington responsible for creating these restrictions. From a political standpoint, what matters is not what works out best for the country over all. What matters is how vocal and how much political muscle one sector has relative to another.

Such economically short-sighted and nationally counterproductive policies are by no means confined to the steel industry. If a million new and well-paying jobs are created in companies scattered all across the country, that carries less weight politically than if half a million jobs are lost in one industry where labor unions and employer associations are able to raise a clamor. When the million new jobs represent a few dozen here and there in innumerable businesses scattered from coast to coast, there is not enough concentration of economic interest and political clout in one place to make it worthwhile to mount a counter-campaign. Therefore laws are often passed by Congress restricting international trade for the benefit of some concentrated and vocal constituency, even though these restrictions may cause far more losses of jobs nationwide.

INTERNATIONAL TRADE RESTRICTIONS

While there are many advantages to international for the world as a whole and for individual countries as a whole, like all forms of economic efficiency, at home or abroad, it displaces less efficient ways of doing things. Just as the advent of the automobile inflicted losses on the horse-and-buggy industry and the spread of giant supermarket chains drove many small neighborhood stores out of business, so imports of things in which other countries have a comparative advantage create losses of profits and jobs in the corresponding domestic industry.

Despite offsetting economic gains that typically far outweigh the losses, politically it is almost inevitable that there will be loud calls for government protection from foreign competition through various restrictions against imports. Many of the most long-lived fallacies in economics have grown out of attempts to justify these international trade restrictions. Although Adam Smith destroyed most of these fallacies more than two centuries ago, as far as economists are concerned, these fallacies remain politically potent today.

Some people argue, for example, that we cannot compete with countries whose wages are much lower than ours. Poorer countries, on the other hand, may say that they must protect their "infant industries" from competition with more developed industrial nations until the local industries acquire the experience and know-how to compete on even terms. In all countries, there are complaints that other nations are not being "fair" in their laws regarding imports and exports.

A frequently heard complaint of unfairness, for example, is that some countries "dump" their goods on the international market at artificially low prices, losing money in the short run in order to gain a larger market share that they will later exploit by raising prices after they achieve a monopolistic position.

In the complexities of real life, seldom is any argument right 100 percent of the time or wrong 100 percent of the time. When it comes to arguments for international restrictions, however, most of the arguments are fallacious most of the time. Let us examine them one at a time, beginning with the high-wage fallacy.

The High-Wage Fallacy

In a prosperous country such as the United States, a fallacy that sounds very plausible is that American goods cannot compete with goods produced by low-wage workers in poorer countries. But, plausible as this may sound, both history and economics refute it. Historically, high-wage countries have been exporting to low-wage countries for centuries. Britain was the world's greatest exporter in the nineteenth century and its wage rates were much higher than the wage rates in many, if not most, of the countries to which it sold.

Economically, the key flaw in the high-wage argument is that it confuses wage rates with labor costs—and labor costs with total costs.

When workers in a prosperous country receive twice the wage rate as workers in a poorer country and produce three times the output per man-hour, then it is the high-wage country which has the lower labor costs. That is, it is cheaper to get a given amount of work done in the more prosperous country simply because it takes less labor, even though individual workers are paid more. The higher-paid workers may be more efficiently organized and managed, or have far more or better machinery to work with. There are, after all, reasons why one country is more prosperous than another and often that reason is that they are more efficient at producing output.

Higher wage rates per unit of time are not the same as higher costs per unit of output. It may not even mean higher labor costs per unit of output—and labor costs are not the only costs.

The cost of capital and management are a considerable part of the cost of the product. In some cases, capital costs exceed labor cost, especially in industries with high fixed costs, such as electric utilities and telephone companies. A prosperous country usually has a greater abundance of capital and, because of supply and demand, capital tends to be cheaper than in poorer countries where capital is more scarce and earns a correspondingly higher rate of return.

When Russia began a large-scale industrialization in the 1890s, foreign investors could earn 17.5 percent per year—until so many invested in Russia that the rate of return fell below 5 percent by 1900. Poorer countries with high capital costs would have difficulty competing with richer countries with lower capital costs, even if they had a real advantage in labor costs, which they often do not.

Against this background, it may be easier to understand why dire predictions of a "giant sucking sound" as American jobs would go to Mexico in the wake of the North American Free Trade Agreement of 1993 turned out to be completely wrong. The number of American jobs increased and the unemployment rate in the United States fell to record lows. This did not come at the expense of Mexico, however. Both countries gained for the same reasons that countries have gained from international trade for centuries—absolute advantage and comparative advantage.

At any given time, it is undoubtedly true that some industries will be adversely affected by foreign imports, just as they are adversely affected by every other source of cheaper products. These other sources of greater efficiency are at work all the time, forcing industries to modernize, downsize or go out of business. Yet, when this happens because of foreigners, it can be depicted politically as a case of our country versus Japan or Mexico, when in fact it is the old story of domestic special interests versus consumers.

During periods of unemployment, politicians are especially likely to be under great pressure to come to the rescue of particular industries by restricting imports that compete with them. One of the most tragic examples of such restrictions occurred during the worldwide depression of the 1930s, when tariff barriers and other restriction went up around the world. Just as free trade provides economic benefits to all countries simultaneously, so trade restrictions reduce the efficiency of all countries simultaneously, lowering standards of living, without producing the increased employment that was hoped for.

At any given time, a protective tariff or other import restriction may provide immediate relief to a particular industry and thus gain the financial and political support of corporations and labor unions in that industry. But, like many political benefits, it comes at the expense of others who may not be as organized, as visible, or as vocal. Economists have long blamed the international trade restrictions around the world for needlessly prolonging the worldwide depression of the 1930s. Economists, however, do not have many votes. Nor do many of the voters know much economics.

Chapter 20

International Transfers
of Wealth

One of the things that keeps people thinking of international trade as some kind of contest between nations, with winners and losers, is the practice of regarding "deficits" and "surpluses" in the international balance of trade as if they represented a major problem or benefit. The trade itself can be very beneficial, as a means of adding to the total supply of goods and services available to the countries which engage in it, but these benefits do not depend on whether a given country has more exports than imports or vice-versa.

The great Supreme Court Justice Oliver Wendell Holmes said: "Think things, not words." Nowhere is that more important than when discussing international trade, where there are so many misleading and emotional words used to describe and confuse things that are not difficult to understand in themselves. The terminology used to describe an export surplus as a "favorable" balance of trade and an import surplus as an "unfavorable" balance of trade goes back for centuries.

At one time, it was widely believed that an import surplus impoverished a nation because the difference between imports and exports had to be paid in gold, and the loss of gold was seen as a loss of national wealth. However, as early as 1776, Adam Smith's classic *The Wealth of Nations* argued that the real wealth of a nation consists of its goods and services, not its gold supply. Too many people have yet to grasp this, even at the beginning of the twenty-first century. If the goods and services available to the American people are greater as a result of international trade,

then Americans are wealthier, not poorer, regardless of whether
there is a "deficit" or a "surplus" in the international balance
of trade.

If Americans buy more Japanese goods than the Japanese buy
American goods, then Japan gets American dollars to cover the
difference. Since Japan is not just going to collect these dollars as
souvenirs, it usually turns around and invests them in the American economy. In most cases, the money never leaves the United
States. The Japanese simply buy investment goods—Rockefeller
Center, for example—rather than consumer goods. American dollars are worthless to the Japanese if they do not spend them on
something. In gross terms, international trade has to balance, in
order to make any economic sense. But it so happens that the conventions of international accounting count imports and exports in
the "balance of trade," but not things which don't move at all, like
Rockefeller Center.

In some years, the best-selling car in America has been a
Honda or a Toyota, but no automobile made in Detroit has ever
been the best-selling car in Japan. The net result is that Japanese
automakers receive many millions of dollars in American money
and Japan has a net surplus in its trade with the United States. But
what do the makers of Hondas and Toyotas do with all that
American money? One of the things they do is build factories in
the United States, employing thousands of American workers to
manufacture their cars closer to their customers, so that Honda
and Toyota do not have to pay the cost of shipping cars across the
Pacific Ocean. Their American employees have been paid sufficiently high wages that they have repeatedly voted against joining labor unions in secret ballot elections.

Looking at *things*, rather than words, there is little here to be
alarmed about. What alarms people are the words and the accounting rules which produce numbers to fit those words. A
country's total output consists of both goods and services—
houses and haircuts, sausage and surgery—but the international
trade balance consists only of physical goods that move. The
American economy produces more services than goods, so it is
not surprising that we import more goods than we export—and
export more services than we import.

American know-how and American technology are used by other countries around the world and these countries of course pay us for these services. For example, most of the computers in the world run on operating systems created by Microsoft. But their payments to Microsoft and other American companies for their services are not counted in the international balance of trade, since trade includes only goods. This is just an accounting convention. Yet the American "balance of trade" is reported in the media as if this partial picture were the whole picture and the emotionally explosive word "deficit" sets off alarms.

When you count all the money and resources moving in and out of a country for all sorts of reasons, then you are talking about the international "balance of payments"—regardless of whether the payments were made for goods or services. While this is not as misleading as the balance of trade, it is still far from being the whole story, and it has no necessary connection with the health of the economy. Ironically, one of the rare balance of payments surpluses for the United States in recent years was followed by the 1992 recession.

According to the accounting rules, when people in other countries invest in the United States, that makes us a "debtor" to those people, because we owe them the money that they put here, since it was not sent as a gift. When people in many countries around the world feel more secure in putting their money in American banks or investing in American corporations, rather than relying on their own banks and corporations, then vast sums of money from overseas find their way to the United States.

Foreigners invested $12 billion in American businesses in 1980 and this rose over the years until they were investing more than $200 billion annually by 1998. Looked at in terms of *things*, there is nothing wrong with this. It creates more jobs for American workers and creates more goods for American consumers. Looked at in terms of *words*, however, this is a growing debt to foreigners. Incidentally, contrary to popular fears that Japan was buying up America, the largest share of foreign direct investment in the United States in 1998 was Great Britain's 19 percent, compared to Japan's 16 percent. Britain was also the largest recipient of Ameri-

can direct investment abroad, receiving 18 percent of such investments, with Canada being next at 11 percent.

The more prosperous and secure the American economy is,
the more foreigners are likely to want to send their money here
and the higher our annual balance of payments "deficits" and accumulated international "debt" rises. Hence it is not at all surprising that the long prosperity of the U. S. economy in the 1990s was
accompanied by record levels of international deficits and debts.
The United States was where the action was and this was where
many foreigners wanted their money to be, in order to get in on
the action. This included foreign businesses merging with American businesses or buying them. As an official publication of the
Commerce Department put it:

> Total acquisition activity by foreign direct investors was at record
> levels . . . A general factor behind the surge in acquisitions was the
> desire to reduce costs through economies of scale in response to
> heightened global competition. In addition, the desire of foreign
> investors to gain access to the advanced and growing technologi-
> cal capability of the United States led to a number of acquisitions
> of telecommunication and information-related businesses.

International mergers and acquisitions have been on such a
large scale that, in 1995, 32 percent of all American exports went
to foreign companies affiliated with American companies and 38
percent of imports to the United States came from foreign companies affiliated with American companies.

The late distinguished economist Herbert Stein and a fellow
economist co-author put it best: "If all transactions are accounted
for, there can be no deficit in the balance of payments." Money does
not disappear into thin air, nor do foreign recipients of American
dollars let the money sit idle—and they know that the best place to
put American dollars is in the United States. However, because accounting conventions count some kinds of cash flows, but not others, there can be "deficits" and "surpluses." For example, when
flows of foreign investments into the United States are not counted,
then the United States can have a deficit and run up "debts"—according to accounting conventions. Such capital inflows doubled

between 1988 and 1998. The "debts" generated by such activities are more like what happens when you deposit money in a bank, rather than like what happens when you simply charge things on a credit card. Every time you deposit a hundred dollars in a bank, that bank goes a hundred dollars deeper in debt, because it is still your money and they owe it to you.

Some people might become alarmed if they were told that the bank in which they keep their life's savings was going deeper and deeper into debt every year. But such worries would be completely uncalled for, since the bank's growing debt means only that many other people are also depositing money in that same bank. Alarmists are unlikely to try to scare people by saying that American banks are going deeper into debt, because the banks themselves would correct the misconception and discredit the alarmists. But when similar fears are stirred up because the United States is in debt to foreign countries, such misconceptions are less likely to be dispelled, because there is less likely to be someone on hand with a vested interest in correcting the record and sufficient credibility to do so.

For most of its history, the United States has been a debtor nation—and has likewise had the highest standard of living in the world. One of the things that helped develop the American economy and changed the United States from a small agricultural nation to an industrial giant was an inflow of capital from Western Europe in general and from Britain in particular. These vast resources enabled the United States to build canals, factories and transcontinental railroads to tie the country together economically.

As of the 1890s, for example, foreign investors owned about one-fifth of the stock of the Baltimore & Ohio Railroad, more than one-third of the stock of the New York Central, more than half the stock of the Pennsylvania Railroad and nearly two-thirds of the stock of the Illinois Central. Obviously, foreign investors would never have sent their money here unless they expected to get it back with interest and dividends. Equally obviously, American entrepreneurs would never have agreed to pay this interest and these dividends to them unless they expected these investments to produce big enough returns to cover these payments and still leave a profit for the American enterprises.

This all worked out largely as planned, for generations on end. But this meant that the United States was officially a debtor nation for generations on end. Only as a result of lending money to European governments during the First World War did the United States become a creditor nation. Since then we have been both, at one time or another. But these have been accounting details, not determinants of American prosperity or problems.

Neither the domestic economy nor the international economy is a zero-sum game, where some must lose what others win. Everyone can win when investments create a growing economy. There is a bigger pie, from which everyone can get bigger slices. The massive infusion of foreign capital contributed to making the United States the leading industrial nation by 1913, when it produced more than one-third of all the manufactured goods in the world.

The situation is very different in some less fortunate countries today, even when the words used in accounting are the same. In these poorer countries, when exports will not cover the cost of imports and there is no high-tech know-how to export, the government must borrow money from some other country or from some international agency, in order to cover the difference. These are genuine debts and causes for genuine concern. But the mere fact of a trade deficit does not by itself create a crisis in a country like the United States, though political and journalistic rhetoric can turn it into something to alarm the public.

In general, international deficits and surpluses have had virtually no correlation with the performance of most nations' economies. Germany and France have had international trade surpluses while their unemployment rates were in double digits. Japan's postwar rise to economic prominence on the world stage included years when it ran deficits, as well as years when it ran surpluses. The United States was the biggest debtor nation in the world during its rise to industrial supremacy, became a creditor as a result of lending money to its European allies during the First World War, and has been both a debtor and a creditor at various times since. Through it all, the American standard of living has remained the highest in the world, unaffected by whether it was a creditor or a debtor nation.

Deficits and debts are accounting concepts. What matters economically is what is done with the resources involved. Even the biggest and richest corporations have debts, since they sell bonds as well as stocks. Prosperous countries likewise attract investments from other countries. When these investments pay off, they make both the creditor and the debtor wealthier than before.

This is wholly different from a poor country which has received loans from foreign governments or international agencies, precisely because its economic prospects cannot attract investments through the marketplace. As far as accounting is concerned, these debts are all the same. But that is why economics differs from accounting—and why the facts often differ greatly from what is said in politics and the media.

KINDS OF TRANSFERS

International transfers of wealth take a variety of forms. Some people working abroad send money back to their families at home. Companies send investments to other countries and later, if things work out as hoped, they receive profits back from those countries. Nations have conquered other nations and transferred the wealth of the conquered people to the conqueror's country. In more recent times, some of the wealthier countries have donated foreign aid to some of the poorer countries.

As with other aspects of economics, the basic principles involved in international movements of wealth are not complicated. However, much confusion has been spread about these international transactions as a result of economic illiteracy, politics and journalistic hype.

Remittances

Emigrants working in foreign countries often send back money to their families to support them. During the nineteenth and early twentieth centuries, Italian emigrant men were particularly noted for living in terrible conditions and even skimping on food, in order to send money back to their families in Italy. Most

of the people fleeing the famine in Ireland during the 1840s trav-
eled across the Atlantic with their fares paid by members of their
families already living in the United States.

In the late twentieth century, there were so many emigrants
working in so many countries abroad, and sending money home,
that their remittances exceeded all the foreign aid from all the
government agencies in the world combined. Most of Pakistan's
international trade deficit was covered by remittances from Pakistanis working abroad and Jordan received more money from
Jordanians living overseas than it did from all its exports.

At one time, overseas Chinese living in Malaysia, Indonesia
and other Southeast Asian nations were noted for sending money
back to their families in China. Politicians and journalists often
whipped up hostility against the overseas Chinese by claiming
that such remittances were impoverishing their countries for the
benefit of China. In reality, the Chinese created many of the enterprises —and sometimes whole industries—in these Southeast
countries. What they were sending back to China was a fraction of
the wealth they had created and added to the wealth in the countries where they were now living.

Similar charges were made against the Lebanese in West
Africa, the Indians and Pakistanis in East Africa, and other groups
around the world. The underlying fallacy in each case was due to
ignoring the wealth created by these groups, so that the countries
to which they immigrated had more wealth—not less—as a result
of their being there. Sometimes the hostility generated against
these groups has led to their leaving these countries or being expelled, leading to economic declines after their departure.

Imperialism

Genuine plunder of one nation or people by another has been
all too common throughout human history. Alexander the Great
looted the treasures of the conquered Persians. Spain took gold
and silver by the ton from the conquered indigenous peoples of
the Western Hemisphere and forced some of them into mines to
dig up more. Julius Caesar was one of many Roman conquerors to

march in triumph through the eternal city, displaying the riches and slaves he was bringing back from his victories abroad.

Although imperialism is one of the ways in which wealth can be transferred from one country to another, there are also non-economic reasons for imperialism which have caused it to be persisted in, even when it was costing the conquering country money on net balance. Military leaders may want strategic bases, such as the British base at Gibraltar or the American base at Guantanamo Bay in Cuba. Nineteenth century missionaries urged the British government toward acquiring control of various countries in Africa where there was much missionary work going on—such urgings often being opposed by chancellors of the exchequer, who realized that they would never get enough money out of these poor countries to repay the costs of establishing and maintaining a colonial regime there.

Some private individuals like Cecil Rhodes might get rich in Africa, but the costs to the British taxpayers exceeded even Rhodes' fabulous fortune. In other countries as well, particular individual or corporate special interests might make money in conquered lands where the government lost money. However, even the business interests often lost money in the colonies. During the era before the First World War, when Germany had colonies in Africa, only 4 of its 22 enterprises with cocoa plantations there paid dividends, as did only 8 of 58 rubber plantations and only 3 out of 49 diamond mining companies.

Most major industrial nations sent only trivial percentages of their exports or investments to their conquered colonies in the Third World and received imports that were similarly trivial compared to what these industrial nations produced themselves or purchased as imports from other industrial countries. At the height of the British Empire in the early twentieth century, the British invested more in the United States than in all of Asia and Africa put together. Quite simply, there was more wealth to be made from rich countries than from poor countries. For similar reasons, throughout most of the twentieth century the United States invested more in Canada than in Asia and Africa put together. Only the rise of prosperous Asian industrial nations in the latter part of the twentieth century attracted more American investors to that part of the world.

Perhaps the strongest evidence against the economic significance of colonies in the modern world is that Germany and Japan lost all their colonies and conquered lands as a result of their defeat in the Second World War—and both countries reached unprecedented levels of prosperity thereafter. A need for colonies was a particularly effective political talking point in pre-war Japan, which had very few natural resources of its own. But, after its dreams of military glory ended with its defeat, Japan simply bought whatever natural resources it needed from those countries that had them.

Imperialism has often caused much suffering among the conquered peoples. But, in the modern industrial world at least, imperialism has seldom been a major source of international transfers of wealth.

While investors have tended to invest in more prosperous nations, making both themselves and these nations wealthier, some people have depicted investments in poor countries as somehow making the latter even poorer. The Marxian concept of "exploitation" was applied internationally in Lenin's book *Imperialism*, where investments by industrial nations in non-industrial countries were treated as being economically equivalent to the looting done by imperialist conquerors. Tragically, however, it is in precisely those less developed countries where little or no foreign investment has taken place that poverty is at its worst.

Wealthy individuals in poor countries often invest in richer countries, where their money is safer from political upheavals and confiscations. Ironically, poorer countries are thus helping richer industrial nations to become still richer. Meanwhile, theories of economic imperialism depict international investments as being the equivalent of imperialist looting. Under the influence of such theories, or in response to popular belief in such theories, governments in poorer countries have often pursued policies which discouraged investments from being made there by foreign investors.

By the late twentieth century, however, the painful economic consequences of such policies had become sufficiently apparent to many people in the Third World that some governments—in Latin

America and India, for example—began moving away from such policies, in order to gain some of the benefits received by other countries which had risen from poverty to prosperity with the help of foreign investments. Economic realities had finally broken through ideological beliefs, though generations suffered needless deprivations before basic economics was finally accepted.

Foreign Aid

What is called "foreign aid" are transfers of wealth from foreign governmental organizations to the governments of poorer countries. The term "aid" assumes *a priori* that such transfers will in fact aid the poorer countries' economies to develop. In some cases it does, but in other cases foreign aid simply enables the existing politicians in power to enrich themselves through graft and to dispense largess strategically to others who help to keep them in power. Because it is a transfer of wealth to governments, as distinguished from investments in the private sector, foreign aid has encouraged many countries to set up government-run enterprises that have failed.

Perhaps the most famous foreign aid program was the Marshall Plan, which transferred wealth from the United States to various countries in Western Europe after the end of World War II. It was far more successful than later attempts to imitate it by sending foreign aid to Third World countries. Western Europe's economic distress was caused by the devastations of the war. Once the people were fed and the infrastructure rebuilt, Western Europe simply resumed the industrial way of life which they had achieved—indeed, pioneered—before. That was wholly different from trying to create all the industrial skills that were lacking in poorer, non-industrial nations.

Even massive and highly visible failures and counterproductive results from foreign aid have not stopped its continuation and expansion. The vast sums of money dispensed by foreign aid agencies such as the International Monetary Fund and the World Bank give the officials of these agencies enormous influence on the governments of poorer countries, regardless of the success or failure of the programs they suggest or impose as preconditions for receiving the money. In short, there is no economic bottom line to determine which actions, policies, organizations or individuals could survive the weeding out process that takes place through competition in the marketplace.

In addition to the "foreign aid" dispensed by international agencies, there are also direct government-to-government grants of money, shipments of free food, and loans which are made available on terms more lenient than those available in the financial markets and which are periodically "forgiven" or allowed to default. Thus American government loans to the government of India and British government loans to a number of Third World governments have been simply cancelled, converting these loans into gifts.

Sometimes a richer country takes over a whole poor society and heavily subsidizes it, as the United States did in Micronesia. So much American aid poured in that many Micronesians abandoned economic activities on which they had supported themselves before, such as fishing and farming. If and when the Americans decide to end such aid, it is not at all certain that the skills and experience that Micronesians once had will remain sufficiently widespread to allow them to become self-sufficient again.

Beneficial results of foreign aid are more likely to be publicized by the national or international agencies which finance these ventures, while failures are more likely to be publicized by critics, so the net effect is not immediately obvious. One of the leading development economists of his time, Professor Peter Bauer of the London School of Economics, has argued that, on the whole, "official aid is more likely to retard development than to promote it." Whether that controversial conclusion is accepted or rejected, what is more fundamental is that terms like "foreign aid" not be allowed to insinuate a result which may or may not turn out to be substantiated by facts and analysis.

THE INTERNATIONAL MONETARY SYSTEM

Wealth may be transferred from country to country in the form of goods and services, but by far the greatest transfers are made in the form of money. Just as a stable monetary unit facili-

tates economic activity within a country, so international economic activity is facilitated when there are stable relationships
between one country's currency and another's. It is not simply a
question of the ease or difficulty of translating dollars into yen or
francs. It is a far more important question of knowing whether an
investment made in the United States, Japan, or France today will
be repaid a decade or more from now in money of the same
value—whether measured in purchasing power or in the currency originally invested.

Where currencies fluctuate relative to one another, anyone
who engages in any international transactions becomes a speculator. Even a tourist who buys souvenirs in Mexico or on a
Caribbean cruise will have to wait until the credit card bill arrives
to discover how much the item they paid 30 pesos for will cost
them in U.S. dollars. It can turn out to be either more or less than
they thought. Where millions of dollars are invested overseas, the
stability of the various currencies is urgently important. It is important not simply to those whose money is directly involved, it
is important in maintaining the flows of trade and investment
which affect the material wellbeing of the general public in the
countries concerned.

During the era of the gold standard, which began to break
down during the First World War and ended during the Great
Depression of the 1930s, various nations made their national currencies equivalent to a given amount of gold. An American dollar, for example, could always be exchanged for a fixed amount of
gold from the U. S. government. Both Americans and foreigners
could exchange their dollars for a given amount of gold. Therefore any foreign investor putting his money into the American
economy knew in advance what he could count on getting back if
his investment worked out. No doubt that had much to do with
the vast amount of capital that poured into the United States from
Europe and helped develop it into the leading industrial nation
of the world.

Other nations which made their currency redeemable in fixed
amounts of gold likewise made their economies safer places for
both domestic and foreign investors. Moreover, their currencies
were also automatically fixed relative to the dollar and other cur-

rencies from other countries that used the gold standard. As Nobel Prizewinning monetary economist Robert Mundell put it, "currencies were just different names for particular weights of gold." During that era, financier J. P. Morgan could say, "money is gold, and nothing else."

Various attempts at stabilizing international currencies against one another have followed the disappearance of the gold standard. Some nations have made their currencies equivalent to a fixed number of dollars, for example. Various European nations have created their own international currency, the Euro, and the Japanese yen has been another stable currency widely accepted in international financial transactions.

With the spread of electronic transfers of money, reactions to any national currency's change in reliability can be virtually instantaneous. Any government that is tempted toward inflation knows that money can flee from their economy literally in a moment. The discipline this imposes is different from that once imposed by a gold standard, but whether it is equally effective will only be known when future economic pressures put the international monetary system to a real test.

Chapter 21

An Overview

Although the basic economics of international economic transactions is not rocket science, it does take a little more thought than some other economic principles. However, this alone is not enough to explain all the confusion that reigns on the subject. People with special interests to protect, or ideological visions to which they are committed, find international trade and international wealth movements a fertile field for bamboozling a public that has few reasons to pay much attention to international economics.

Most Americans' lives are not likely to be changed in any obvious and fundamental way by international trade or international financial activities. While there are many imported products in the American economy, these are typically products that Americans also make today or have made in the past and could make in the future, if there were no international trade.

There are, however, some important consequences of international economic events that may not be obvious. As already noted, the severe tariff restrictions put in place early in the Great Depression of the 1930s have been regarded by many economists as needlessly worsening and extending the worldwide depression. The last thing needed when the national income is going down is a policy that makes it go down faster, by denying consumers the benefits of being able to buy what they want at the lowest price available.

Even in normal times, the losses associated with producing many goods domestically at higher costs would add up to a loss of real purchasing power and the standard of living dependent on it. Virtually all high-quality cameras in America—cameras with interchangeable lenses, for example—are imported, and it has been decades since such cameras were manufactured in the United States. Many cars, computers, television sets, and other products sold in the United States—including some with American brand names—are imported. In short, while international trade does not play as large a role in the economy of the United States as in some other economies, its effects are nevertheless larger than may be apparent to the general public.

Just as trade restrictions such as the Hawley-Smoot tariffs of the 1930s damaged the already ailing economy of the Great Depression, the North American Free Trade Agreement of 1993 helped enhance the prosperity of the 1990s, creating more jobs and reducing unemployment to record low levels, despite the cries of protectionists that NAFTA would lead to a massive flight of jobs from America to low-wage countries elsewhere. In short, international economic activities matter to Americans, though not to the same extent as to the peoples of other countries whose international trade is a much larger percentage of their national economic activity. Britain, for example, has not fed itself from its own agriculture in more than a century, so it is heavily dependent on international trade just to have something to eat, quite aside from the many other benefits it receives.

Whatever the complications of international economic activities, the fundamental fact in international markets is the same as that in domestic markets: Exchanges continue to take place only to the extent that both parties benefit. Opponents of free trade try to depict it as harmful and to appeal to a sense of "us" against "them," as if other countries are in some way making Americans worse off by selling them things that they want to buy.

Sometimes this approach is buttressed by claims that this or that foreign country is being "unfair" in its restrictions on imports from the United States. But the sad fact is that all countries impose "unfair" restrictions on imports, usually in response to some internal special interests. However, here as elsewhere, we have to make our choices among alternatives actually available. Other countries' restrictions deprive both them and us of some of the benefits of international trade. If we do the same in response, it will deprive both of us of still more benefits. If we let them "get away with it," this will minimize the losses on both sides.

International trade is not a favor we bestow on other nations, despite laws about giving or withholding "most favored nation" treatment to this or that country in its trade with the United States. International trade is not a contest, despite talk about who "wins" or "loses" in this trade. Anybody who loses stops trading. The real losses occur when the public allows this kind of rhetoric to lead them astray from the basic fundamentals of economics.

International trade is like anything else that allows goods and services to be produced more cheaply or better. It benefits the consumers while harming profits and employment among those who produce more costly or more obsolete products. Protecting the less efficient producer makes no more sense internationally than it does domestically. Whatever jobs are saved In either case do not represent net savings for the economy as a whole, but only the saving of some jobs by sacrificing others, along with sacrificing the consumer. When particular jobs and businesses succumb to more efficient competition, whether domestic or international, resources which have alternative uses can go to those alternative uses and add to the national output. It is not a zero-sum game.

The transfer of wealth internationally through market transactions allocates the resources of the world in much the same way that such transfers allocate resources domestically. In both cases, it is like water seeking its own level. If investments with a given degree of risk are paying off at a higher rate in Taiwan than in Sweden, then American or British or German capital will flow to Taiwan and not to Sweden, thereby raising the level of productivity in the world as a whole and raising standards of living internationally. Money and the resources it represents become, as it were, citizens of the world.

Such economic benefits are often not welcome politically, however. While comparative advantage and free trade allow all nations to share in the world prosperity promoted by free movements of resources, not all industries in all nations prosper. Those sectors of particular economies that are unable to match the competition in efficiency stand to lose money and jobs, and may even be threatened with bankruptcy. Seldom will they go quietly. Representatives of industries and regions that stand to lose business and jobs because of international competition are almost certain to seek restrictions on imported goods or resources which threaten their particular wellbeing, however beneficial such international transactions may be to the population as a whole.

International movements of goods and investments also restrict the range of options available to particular governments. As noted in Chapter 16, governments have for centuries transferred wealth from the people to themselves by the simple process of issuing inflationary amounts of money and spending the newly created money for whatever the government wanted to finance. With free international movements of wealth—at instantaneous speeds with computerized banking—money and the resources they represent tend to be transferred out of countries whose governments are conducting such clandestine confiscations. Other economically counterproductive policies tend likewise to cause domestic wealth to flow out of a country and foreign wealth to stop coming in.

Political leaders have far more control when wealth flows into their countries in the form of "foreign aid"—that is, transfers from national or international agencies to governments. The alternative of receiving wealth from abroad via the marketplace would require satisfying foreign investors that a project was likely to succeed and that the local legal and political system was one they could rely on when time came to take their earnings out or to take their whole investment out if they wished.

Showy projects with only a political pay-off for the government—a sports stadium, a glitzy plaza, or a national airline in a country without enough passengers to enable it to pay for itself—can all be financed by foreign aid but are unlikely to be financed by international investors. Moreover, government officials can be more generous with themselves and their followers and favorites when it comes to appropriating foreign aid money for personal use, including putting it in Swiss banks.

In short, countries with inefficient economies and corrupt governments are far more likely to receive foreign aid than to receive investments from people who are risking their own money. Put differently, the availability of foreign aid reduces the necessity for a country to restrict its investments to economically viable projects or to reduce its level of corruption. Far more wealth may be available internationally for the economic development of a poor country and yet that country's government may prefer to receive a smaller amount through foreign aid, since government officials themselves benefit more from this smaller amount than from a larger amount of wealth that would have preconditions which negatively affect these officials' wellbeing, even if it would enhance the economic wellbeing of their country as a whole.

An intermediary form of wealth transfer is an investment from private sources that is guaranteed by their own government, which stands ready to reimburse them with taxpayers' money should their overseas investment prove unprofitable or the profits uncollectible. Thus when the Mexican government was on the verge of defaulting on its loans from American banks in 1986, the American government lent them the money to pay off these banks and other investors. Obviously , if these banks had been forced to take huge losses, they would have become more wary of risky investments in the future and in other countries. As we have seen in other contexts, losses play as important a role in the economy as profits, though they are not nearly as popular. Artificially preventing losses is reducing incentives to allocate resources efficiently.

Part VII:
POPULAR
ECONOMIC
FALLACIES

Chapter 22

"Non-Economic" Values

Now that you know some of the basics of economics, it may be much easier to see through some popular notions that sound good but will not stand up under scrutiny. The next few chapters contain just a sampling of such notions.

One of the last refuges of someone whose pet project or theory has been exposed as economic nonsense is to say: "Economics is all very well, but there are also *non-economic* values to consider." Presumably, these are supposed to be higher and nobler concerns that soar above the level of crass materialism.

Of course there are non-economic values. In fact, there are *only* non-economic values. Economics is not a value in and of itself. It is only a way of weighing one value against another. Economics does not say that you should make the most money possible. Many professors of economics could themselves make more money in private industry. Anyone with a knowledge of firearms could probably make more money working as a hit man for organized crime. But economics does not urge you toward such choices.

Adam Smith, the father of laissez-faire economics, gave away substantial sums of his own money to less fortunate people, though he did so with such discretion that this fact was discovered only after his death, when his personal records were examined. Henry Thornton, one of the great monetary economists of the nineteenth century, regularly gave away more than half his annual income before he married and had a family to support, though he continued to give large donations to humanitarian causes afterwards.

What lofty talk about "non-economic values" usually boils down to is that some people do not want their own particular values weighed against anything. If they are for saving Mono Lake or preserving some historic building, then they do not want that weighed against the cost—which is to say, ultimately, against all the other things that might be done instead with the same resources.

For such people, there is no point considering how many Third World children could be vaccinated against fatal diseases with the money that is spent saving Mono Lake or preserving a historic building. We should vaccinate those children *and* save Mono Lake *and* preserve the historic building—as well as doing innumerable other good things, according to this way of looking at the world. To people who think (or rather, react) in this way, economics is at best a nuisance that stands in the way of doing what they have their hearts set on doing. At worst, economics is seen as a needlessly narrow, if not morally warped, way of looking at the world.

Such condemnations of economics are due to the fundamental fact that economics is the study of the use of scarce resources which have alternative uses. We might all be happier in a world where there were no such constraints to force us into choices and trade-offs that we would rather not face. But that is not the world that human beings live in—or have ever lived in, during thousands of years of recorded history. In the world that people live in, and are likely to live in for centuries to come, trade-offs are inescapable. Even if we refuse to make a choice, circumstances will make choices for us, as we run out of many important things that we could have had, if only we had taken the trouble to weigh alternatives.

Lofty talk about "non-economic values" too often amounts to very selfish attempts to impose one's own values, without having to weigh them against other people's values. Taxing away what other people have earned, in order to finance one's own moral adventures, is often depicted as a humanitarian endeavor, while allowing others the same freedom and dignity as oneself, so that they can make their own choices with their own earnings, is considered to be pandering to "greed." Greed for power is no less dangerous than greed for money, and has shed far more blood in the process. Political authorities have often had "non-economic values" that were devastating to the general population.

SAVING LIVES

Perhaps the strongest arguments for "non-economic values" are those involving human lives. Many highly costly laws, policies, or devices designed to safeguard the public from lethal hazards are defended on grounds that "if it saves just one human life" it is worth whatever it costs. Powerful as the moral and emotional appeal of such pronouncements may be, they cannot withstand scrutiny in a world where scarce resources have alternative uses.

One of those alternative uses is saving other human lives in other ways. Few things have saved as many lives as the simple growth of wealth. An earthquake powerful enough to kill a dozen people in California will kill hundreds of people in some less affluent country and thousands in a Third World nation. Greater wealth enables California buildings, bridges, and other structures to be built to withstand far greater stresses than similar structures can withstand in poorer countries. Those injured in an earthquake in California can be rushed more quickly to far more elaborately equipped hospitals with larger numbers of more highly trained medical personnel.

This is just one of innumerable ways in which wealth saves lives. There have been various calculations of how much of a rise in national income saves how many lives. Whatever the correct figure—X million dollars to save one life—anything that prevents national income from rising that much has, in effect, cost a life. If some particular safety law, policy, or device costs 5X million dollars, either directly or in its inhibiting effect on economic growth, then it can no longer be said to be worth it "if it saves just one human life" because it does so at the cost of 5 other human lives. There is no escaping trade-offs, so long as resources are scarce and have alternative uses.

THE MARKET

The very language in which many issues are discussed opens the way to confusing economics with some materialistic preoccupation that violates human considerations. Many economists and others speak of "the market" as a shorthand way of referring to a set of conditions in which individuals make their own choices in light of their own respective values. But this language leads some who hear it to imagine that "the market" is some impersonal and amoral idol, on whose altar we are sacrificing moral and humane concerns. In reality, the market is merely a mechanism through which millions of human beings express their own preferences and values, rather than have some elite with political power impose that elite's preferences and values on all.

Once we realize that scarcity and trade-offs are inescapable, the only questions remaining are who is to make those trade-offs and through what mechanisms. Individual freedom, competition and prices add up to what is loosely called "the market." But the market is not a thing located at a place. Markets in that crude and simple-minded sense have existed even in Communist countries. What distinguishes "the market" as economists use the term are (1) individual free choice and (2) the guidance provided by prices which result from millions of people interacting with one another as they exercise that free choice. To say "the market decides" is only to say that these millions of people decide, instead of having others' decisions imposed on them. Like economics, the market is not some separate entity with its own values. It is people making their own choices.

"UNMET NEEDS"

One of the most common—and certainly one of the most pro-found—misconceptions of economics involves "unmet needs." Politicians, journalists, and academicians are almost continuously pointing out unmet needs in our society that should be supplied by some program or other. Most of these are things that most of us wish our society had more of.

What is wrong with that? Let us go back to square one. If economics is the study of the use of scarce resources which have alternative uses, then it follows that there will always be unmet needs. Some particular desires can be singled out and met 100 percent, but that only means that other desires will be even more unfulfilled than they are now.

Anyone who has driven in most big cities will undoubtedly feel that there is an unmet need for more parking spaces. But, while it is both economically and technologically possible to build cities in such a way as to have a parking space available for anyone who wants one, anywhere in the city, at any hour or the day or night, does it follow that we should do it?

The cost of building vast new underground parking garages, or of tearing down existing buildings to create parking garages above ground, or of designing new cities with fewer buildings and more parking lots, would all be astronomical. What other things are we prepared to give up, in order to have this automotive heaven? Fewer hospitals? Less police protection? Fewer fire departments?

Are we prepared to put up with even more unmet needs in these areas? Maybe some would give up public libraries in order to have more places to park. But, whatever choices are made and however it is done, there will still be more unmet needs elsewhere, as a result of meeting an unmet need for more parking spaces.

We may differ among ourselves as to what is worth sacrificing in order to have more of something else. The point here is more fundamental: Merely demonstrating an unmet need is not sufficient to say that it should be met—not when resources are scarce and have alternative uses.

What might appear to be cheaper, when measured only in government expenditures, would be to restrict or forbid the use of private automobiles in cities, adjusting the number of cars to the number of parking spaces, instead of vice-versa. But this saving in government expenditures would have to be weighed against the vast private expenditures currently devoted to the purchase, maintenance, and parking of automobiles in cities. Obviously these expenditures would not have been undertaken in the first place if those who pay these prices (as well as the costs of personal aggravation that go with driving in a city) did not find the benefits to be worth it to them.

To go back to square one again, *costs are foregone opportunities*, not government expenditures. Forcing thousands of people to forego opportunities for which they have willingly paid vast amounts is a cost that may outweigh the savings from not having to build more parking spaces or do the other things necessary to accommodate cars in cities. None of this says that we should have more or fewer parking spaces in cities. What it says is that the way this issue—and many others—is presented makes no sense in a world of scarce resources which have alternative uses. That is a world of trade-offs, not solutions—and whatever trade-off is decided upon will still leave unmet needs.

So long as we respond gullibly to political rhetoric about unmet needs, we will arbitrarily choose to shift resources to whatever the featured unmet need of the day happens to be and away from other things. Then, when another politician—or perhaps even the same politician at a later time—discovers that robbing Peter to pay Paul has left Paul worse off, and wants to help him meet his unmet needs, we will start shifting resources in another direction. In short, we will be like a dog chasing his tail and getting no closer, no matter how fast he runs.

This is not to say that we have the ideal trade-offs already and should leave them alone. Rather, it says that whatever trade-offs we make should be seen from the outset as trade-offs—not meeting unmet needs.

The very word "needs" arbitrarily puts some desires on a higher plane than others, as categorically more important. But, however urgent it may be to have *some* food and water, in order to sustain life itself, nevertheless—beyond some point—both become not only unnecessary but even counterproductive and dangerous. Widespread obesity among Americans shows that food has already reached that point and anyone who has suffered the ravages of flood (even if it is only a flooded basement) knows that water can reach that point as well. In short, even the most urgent needs remain needs only within a given range. We cannot live half an hour without oxygen but even oxygen beyond some concentration level can promote the growth of cancer and has been known to make newborn babies blind for life. There is a reason why hospitals do not use oxygen tanks willy-nilly.

In short, nothing is a "need" categorically, regardless of how urgent it may be to have at particular times and places and in particular amounts. Unfortunately, most laws and government policies apply categorically, if only because of the dangers in leaving every official to become a petty despot in interpreting what these laws and policies mean and when they should apply. In this context, calling something a "need" categorically is playing with fire. Many complaints that some basically good government policy has been applied stupidly may fail to address the underlying problem of categorical laws in an incremental world. There may not have been any intelligent way to apply categorically a policy designed to meet desires whose benefits vary incrementally and ultimately cease to be benefits.

By its very nature, as a study of the use of scarce resources which have alternative uses, economics is about incremental trade-offs—not about "needs" or "solutions." That may be why economists have never been as popular as politicians who promise to solve our problems and meet our needs.

WHAT IS "WASTE"?

Although efficiency is what economics is all about, there are many false notions as to what constitutes "efficiency." Some think that it can be reduced to output per man-hour or to more miles per gallon or larger crops per acre. It cannot.

Efficiency is inescapably bound up with what people want—and at what cost. Even an apparently scientific question like the efficiency of an automobile engine rests ultimately on what you want the car to do. Otherwise, all automobile engines are 100 percent efficient, in the sense that all the energy they get from fuel is used, whether in moving the car forward, overcoming internal friction in the engine, shaking the car body randomly, generating heat that is radiated out into the air, etc. It is only after you define what you want as moving the car forward that the efficiency of different engines can be compared in terms of what percentage of their power is used for that particular purpose.

When a third party defines efficiency for other people, that often conflicts with what those other people prefer in their own individually differing circumstances. For example, there have been many laments about Americans using gasoline in "wasteful" ways during the 1980s and 1990s, as contrasted with their more "fuel-efficient" behavior in the 1970s. But the reason for the change was that the real price of gasoline was lower in the 1980s and 1990s, reflecting large increases in both the immediate supply and the known reserves of petroleum in the world. Consumers were responding to the changing realities conveyed by prices, rather than to the fashionable but unproven alarms conveyed by words in the media and in politics.

During the 1970s, an international oil cartel—the Organization of Petroleum Exporting Countries (OPEC)—deliberately cut back on petroleum production, disrupting economies around the world. In the United States, government price controls turned a minor adjustment into a major shortage. By the 1990s, new discoveries of petroleum deposits and the weakening of the OPEC cartel had the world awash in oil, with the real prices of gasoline hitting all-time lows.

It is not wasteful to increase one's use of resources that have become more abundant. That is precisely what is supposed to happen in a price-coordinated economy because that is the most efficient behavior, with efficiency defined as the most effective way of satisfying people's desires.

Waste is no more objectively definable than its opposite, efficiency. The arbitrary assumption that it is serves only to let third parties impose their definitions on other people, who obviously would not be doing the things that observers define as wasteful if they themselves did not see matters differently.

Some consider it a "waste" not to recycle aluminum cans or newspapers, but studies have shown that recycling uses up more resources than it saves. About 10 percent of the entire crust of the Earth consists of aluminum, and the trees that newspapers are made from automatically recycled themselves for thousands of years before human being figured out how to plant seeds. If there were a genuine threat of running out of aluminum, its price today would reflect that future scarcity through the mechanisms of "present value" discussed in Chapter 12, and people would automatically find it financially worthwhile to recycle aluminum cans. The fact that it is not financially worthwhile reflects an underlying reality that is very different from the fashionable hysteria behind public exhortations and politically-imposed policies.

Chapter 23

Prices and
Purchasing Power

There seem to be almost as many fallacies about prices as there are prices. For example, it is common to hear that the same thing is sold at very different prices by different sellers. While this can happen, usually this involves defining things as being "the same" when they are not. Other fallacies include the notion that "greedy" sellers are responsible for rising prices or that "predatory" businesses destroy competition by selling below cost and bankrupting their rivals, so that they can then raise prices to monopolistic levels afterward. While these are only a small sample, looking at them closely may illustrate how easy it is to create a plausible-sounding fallacy and get it accepted by many otherwise intelligent people, who simply do not bother to scrutinize the logic or the evidence.

DIFFERENT PRICES FOR THE "SAME" THING

Physically identical things are often sold for different prices, usually because of accompanying conditions that are quite different. As noted in Chapter 6, two airline passengers sitting side by side in the same plane may have paid very different fares because one bought a guaranteed reservation, while the other was a standby who got on board when there happened to be space available. What they really bought were two very different probabilities of getting on board that plane. Only in retrospect did they end up with the same thing—but people do not act in retrospect. As of the time they acted, they bought very different things. Similarly, someone who wins an automobile with a $20 lottery ticket can end up with the same car for which someone else paid $20,000. But one bought a low probability of getting a car and the other bought a virtual certainty. The car they ended up with may be the same but what they bought was not the same.

The Post Office has run a massive advertising campaign claiming that its two-day delivery service, Priority Mail, costs much less than the competing two-day delivery services of Federal Express or United Parcel Service. The only problem with this claim is that almost all Federal Express or UPS two-day packages actually get delivered in two days, while little more than one-third of the long-distance Priority Mail arrives in two days. In other words, the more expensive service is more reliable, which was why it is more expensive. The Post Office ads were comparing apples and oranges.

It is also possible to be comparing apples and oranges when the products themselves are in fact physically identical. Sometimes different brands of the same goods or services are thought to differ only by brand name and brands in general may be thought to serve no useful purpose. Both these special situations deserve closer attention.

"Identical" Products

Discount stores often sell the same camera for a lower price than a camera store charges. But the people in a camera store are usually more knowledgeable about photography than people who work in discount stores, and more knowledgeable people usually have higher salaries that have to be paid out of higher prices. Camera stores usually also have a larger inventory of different cameras and accessories, and larger inventories of merchandise have a cost, just as a larger inventory of knowledge has a cost.

The value of these higher-cost features varies with the particular customer and that customer's own knowledge and desires. This becomes painfully apparent when someone who has bought a new camera has trouble operating it and goes back to the seller to get advice on how to use it. If the clerk in a discount house does not know enough to solve the customer's problem, the bargain camera may turn out to be no bargain, after all. Moreover, if the discount-house customer then goes to a camera store salesman to seek advice, he may find the salesman less than wholly sympathetic to some other store's customer.

Another way in which the accompanying knowledge is an integral part of the value of the physical product is in making the initial choice of camera. If a camera store sells a particular make and model of camera for $300 and the discount house sells it for $280, it may still pay to go to the camera store where another make and model of camera is available for $250 that does what you want to do just as well or better. The more expensive camera may have features that mean nothing to you but is no better, and perhaps not as good, for the kinds of pictures you want to take. If the camera store's larger selection and more knowledgeable sales staff enables you to buy only what meets your own needs, there may be financial savings there, as well as better advice on operating the camera, even if the discount house charges a lower price for each particular camera that both stores carry.

On the other hand, if the customer happens to be very knowledgeable about photography, then it may be unnecessary to consult the sales staff at either store, whether in making a selection or in knowing how to use the camera. In that case, buying at the discount house can mean real savings. Similarly, if the camera being bought is so simple that anybody can figure it out, then there is no need to pay for expertise that is not needed. Apparently most people do not feel the need to buy cameras from a camera store. More than half buy them from discount houses and another 19 percent buy them from mail order houses.

The point here is not to claim that it is generally better or generally worse to buy cameras at a camera store or at a discount house. Instead, the point is that what is being sold in the two places is not the same, even when the cameras themselves are physically identical. The stores are charging different prices because they are supplying different things which have different costs to the seller, as well as to the buyer.

Other products in other stores may also be physically identical and yet sell for different prices reflecting different accompanying circumstances. Groceries are likely to cost more in a remote community, hundred of miles from the supplier's warehouse, or in a high-crime neighborhood, where the cost of iron grates or armed guards, as well as higher rates of shoplifting and vandalism, have to be recovered from the prices charged the customers.

Goods sold in attractively decorated stores with polished and sophisticated sales staffs, as well as easy return policies, are likely to cost more than the physically identical products sold in a stark warehouse store with a no-refund policy. Christmas cards can be bought for much lower prices on December 26th than on December 16th, even though the cards are physically identical to what they were when they were in great demand before Christmas.

Mistakes or miscalculations may sometimes cause the same thing to be sold for different prices under comparable conditions temporarily, but competition usually makes this a passing phenomenon. When customers go where prices are lower, those whose prices are higher have little choice but to lower their prices, if they are not offering some offsetting advantages along with the same physical product. Where there are permanently different prices for things that are truly the same, the higher-price seller usually ends up going out of business.

Brand Names

Brand names are another way of economizing on scarce knowledge. When you drive into a town you have never seen before and want to get some gasoline for your car or eat a hamburger, you have no direct way of knowing what is in the gasoline that some stranger at the filling station is putting into your tank or what is in the hamburger that another stranger is cooking for you to eat at a roadside stand that you have never seen before. But, if the filling station's sign says Chevron and the restaurant's sign says McDonald's, then you don't worry about it. At worst, if something terrible happens, you can sue a multi-billion-dollar corporation. You know it, the corporation knows it, and the local dealer knows it. That is what reduces the likelihood that something terrible will happen.

On the other hand, imagine if you pull into a no-name filling station in some little town and the stranger there puts something into your tank that messes up your engine or—worse yet—if you eat a no-name hamburger that sends you to the hospital. Your chance of suing the local dealer business owner successfully, (perhaps before a jury of his friends and neighbors) may be considerably less. Moreover, even if you should win, the chances of collecting enough money to compensate you for all the hassle you have been through is more remote.

Brand names are not guarantees. But they do reduce the range of uncertainty. If a hotel sign says Hyatt Regency, chances are you will not have to worry about whether the bed sheets in your room were changed since the last person slept there. If the camera you buy is a Leica, it is unlikely to jam up the first time you wind the film. Even if you stop at a dingy and run-down little store in a strange town, you are not afraid to drink a soda they sell you, if it is a bottle or can of Coca Cola or Seven-Up. Imagine, however, if the owner of this unsavory little place mixed you a soda at his own soda fountain. Would you have the same confidence in drinking it?

Like everything else in the economy, brand names have both benefits and costs. A hotel with a Hyatt Regency sign out front is likely to charge you more for the same size and quality of room, and accompanying service, than you would pay for the same things in some locally-run independent hotel *if you knew where to look*. Someone who regularly stops in this town on business trips might well find a locally-run hotel that is a better deal. But it is as rational for you to look for a brand name when passing through for the first time as it is for the regular traveller to go where he knows he can get the same things for less.

Since brand names are a substitute for specific knowledge, how valuable they are depends on how much knowledge you already have about the particular product or service. Someone who is very knowledgeable about photography might be able to get a bargain on an off-brand camera or lens, or even a second-hand camera or lens. But that same person might be well advised to stick to well known brands of new stereo equipment, if his knowledge in that field falls far short of his expertise in photography.

Many critics of brand names argue that the main brands "are all alike." Even when that is so, the brand names still perform a valuable function. All the brands may be better than they would have to be if the product were sold under anonymous or generic labels. Both Kodak and Fuji film have to be better than they would have to be if boxes simply said "Film," without any reference to the manufacturer. But, when film is sold with brand names on the boxes, Kodak knows that it will lose millions of dollars in sales if it falls behind Fuji in quality and Fuji knows that it will lose millions if it falls behind Kodak.

Even when the various brands of a product are made to the same formula by law, as with aspirin, quality control is promoted when each producer of each bottle of aspirin is identified than when the producer is anonymous. Moreover, the best-known brand has the most to lose if some impurity gets into the aspirin during production and causes anyone injury or death. This is especially important with foods and medicines. McDonald's not only has to meet the standards set by the government, it has to meet the standards set by the competition of Wendy's and Burger King. If Campbell's soup were identified on the label only as "soup" (or "Tomato Soup," "Clam Chowder," etc), the pressures on all canned soup producers to maintain both safety and quality would be less.

One of the A & P grocery chain's big advantages during its heyday was that it produced many items itself and sold them under its own brand name. This not only saved A & P the vast amounts of advertising money usually needed to get any new product known and accepted by the public, it saved the economy the costs associated with the use of one of its most scarce resources, knowledge. Consumers were able to rely on some new and unknown product simply because it had an A & P label on it.

For example, A & P itself baked much of the bread sold in its stores—half a billion loaves a year. While this bread was accepted on faith by the public, if A & P had taken advantage of this trust to sell low-quality bread made with cheaper ingredients, it would not only have lost sales of bread after the public discovered that its trust was misplaced, the value of A & P's brand name on other products would also have been tarnished—and many millions of dollars lost as a result. Most consumers have no knowledge of what it takes to make a good loaf of bread, but A & P did, and its brand name gave it an incentive to use its knowledge to do so.

Thus the knowledge of the few served the interest of the many, as a result of brand names and a competitive market economy. In countries where there are no brand names, or where there is one producer created or authorized by the government, the quality of the product or service tends to be notoriously low. During the days of the Soviet Union, the country's only airline, Aeroflot, became the epitome of bad service and rudeness to passengers. After the dissolution of the Soviet Union, a new privately financed airline began to have great success, in part because its passengers appreciated being treated like human beings for a change. The management of the new airline declared that its employment policy was that it would not hire anyone who had ever worked for Aeroflot. Similarly, one of the reasons for the great success of McDonald's in Moscow—the largest McDonald's in the world, with lines of people waiting to get into it—is that it was being compared to the previous bad quality of service in Soviet restaurants, not to Wendy's or Burger King.

Competition in the marketplace affects not only price but quality. Brand names make the competitors responsible for both.

VOLITIONAL PRICING

High prices are often blamed on the "greed" of sellers, as if they can set prices by an act of will. In some trivial sense, they can. Any of us can set the price of his own labor at a million dollars a year, but that will not make us millionaires. Obviously, it doesn't matter what we charge, unless others to agree to pay it. That is not likely to happen in a world ruled by supply and demand, except for individuals whose rare talents cause them to be in huge demand and in very short supply.

"Greed" is seldom even defined. Virtually everyone would prefer to get a higher price for what he sells and pay a lower price for what he buys. Would you pay a dollar for a newspaper that was available for fifty cents? Or offer to work for half of what an employer was willing to pay you? Would adding a string of zeros to prices or salaries change the principle or the definition of greed? It is hard to see why it should.

But, if everybody is greedy, then the word is virtually meaningless. If it refers to people who desire far more money than most others would aspire to, then the history of most great American fortunes—Ford, Rockefeller, Carnegie, etc.—suggests that the way to amass vast amounts of wealth is to figure out some way to provide goods and services at *lower* prices, not higher prices.

Richard Sears was ferociously determined to overtake Montgomery Ward and worked tirelessly for incredible hours toward that end, taking risks that bordered on the reckless. He sought out every way of cutting costs, so that he could undercut Ward's prices, and every way of attracting customers away from all his rivals. He did all this, not because he did not have enough money to live on, but because he wanted more. If that is our definition of "greed," then he was greedy. More important, in this case as in many others, it was precisely greed that led to *lower* prices. That was how Sears overtook Montgomery Ward and replaced it as the leading retailer in the country at the beginning of the twentieth century. In later years, that is how Wal-Mart overtook Sears.

When prices go up, it is far more likely to be due to supply and demand than to greed. In most cases, the only direction in which a business can move and maintain its prices by an act of will is down—and they can do this only if they have managed to bring their costs done to a level that enables them to make money at these lower prices. To force prices up by an act of will is to allow rivals to undersell you and take away your customers.

If it is greed to want vast amounts of money, then that objective is far more readily reached through low prices and a mass market. Today, Wal-Mart makes far more millions of dollars in profits than stores that cater to the rich. There is probably not a snooty upscale restaurant anywhere that makes the kind of money that McDonald's brings in every year from its nearly 25,000 outlets around the world.

Each individual rich person, by definition, has more money than average, but they are so overwhelmingly outnumbered by people who are not rich that more money is usually made serving a mass market. There is a reason why advertisers pay far more money to run their commercials during broadcasts of Super Bowls than during broadcasts of operas or ballets. Aficionados of opera or ballet may average higher incomes than football fans, but the big money is to be made selling to football fans, simply because there are so many of them.

As noted in chapter 4, no company would ever go bankrupt if it could simply raise its prices to cover whatever its costs happened to be. In reality, far more businesses go belly up than survive. That should be the decisive evidence against volitional pricing.

"PREDATORY" PRICING

One of the popular fallacies that has become part of the tradition of anti-trust law is "predatory pricing." According to this theory, a big company that is out to eliminate its smaller competitors and take over their share of the market will lower its prices to a level that dooms the competitor to unsustainable losses and forces it out of business. Then, having acquired a monopolistic position, it will raise its prices—not just to the previous level, but to new and higher levels in keeping with its new monopolistic position. Thus, it recoups its losses and enjoys above-normal profits thereafter, at the expense of the consumers.

One of the most remarkable things about this theory is that those who advocate it seldom provide concrete examples of when it actually happened. Perhaps even more remarkable, they have not had to do so, even in courts of law, in anti-trust cases.

Both the A & P grocery chain in the 1940s and the Microsoft Corporation in the 1990s have been accused of pursuing such a practice in anti-trust cases, but without a single example of this process having gone to completion. Instead, their current low prices (in the case of A & P) and the inclusion of a free Internet browser in Windows software (in the case of Microsoft) have been interpreted as directed toward that end—though not with actually having achieved it. Since it is impossible to prove a negative, the accused company cannot disprove that it is pursuing such a goal, and the issue simply becomes a question of whether those who hear the charge choose to believe it.

At one time, it was claimed that the Standard Oil Company gained its dominant position in the petroleum industry this way.

Later scholarly research, however, discredited even this one example. Yet the theory has continued to be advocated, with concrete examples being neither asked nor given. But this is more than just a theory without evidence. It is a fallacy in that it makes no economic sense.

A company that sustains losses by selling below cost to drive out a competitor is following a very risky strategy. The only thing it can be sure of is losing money initially. Whether it will ever recover enough extra profits to make the gamble pay off in the long run is problematical. Whether it can do so and escape the antitrust laws is even more problematical—and these laws can lead to millions of dollars in fines and/or the dismemberment of the company. But, even if our would-be predator manages somehow to overcome these problems, it is by no means clear that eliminating existing competitors will mean eliminating competition.

Even when a rival firm has been forced into bankruptcy, its physical equipment and the skills of the people who once made it viable do not vanish into thin air. A new entrepreneur can come along and acquire both—perhaps at low distress sale prices, enabling the new competitor to have lower costs than the old and hence be a more dangerous rival.

As an illustration of what can happen, back in 1933 *The Washington Post* went bankrupt, though not because of predatory pricing. However, this bankruptcy did not cause the printing equipment, the building, or the reporters to disappear. All were acquired by publisher Eugene Meyer, at a price that was less than one-fifth of what he had bid unsuccessfully for the same newspaper just four years earlier. In the decades that followed, under new ownership and management, *The Washington Post* grew to become the largest newspaper in the nation's capital, while its rivals disappeared one by one, until it was the only major newspaper in town in 1978.

Bankruptcy can eliminate particular owners and managers, but it does not eliminate competition in the form of new people, who may either take over an existing bankrupt enterprise or start their own new business from scratch in the same industry. The fallacy of "predatory pricing" includes another fallacy—confusing existing competitors with competition. Competition is a condition in the market in which there is no way to keep out those who wish to enter an industry. Even elimination of all current competitors will not destroy competition, if the resulting higher profits of the surviving monopoly attract new competitors.

PURCHASING POWER

Some of the oldest fallacies in economics—refuted by economists more than two centuries ago—revolve around fears that there will not be enough "purchasing power" to buy all the vast and growing array of things being produced. And, if it is impossible to sell everything that it being produced, it will likewise be impossible to keep the workers fully employed.

Government social programs or even the building of military bases are often proclaimed by politicians to be adding to the country's purchasing power, when in fact they are simply *transferring* purchasing power from taxpayers, with no net increase for the economy as a whole. Sometimes it is even claimed that the government money spent "multiplies" its economic effects by being spent and re-spent again and again as it circulates through the community. But if that same money had not been taken from the taxpayers, it would have been spent and re-spent somewhere else. Similarly, if private businesses had used that same money for investment, it would have been re-spent by those from whom the investors bought machinery or desks or whatever else they might buy.

At various times it has been thought that people who save are depriving the economy of purchasing power and thus endangering other people's jobs. But money that is saved does not vanish into thin air. It is lent out by banks and other financial institutions, being spent by different people for different purposes, but still remaining just as much a part of purchasing power as if it had never been saved.

Some have argued that workers do not receive enough pay to "buy back" what they have produced, while the wealthier classes do not spend all of their income, leaving a gap between the value of total output and the purchasing power available to buy it. But, as already noted, money that is saved and invested is just as much purchasing power as money that is spent for consumer goods. All this was argued out in the early nineteenth century, in controversies over what became known as Say's Law—that supply creates its own demand. Yet the idea that purchasing power is deficient under capitalism has never completely died out, despite being refuted both theoretically and empirically by economists centuries ago.

In the crudest form of the purchasing power fallacy, the enormous increase in output resulting from the industrial revolution led many in the eighteenth and nineteenth centuries to wonder how the economy could possibly absorb such unprecedentedly large and growing production. What would happen when all the needs of human beings had been met, as seemed imminent to some at the time, and the machines and workers kept producing more?

As history unfolded, this proved to be one of many non-problems with which imaginative members of the intelligentsia have managed to torture themselves, and alarm others, over the centuries. (Declining IQs, exhaustion of natural resources, overpopulation, and global warming are others) The sating of human desires, which some feared in the early nineteenth century, still seems remote today, even though we have an abundance of such things as refrigerators, computers, and television sets that were not even dreamed of then.

More is involved here than the simple fact that the danger that was feared never materialized. Ingenious alarmists can always argue that the disaster they foretold has merely been "postponed" by good fortune that cannot last forever. In short, the empirical argument against a failure of purchasing power is not enough. What must be understood is why such a theory is invalid logically.

What a group of French economists known as Physiocrats showed in the late eighteenth century was that the production of goods and services automatically generates the purchasing power needed to buy those goods and services. When the economy creates another hundred million dollars worth of output, that is also another hundred million dollars worth of wealth that can be used to buy this or other output. Production is ultimately bought with other production, using money as a convenience to facilitate the transactions.

At any given moment, there may be too many belts or radios to sell at prices that will cover the costs of making them. Their producers will lose money and therefore be forced to cut back production, hiring fewer workers as a result. But, as noted in Chapter 15, it is a fallacy to assume that what is true for a part of the national economy is necessarily true for the whole. So long as resources are scarce and have alternative uses, the fact that they are being wasted in one sector only means that there are other sectors that could put those same resources to better use.

Business losses and unemployment in the sectors that are producing output that is worth less than its cost of production are precisely what causes these resources to be transferred to other sectors. It is the assumption that the overproduction found in particular sectors can also be found in the economy as a whole that is the fallacy of composition.

One of the things that has lent an appearance of plausibility to theories of "overproduction" or a deficiency of purchasing power has been a recurrence of periods of economic downturn, known as recessions or depressions. During the Great Depression of the 1930s, for example, there was a massive increase of unemployment, along with business losses for the economy as a whole. The greatly reduced money supply of 1932 was incapable of buying the amount of output that had been produced during the boom years that ended in 1929. More precisely, the 1932 money supply was incapable of buying the 1929 level of output *at 1929 prices*. Prices began declining as a result of unsold goods, but prices not fall fast enough or far enough to restore immediately the full production needed to create full employment.

Major malfunctions of the monetary system, including both massive bank failures and counterproductive policies by the Federal Reserve Board, as well as restrictive tariffs that disrupted international trade, and amateurish tinkering with the economy by both the Hoover and Roosevelt administrations, turned a problem into a catastrophe. In this situation, Keynesian economics emerged to re-introduce theories of insufficient purchasing power, though in a more sophisticated form.

John Maynard Keynes argued that government spending could put more money back into circulation and restore the economy to full employment faster than by waiting for prices to fall into balance with the reduced amount of money in circulation. But Keynes never claimed that the economy had just produced too much. Nor is there any reason to believe that he would have been surprised to see several times as high a level of national output selling with no problems in later years.

Whatever the merits or demerits of Keynesian economics, which once reigned supreme but was fading fast by the end of the twentieth century, discussions of purchasing power in politics and in the media have been far cruder than anything said by Keynes himself. For example, President Herbert Hoover and then Franklin D. Roosevelt both tried to keep wage rates from falling, as a means of maintaining the purchasing power of workers, as well as for humanitarian reasons. But there was no way to keep employing the same number of workers as before, at the same wage rates as before, when the money supply was one-third smaller. Similar government attempts to keep particular prices up, both in agriculture and in industry, ignored the fact that prices had to come down in the economy as a whole if everything was to be purchased with a smaller money supply.

Scary as it may seem, neither president understood this much basic economics. Moreover, it did not just seem scary, it *was* scary, because the livelihoods of millions of Americans were at risk and many suffered disastrously. Although some have tried to depict FDR as the man who got us out of the Great Depression, all previous depressions had ended much sooner, without any major government intervention. This was in fact the first depression in which the federal government intervened so much, first under Hoover and then even more so under Roosevelt.

Some economists, including Nobel Prize winner Milton Friedman, have argued that it was precisely government policies that kept the economy from recovering as quickly as it had before, when left alone.

Chapter 24

Business and Labor

Those who favor government intervention in the economy often depict those who prefer free competition as pro-business apologists. This has been profoundly wrong for at least two centuries.

Adam Smith, the eighteenth-century father of free-market economics, was so scathingly critical of businessmen that it would be impossible to find a single favorable reference to them in his 900-page classic, *The Wealth of Nations*.[1] Instead, Smith warned against "the clamour and sophistry of merchants and manufacturers," whom he characterized as people "who seldom meet together, even for merriment and diversion, but the conversation ends in a conspiracy against the public, or in some contrivance to raise prices." Any suggestions about laws and policies coming from such people, he said, ought to be "carefully examined, not only with the most scrupulous, but with the most suspicious attention."

In the nineteenth century, the next great classical economist in the free-market tradition, David Ricardo, spoke of businessmen as "notoriously ignorant of the most obvious principles" of economics. Knowing how to run a business is not the same as understanding the larger and very different issues involved in understanding how the economy as a whole affects the population as a whole. Skepticism about the business community has remained part of the tradition of free-market economists throughout the twentieth century as well, with Milton Friedman's views being very similar to those of Adam Smith on this point.

---

[1] When I taught economics, I used to offer to give an A to any student who could find a favorable reference to businessmen in *The Wealth of Nations*. None ever did.

Free market competition has often been opposed by the business community, from Adam Smith's time to our own. It was business interests which promoted the pervasive policies of government intervention known as "mercantilism" in the centuries before Smith and others made the case for ending such intervention and establishing free markets.

After free market principles gained wider acceptance in the nineteenth and twentieth centuries, business leaders were of course prepared to invoke those principles for political reasons, whenever it suited their particular purposes of the moment. But business leaders and organizations have proven equally willing to seek government intervention to keep out foreign competition, bail out failing corporations and banks, and receive billions of dollars in agricultural subsidies, ostensibly for the sake of saving family farms, but in reality going disproportionately to big corporations. When President Richard Nixon imposed the first peacetime wage and price controls in 1971, he was publicly praised by the chairman of General Motors, and cooperation with these policies was urged by the National Association of Manufacturers and the U. S. Chamber of Commerce. Businesses themselves have pushed for laws making it harder for outside investors to take over a corporation and replace its management. Business leaders are not wedded to a free market philosophy or any other philosophy. They promote their own self-interest any way that can, like other special interest groups. Economists and others who are in fact supporters of the free market have known that at least as far back as Adam Smith.

As noted in earlier chapters, the efficient uses of scarce resources by the economy as a whole depends on a system that features both profits and losses. Businesses are interested only in the profit half. If they can avoid losses by getting government subsidies, tariffs and restrictions against imports, or domestic laws that stifle competition in various agricultural products, they will do so. Losses, however, are essential to the process that shifts resources to those who are providing what consumers want at the lowest prices—and away from those who are not.

The American computer industry is a classic example. Over a period of more than a decade, the prices of computers have declined by an average of more than 30 percent *annually*. Meanwhile, the advances in computer chip design have led to a 30 percent annual increase in the power to process millions of pieces of information per second. Yet, during this incredible era of progress, some computer companies have operated at huge losses, while others have profited greatly. Data General lost $59 million dollars in one year, UNISYS lost $436 million and IBM lost $18 billion in two years. Resources were shifting to other firms that were providing more of what the consumers wanted at lower prices. Symbolic of these changes is that Microsoft's Bill Gates, once just a subcontractor to IBM, became the richest man in America while IBM was losing billions of dollars money and laying off more than 100,000 employees. It was all part of the same process.

Much the same story could be told of the airline industry. Between the last year of federal regulation in 1977 and twenty years later in 1997, the average air fare dropped by 40 percent and the average percentage of seats filled on planes rose from 56 percent to 69 percent, while more passengers than ever were carried more safely than ever. Meanwhile, whole airlines went bankrupt. That was the cost of greater efficiency. It has been estimated that, during the era of federal regulation, government intervention in the market had caused costs and fares to be to percent higher than they would have been in a free market. When the protection of federal regulation was removed, those airlines which could not survive with lower fares and rising fuel costs went out of business.

Even people who understand the need for competition, and for both profits and losses, nevertheless often insist that it should be "fair" competition. But this is a slippery word that can mean almost anything. For many years, there were federal "fair trade" laws designed to prevent chain stores from selling merchandise below list price and thus driving smaller sellers out of business. With international trade likewise, there are those who say that they are for free trade, provided that it is "fair" trade. Here too, it means artificially keeping prices higher than they would be in the absence of government intervention, so that companies with higher costs of doing business can survive. Like discussions of fairness in other contexts besides economics, this kind of reasoning ignores the costs imposed on third parties—in this case, the consumers who pay needlessly high prices to keep less efficient businesses using scarce resources which have alternative uses.

Businesses are often praised for what they do worst and denounced for what they do best. The greatest contribution that a business makes to the economy and the society is in producing the most goods with the least resources, including labor. But nothing will get a corporation denounced more widely than laying off workers. On the other hand, nothing gets more public praise than business' giving away the stockholders' money to fashionable causes, many of which undermine the free market and the free society on which business itself depends.

Some people consider it a valid criticism of corporations that they are "just in business to make profits." By this kind of reasoning, workers are just working to earn their pay. In the process, however, they produce all the things that give their fellow Americans the highest standard of living in the world. What matters is not the motivation but the results. In the case of business, the real question is: What are the *preconditions* for earning a profit?

One precondition is that profit-seeking corporations cannot squander scarce resources the way Soviet enterprises did. Corporations operating in a market economy have to pay for all their inputs—whether labor, raw materials, or electricity—and they have to pay as much as others are willing to bid for them. Then they have to sell their own end product—at a price as low as their competitors are charging. If they fail to do this, they fail to make a profit. And if they keep on failing to make a profit, either the management will be replaced or the whole business will be replaced by some competitor who is more efficient.

Sometimes the charge is made that profits are short-run gains, with the implication that they come at the expense of longer-term considerations. But future values are reflected in the present value of a business' assets. A factory that runs full blast to make a profit today, while neglecting the maintenance and repair of its machinery will immediately see a decline in the value of its property and of its stockholders' stock. It is in the *absence* of a profit-and-loss economy that there are few incentives to maintain the long-run productivity of an industrial enterprise or a collective farm, as in the Soviet Union. What happens to the enterprise after the current management's tenure is over is of little concern in a system where there are no profits and no present values to influence decisions.

The case for a free market is not that it benefits business, but that it benefits consumers. It is a sad commentary on our times when that case is not debated on its own merits, but instead the motives of those who make that case are impugned and they are presumed to be agents or apologists for business interests who are in fact often opposed to free markets.

NON-PROFIT ORGANIZATIONS

We have seen that the role of profit-seeking businesses is better understood when they are recognized as profit-and-loss businesses, with all the pressures and incentives created by these dual potentialities. By the same token, what are called "non-profit organizations" can be better understood when they are seen as non-profit *and non-loss* institutions—that is, institutions which operate free of the constraints of a bottom line.

This does not mean that they have unlimited money. It does mean that, with whatever money they do have, non-profit organizations are under very little pressure to achieve their institutional goals to the maximum extent possible with the resources at their disposal. Those who supply those resources include the general public, who cannot closely monitor what happens to their donations, and those whose money provided the endowments—$13 billion at Harvard, for example—that help finance non-profit institutions. Much or most of these endowments were left by people now dead, who cannot monitor at all.

Non-profit organizations have additional sources of income, including fees from those who use their services, such as visitors to museums and audiences for symphony orchestras. These fees are in fact the main source of the more than half a trillion dollars in revenue received annually by non-profit organizations in America. However, these fees do not cover the full costs of their operation —which is to say, the recipients are receiving goods and services that cost more than these recipients are paying and some are receiving them free. Such subsidized beneficiaries cannot impose the same kind of economic discipline as the customers of a profit-and-loss business who are paying the full cost of everything they get.

Under these conditions, the goals of those individuals in charge of a non-profit institution can be substituted for the institution's ostensible goals or the goals of their donors or founders. It has been said, for example, that Henry Ford and John D. Rockefeller would turn over in their graves if they knew what kinds of things are being financed today by the foundations which bear their names. While that is ultimately unknowable, it is known that Henry Ford II resigned from the board of the Ford Foundation in protest against what the foundation was doing with the money left by his grandfather. More generally, it is now widely recognized how difficult it is to establish a foundation to serve a given purpose and expect it to stick to that purpose after the money has been contributed and the donors are dead.

Academic institutions, hospitals and foundations are usually non-profit organizations in the United States, although non-profit institutions cover a wide range and can also engage in activities normally engaged in by profit-seeking enterprises, such as selling Sun Kist oranges or publishing *Nation's Business* magazine.

In whatever activities they engage, non-profit organizations are not under the same pressures to get "the most bang for the buck" as are enterprises in which profit and loss determine their survival. This effects efficiency, not only in the narrow financial sense, but also in the broader sense of achieving avowed purposes. Colleges and universities, for example, can become disseminators of particular ideological views that happen to be in vogue ("political correctness") and restrictors of alternative views, even though the goals of education would be better served by exposing students to contrasting and contending ideas.

Two centuries ago, Adam Smith pointed out how academics running colleges and universities financed by endowments can run them in self-serving ways, being ""very indulgent to one another," so that each academic would "consent that his neighbour may neglect his duty, provided he himself is allowed to neglect his own." Widespread complaints today that professors neglect teaching in favor of research, and sometimes neglect both in favor of leisure or other activities, suggest that the underlying principle has not changed much in more than two hundred years. Tenure guaranteeing lifetime appointments are common in non-profit colleges and universities, but are practically unknown in businesses that must meet the competition of the marketplace.

This is only one of the ways in which the employment policies of non-profit organizations have more latitude than those of enterprises that operate in the hope of profit and under the threat of losses. Before World War II, hospitals were among most racially discriminatory of American employers, even though their avowed purposes would have been better served by hiring the best-qualified doctors, even when those doctors happened to be black or Jewish. Non-profit foundations were also among the most racially discriminatory institutions at that time. The same was true of the academic world, where the first black professor was not hired at a major university until 1940, not long after the first Jewish professor received tenure at Columbia University. It was only in the postwar era, with racial attitudes beginning to change in the wake of the horrors of the Nazi Holocaust, that either group began to have more general access to positions in non-profit organizations.

None of this should suggest that non-profit organizations are oblivious to money. It is just that the purposes for which the money is spent may be quite different from the purposes for which it was donated. Non-profit organizations can be very eager to get more money, and some even skirt the boundaries of their missions and the law to do so. In 1999, for example, non-profit organizations took in about $500 million from sellers of commercial products who were allowed to say or suggest in their advertisements that some foundation or other non-profit organization were favorable toward these products. Commercial endorsements by these tax-exempt organizations are illegal, but denials that these commercial tie-ins were endorsements have usually kept law enforcement officials at bay.

The American Medical Association, for example, collected $600,000 for allowing its logo to be displayed in advertisements for a pharmaceutical drug. Another non-profit organization, The American Cancer Society, pulled in more than a million dollars the same year for allowing the use of its name and logo in advertisements for commercial products, even though it claims that it does not endorse anything. Looked at from the other side, American Express has paid hundreds of millions of dollars to a variety of non-profit organizations for advertising tie-ins.

The fact that some organizations' income is called profit and other organizations' income is not does not change anything economically, however much it may suggest to the unwary that one institution is greedy and the other is not. Many heads of non-profit organizations receive far more money in salary than the average owner of a store or a restaurant receives.

What changes incentives and constraints is the fact that the money received by a profit-and-loss business comes directly from those who use its goods and services, while the money received by a non-profit organization comes primarily from subsidized beneficiaries, from donors and—indirectly—from the taxpayers who pay the additional taxes made necessary by the tax exemptions of non-profit organizations.

The fact that a non-profit organization can provide its services free or below cost virtually assures a market for its output, without being forced to produce that output at the lowest cost. Indeed, the very nature of the output itself can be changed to meet the preferences of the non-profit officials, among other indulgences that are possible with money donated by people who are unlikely to monitor performance as closely as stockholders or financiers who specialize in corporate takeovers.

These illustrations of the financial circumstances peculiar to non-profit organizations are not the whole story. Because of the humanitarian and socially responsible goals of many non-profit institutions, they may attract many people whose idealism makes them conscientious, even when the incentives and pressures are not what they are in a profit-and-loss enterprise. To what extent this offsets the common human temptation to self-indulgence is an empirical question. It should not be forgotten, however, that idealism and self-indulgence are not mutually exclusive, and self-indulgence can easily take the form of promoting one's own ideology, rather than serving the ostensible purposes of the institution.

Here, as elsewhere, we are concerned with the allocation of scarce resources which have alternative uses. Non-profit organizations are therefore examined here in terms of how the built-in incentives and constraints of such institutions affect their economic effectiveness. People tend to respond to incentives and constraints, no matter what kind of organization they are in. Understanding the behavior of these organizations requires understanding the differing incentives and constraints that apply to different kinds of institutions.

THE MYSTIQUE OF "LABOR"

In various forms, the idea has persisted for centuries that labor is what "really" creates the output that we all live on and enjoy. In this view, it is the farmers who feed us and the factory workers who clothe us and provide us with furniture and television sets, while a variety of other workers build the homes we live in. Karl Marx took this vision to its logical conclusion by depicting capitalists, landlords and investors as people who, in one way or another, were enabled by the institutions of capitalism to take away much of what labor had created—that is, to "exploit" labor. Echoes of this vision can still be found today, not only among a relative handful of Marxists but also among non-Marxists or even anti-Marxists, who use such terms as "unearned income" to describe profits, interest, rent and dividends.

This view that there was something special about labor as a source of output and of the value of individual commodities existed before Marx was born—and not only among radicals, but even among such orthodox economists as Adam Smith, the father of laissez-faire economics. The first sentence of Smith's classic *The Wealth of Nations* says: "The annual labour of every nation is the fund which originally supplies it with all the necessaries and conveniences of life which it annually consumes, and which consist always either in the immediate produce of that labour, or in what is purchased with that produce from other nations."

By the late nineteenth century, however, economists had given up the notion that it is primarily labor which determines the value of goods, since capital, management and natural resources all contribute to output and must be paid for from the price of that output. More fundamentally, labor, like all other sources of production costs, was no longer seen as a source of value. On the contrary, it was the value of the goods to the consumers which made it worthwhile to produce those goods—provided that the consumer was willing to pay enough to cover their production costs. This new understanding marked a revolution in the development of economics. It is also a sobering reminder of how long it can take for even highly intelligent people to get rid of a misconception whose fallacy then seems obvious in retrospect.

In one sense, everything we consume is produced by human labor, especially if we broaden the term to include the work of those who plan, manage and coordinate the activities of those who directly lay their hands on the things that are being manufactured or built. Usually, however, the term "labor" or "worker" is reserved for those who are employed by others. Thus, someone who works 35 or 40 hours a week is called a worker, while someone who works 50 or 60 hours a week managing the enterprise is not. Clearly, the amount of work you do is not what makes you a worker or not, as that term is generally used.

If labor were in fact the crucial source of output and prosperity, then we should expect to see countries where great masses of people toil long hours richer than countries where most people work shorter hours, in a more leisurely fashion, and under more pleasant conditions, often including air-conditioning, for example. In reality, we find just the opposite. Third World farmers may toil away under a hot sun and in difficult conditions that were once common in Western nations which have long since gotten soft and prosperous under industrial capitalism.

Put differently, the growth and development of such non-labor inputs as science, engineering and sophisticated investment and management policies, as well as the institutional benefits of a price-coordinated economy, have made the difference and given hundreds of millions of people higher standards of living. Again, this is not something that is difficult to grasp—once the misconceptions have been gotten rid of.

Those misconceptions tend to linger on wherever they can find refuge, even after they have been formally banished by logic and evidence. Official government statistics are still cast in such terms as "unearned income" and "productivity" is defined as output divided by the labor that went into it. International trade is still discussed as if high-wage countries cannot compete successfully with low-wage countries, as if labor were the only cost of production. In reality, high-wage countries have been competing successfully with low-wage countries for centuries, precisely because of advantages in capital, technology and organization.

India was for years forced to ban imports of automobiles from the United States and Japan, in order to protect its own domestically produced cars, made by workers who were paid much less than American or Japanese workers. Consumers in India were for years forced to pay far higher prices for automobiles—and to get on waiting lists to buy them—because the products of their low-wage workers could not compete with automobiles shipped thousands of miles from high-wage countries.[2]

Misconceptions have practical consequences, sometimes needlessly holding down the standard of living of poor people. Antipathy toward "unearned incomes" has led to attempts to control or suppress profits in various countries at various periods of history, with the result of discouraging the investment of capital that those countries have desperately needed to raise the standard of living of their people. In some cases, the more prosperous classes in these poor countries invest their capital abroad, in richer industrial nations that do not tax or restrict capital so much—leading to international transfers of wealth from where it is most needed to where it is least needed, as a result of the domestic politics of envy and resentment, compounded by economic confusion.

What can be seen physically is always more vivid than what cannot be. Those who watch a factory in operation can see the

---

[2]Nor were automobiles the only products for which this was so. Tourists to India have been scrutinized to make sure they were not bringing in computers and other electronic devices to sell while they were there, since such devices were cheaper and better when produced in many more industrial nations with higher wage rates. There is a special irony in these bans on imports of computer products, since Indians in the United States are prominent as engineers and entrepreneurs in California's silicon valley.

workers creating a product before their eyes. They cannot see the investment that made that factory possible in the first place, much less the thinking that went into assessing whether the market for the product was sufficient to justify the expense, or the thinking and trial-and-error experience that made possible the technology with which the workers are working or the massive amounts of knowledge required to deal with ever-changing markets in an ever-changing economy and society.

Many have taken the special role of labor in the direction that Karl Marx took it, leading to the emotionally powerful, but vaguely defined, concept of "exploitation." When differences in prosperity and wealth are attributed to exploitation, whether among individuals or among nations, this serves several important political purposes, however counterproductive it may be economically. First of all, it converts misfortune into victimhood, making others responsible, guilty and fair game for retribution. Far from feeling inferior, the less fortunate can feel morally superior—and entitled to recompense.

These are almost ideal conditions for political mobilization under political and quasi-political leaders, whose own advancement is promoted, whether or not the advancement of those who follow them is helped or hindered. Even those on the sidelines, such as the intelligentsia, can gain great ideological satisfaction from being part of a vanguard of those seeking to redress historic wrongs.

This general pattern has appeared in country after country, even when the particulars of these countries have varied greatly. "Dependency theory" held sway in Latin America for decades, while "post-colonialism" theories were in the ascendancy in Africa and other variations on the exploitation theme appeared in American racial politics and played a role in the expulsions of Indians and Pakistanis from East Africa and the driving out of the "boat people" from Southeast Asia.

Under the influence of "dependency theory," many Latin American nations restricted their economic transactions with wealthier industrial nations of North America and Western Europe, lest these capitalists exploit them. Only after many years of painful economic failures in trying to produce internally the goods which could have been bought more cheaply in the world market did

Latin America's governments abandon dependency theory and the self-destructive economic policies based on it. Perhaps even more remarkable, this theory eventually lost ground even among Latin American intellectuals. Yet what a price was paid in the meantime by those Latin American peoples whose standards of living were needlessly kept lower than they could have been. Misconceptions are more than mere intellectual problems.

Even among those who are conventionally called workers or laborers, much of what they contribute to the economy is not labor but capital—"human capital," as economists call it. It is not so much physical exertion as job skills which constitute the contribution of a machinist, tailor, photographer, chef, pilot, writer, librarian, or entertainer. Most American workers today do not contribute merely work but skills, which is why their incomes increase substantially over their lifetimes. If it were their physical exertions which matter, their capabilities would be greatest in their youth and so would their incomes. But, where it is human capital that is being rewarded, then it is this is far more consistent with their incomes rising with age. As their human capital grows, the profit they receive on that capital grows, even though it is called wages.

A failure to understand the importance of human capital contributed to the defeat of Germany and Japan in World War II. Experienced and battle-hardened fighter pilots represented a very large investment of human capital. Yet the Germans and the Japanese did not systematically take their experienced pilots out of combat missions to safeguard their human capital and have them become instructors who could spread some of their human capital to new and inexperienced pilots being trained for combat. Both followed policies described by the Germans as "fly till you die."

The net result was that, while German and Japanese fighter pilots were very formidable opponents to the British and American pilots who fought against them early in the war, the balance of skills swung in favor of the British and American pilots later in the war, after much of the German and Japanese human capital in the air was lost when their top fighter pilots were eventually shot down and replaced by inexperienced pilots who had to learn everything the hard way in aerial combat, where small mistakes can be fatal. Economic concepts apply even when no money is changing hands. German and Japanese air forces were less efficient at allocating scarce resources which had alternative uses.

Uneasy as some people may be with the idea of thinking of human beings as capital, this is not a denigration but an enhancement of the value of human life. In addition to the intrinsic value of life to each individual, that individual's value to others is highlighted by the concept of human capital. The old military practice of going to great efforts to save cannon in combat, while using soldiers as if they were expendable, has since given way to using very expensive high-tech weapons, as in the Gulf War of 1991, in order to minimize casualties among one's own military personnel, who represent very valuable human capital.

In civilian life as well, human capital is crucial. Those individuals who can contribute only their labor have increasing difficulties finding jobs in a high-tech world, where skills are highly rewarded and there are few jobs left where "a strong back and a weak mind" are sufficient. Machines have increasingly replaced strong backs, even in traditionally arduous occupations such as mining. This economic de-emphasis of physical strength over time has also had the side-effect of reducing or eliminating the advantage of male workers over female workers.

As is so often the case, the economic realities are not very complicated, but there is nevertheless a great difficulty in extricating ourselves from tangled myths and misconceptions. This is especially so when it comes to labor, for people's work has been sufficiently central to their lives to help define who they are, as reflected in the great number of family names which are based on occupations—Smith, Shepherd, Weaver, Taylor, Dyer, Carpenter, Wright, Miller, Brewer, Cook, Butler, and Steward, for example, not to mention such foreign names as Kaufman (merchant) or Bauer (farmer). But, however, emotionally powerful the role of labor may be, it is still part of the general economic pattern of the allocation of scarce resources which have alternative uses.

Chapter 25

An Overview

In addition to whatever you may have learned in the course of this book about particular things such as prices, speculation, or international trade, you should also have learned a more general skepticism about many of the glittering words and fuzzy phrases that are mass produced by the media, by politicians, and by others.

By this time, you may no longer be as ready to believe those who talk about things selling "below their real value" or about how terrible it is for the United States to be "a debtor nation." In the course of reading this book, you may have acquired a certain skepticism about government programs to make this or that "affordable." Statements and statistics about "the rich" and "the poor" may not be unthinkingly accepted any more. Nor should you find it mysterious that so many places with rent control laws also have housing shortages.

However, no listing of economic fallacies can be complete, because the fertility of the human imagination is virtually unlimited. New fallacies are being conceived, or misconceived, while the old ones are being exposed. The most that can be hoped for is to expose some of the more common fallacies and promote both skepticism and an analytical approach that goes beyond the emotional appeals which sustain so many damaging and even dangerous fallacies in politics and in the media.

The importance of economic principles extends beyond things that most people think of as economics. For example, those who worry about the exhaustion of petroleum, iron ore, or other natural resources often assume that they are discussing the amount of physical stuff in the earth, but that assumption changes radically when you realize that statistics on "known reserves" of these resources may tell us more about the interest rate and the costs of exploration than about how much of the resource remains underground. This is one of a whole range of problems and issues which, on the surface, may not seem like economic matters, but which nevertheless look very different after understanding basic economic principles.

Those economic principles are easier to understand than to keep in mind in the midst of slogans and controversies that stir the emotions. For example, nothing is simpler or more in accord with common sense than the economic principle that people tend to buy less at a higher price and more at a lower price. Equally obvious—and equally important—is the tendency of people to supply more at a higher price than at a lower price. Yet the many implications of these two simple principles are often forgotten when discussing such things as rent control or minimum wage laws. These implications are also forgotten when people try to quantify individual or national "needs," disregarding the fact that the amount people will use varies with the price.

It is likewise not difficult to understand that economics is a study of the allocation of scarce resources which have alternative uses. But that too is easy to lose sight of when the media or politicians focus on the plight of particular industries that are losing money and jobs, and call for rescuing these industries from such misfortunes. Those who proclaim that some particular industries or regions of the country are not sharing in the general prosperity—that they are being "left out" or "left behind"—seldom even acknowledge the possibility that the general prosperity itself is in part a consequence of transferring resources from where they are less productive to where they are more productive. Red ink on the bottom line and lay-off notices are among the mechanisms of such transfers.

If you are prepared to sacrifice prosperity for the sake of stability, so be it. All economics can do is make you aware of the consequences of your choices. It cannot tell you what your philosophy or your priorities should be, though it can reveal inconsistencies between goals.

Perhaps more than anything else, an understanding of basic economics can enable us to consider policy issues in terms of the incentives they create and the consequences that follow, rather than simply the goals they proclaim and how wonderful it would be to achieve such goals. Both within government and in the private sector, individuals and organizations tend to respond to the particular incentives facing them by trying to promote their own wellbeing.

When this adversely affects others, it need not be due to "bureaucratic bungling" within government or to "greed" in the private sector. Perfectly rational and decent people tend to respond to the incentives confronting them. Those incentives may need reconsideration more than the individuals need denouncing.

While critics of various programs often point out "unintended consequences" that did more harm than good, many of these consequences were predictable from the outset *if people had looked at the incentives created, rather than the goals proclaimed.*

Very often either history or economics could have told us what to expect, but neither was consulted. It does not matter that a law or policy proclaims its goal to be "affordable housing," "fair trade" or "a living wage." What matters is what incentives are created by the specifics of these laws and how people react to such incentives. These are dry empirical questions which are seldom as exciting as political crusades or moral pronouncements. But they are questions which must be asked, if we are truly interested in the wellbeing of others, rather than in excitement or a sense of moral superiority for ourselves. As historian Paul Johnson has said:

> The study of history is a powerful antidote to contemporary arrogance. It is humbling to discover how many of our glib assumptions, which seem to us novel and plausible, have been tested before, not once but many times and in innumerable guises; and discovered to be, at great human cost, wholly false.

We have seen some of those great human costs—people going hungry in Russia, despite some of the richest farmland on the continent of Europe, people sleeping on cold sidewalks on winter nights in Manhattan, despite far more boarded-up housing units than it would take to shelter them all. A desperate government in eighteenth-century France decreed the death penalty for anyone who refused to accept the money that the revolutionary leaders had issued, in ignorance or disregard of economics. After the astronomical inflation in Germany in the 1920s had destroyed millions of families' life savings, many who were bitterly disappointed with their traditional leaders and institutions turned eventually toward someone who had been just a fringe fanatic before: Adolf Hitler.

No complex or esoteric economic principles would have been required to avoid these and other human tragedies around the world. But it would have required people to stop and think, instead of being swept along by emotions, rhetoric or the political pressures of the moment. For those who are willing to stop and think, basic economics provides the tools for evaluating policies and proposals in terms of logical implications and empirical evidence.

If this book has contributed to that end, then it has succeeded in its mission.

SOURCES

It is neither possible nor necessary to document the source of every statement made in this book. However, there are some key facts which some readers may want to check out or to explore further. Rather than clutter the text with footnotes, in a book intended for the general public, the citations are listed here in an informal way that should nevertheless make it possible to find the original sources.

CHAPTER 1: WHAT IS ECONOMICS?

The article about middle-class Americans began on the front page of Section 3 of the *New York Times* of August 1, 1999 and was written by Louis Uchitelle. The statement that Marxist economist Oskar Lange did not differ fundamentally from Milton Friedman on certain basic propositions and procedures can be verified by reading Oskar Lange, "The Scope and Method of Economics," in the *Review of Economic Studies* (1945–1946), pages 19–32, and comparing that with Milton Friedman's essay "The Methodology of Positive Economics" in his book *Essays in Positive Economics*.

CHAPTER 2: THE ROLE OF PRICES

The quoted statistics and analysis about the Soviet economy are from a book titled *The Turning Point: Revitalizing the Soviet Economy* by two Soviet economists, Nikolai Shmelev and Vladimir Popov, especially pages 128, 130–131, 141. The quote from Friedrich Engels is from his preface to the first German edition of *The Poverty of Philosophy* by Karl Marx, where Marx himself makes similar comments in the text, though not in as lucid language as that used by Engels. Information on Ghana and the Ivory Coast is from a book by W. L. Alpine and James Picket, *Agriculture, Liberalisation and Economic Growth in Ghana and Côte D'Ivoire:1968–1990*, published in Paris in 1996 by the Organisation for Economic Co-Operation and Development. The sales of beef suspected of "mad cow disease" was reported in the *Financial Times* of March 30, 1996. The relationship between housing prices and population changes in upstate New York is discussed was described on page 70 of an article titled "Down-and-Out Upstate," by Jerry Zremski in the Autumn 1999

348 *Sources*

issue of *City Journal*, published by the Manhattan Institute, a think tank in New York.

CHAPTER 3: PRICE CONTROLS

The fact that the housing shortage in the United States occurred when there was no change in the ratio of housing to people is from a book titled *Roofs or Ceilings?* by two economists later destined to win Nobel Prizes, Milton Friedman and George J. Stigler. The book itself has long been out of print, but excerpts from it were included in a collection of writings titled *Rent Control: Costs and Consequences*, edited by Robert Albon and published in 1980 by an Australian think tank, The Centre for Independent Studies, located in Sydney. This particular statement occurs on page 16. The data on housing in San Francisco after the 1906 earthquake are on pages 5 and 6. The facts about rent control in Sweden are from a different article in the same book, "The Rise, Fall and Revival of 'Swedish Rent Control'" by Sven Rydeenfelt. The lack of building in Melbourne under Australian rent control is mentioned on page 125 in another article. The effects of rent control in Paris are from an article by Bertrand de Jouvenal titled "No Vacancies" in a book titled *Rent Control: A Popular Paradox*, published in 1975 by a Canadian think tank, The Fraser Institute. Facts about the effects on rent control in Britain, France, Germany, and the Netherlands are from *Rent Control in North America and Four European Countries* by Joel F. Brenner and Herbert M. Franklin, published by Mercury Press), pages 4, 9, and 69. Many of the facts about rent control and homelessness in the United States are from *The Excluded Americans* by William Tucker (especially pages 19, 162, 275 and Chapter 19, which discusses various elite celebrities living in rent-controlled apartments). The comment from the *New York Times* is from page 40 of an article by John Tierney in their Sunday magazine section of May 4, 1997, titled "At the Intersection of Supply and Demand." The paradox of higher rents in rent-controlled cities is from another study by William Tucker, "How Rent Control Drives Out Affordable Housing," *Policy Analysis* paper number 274, published by the Cato Institute, a think tank in Washington. The decline of the housing stock under rent control in Washington is cited in an article by Thomas Hazlett in a book titled *Resolving the Housing Crisis*, published in 1982 by a San Francisco think tank, the Pacific Institute for Public Policy Research. The quote from an official of the Communist government of Vietnam is from page 422 of *The Fortune Encyclopedia of Economics*, edited by David R. Henderson and published in 1993 by Warner Books. Data on the number of buildings taken over by the city government in New York can be found on page 99 of *The Homeless* by Christopher Jencks, published by Harvard University

Press in 1994. The fact that building resumed in various Massachusetts communities after the state banned local rent control laws can be found in *Rude Awakenings* by Richard W. White, Jr., published in 1992 by ICS Press in San Francisco. The passage describing the cause and effect of price controls during a seventeenth-century local food shortage in Italy is from page 381 of *The Formation of National States in Western Europe*, edited by Charles Tilly and published by the Princeton University Press in 1975. Discussion of the eighteenth-century and nineteenth century local food shortages in India is from *Forty Centuries of Wage and Price Controls* by Robert L. Schuettinger and Eamonn F. Butler, published by the Heritage Foundation, a Washington think tank, in 1979.

CHAPTER 4: AN OVERVIEW

Comparisons of bombing and rent control as means of destroying housing appear on pages 422 and 425 of an article by Walter Block titled "Rent Control" in *The Fortune Encyclopedia of Economics*, edited by David Henderson. The economic problems of the rich "black earth" country of Russia are discussed in Frank Viviano, "Russian Farmland Withers on the Vine: Politics, Mind-set Keep Nation on a Diet of Imports," *San Francisco Chronicle*, October 19, 1998, p. A1 and in Andrew Higgins, "Food Lines," *Wall Street Journal*, October 1998, pp. A1 ff. The steel manufacturer whose equipment automatically shifted from oil to natural gas was mentioned in Steve Liesman and Jacob M. Schlesinger, "Blunted Spike: The Price of Oil Has Doubled This Year; So Where's the Recession?" *Wall Street Journal*, December 13, 1999, where other fuel economy measures are mentioned. See pages A1 ff. Former food-exporting countries which become unable to feed themselves are mentioned in innumerable places, including *Modern Times* by Paul Johnson, pages 724–727 of the 1992 edition. Russian exports of wheat under the czar are shown on page 62 of *The Turning Point* by Soviet economists Nikolai Shmelev and Vladimir Popov. For a painfully enlightening examination of the media's inability to understand basic economic principles during the gasoline crises of the 1970s, and their resulting susceptibility to irrational explanations of what was happening, see Thomas W. Hazlett, *TV Coverage of the Oil Crises: How Well Was the Public Serviced?* (Washington: The Media Institute,1982).

CHAPTER 5: THE RISE AND FALL OF BUSINESSES

The historical sketches of various businesses are based on information from a variety of sources, including innumerable newspaper and magazine articles, as well as books such as *New and Improved: The Story of Mass Marketing in America* written by Richard S. Tedlow and published in

1996 by the Harvard Business School Press, *Forbes Greatest Business Stories of All Time* by Daniel Gross and the editors of *Forbes* magazine, *Masters of Enterprise* by H. W. Brands, *Empire Builders* by Burton W. Folsom, Jr., *The First Hundred Years are the Toughest:What We Can Learn for the Century of Competition Between Sears and Wards* by Cecil C. Hoge, Sr.*A & P* by M. A. Adelman, *The Rise and Decline of the Great Atlantic & Pacific Tea Company* by former A & P executive William L. Walsh and *Made in America* by Sam Walton. The quote about the Soviet economy is from an article by Robert Heilbroner titled "Socialism" in *The Fortune Encyclopedia of Economics*, p. 164. On the misallocation of gasoline, see Stephen Chapman, "The Gas Lines of '79," *The Public Interest*, Summer 1980, p.47; Steven Rattner, "Gas Crisis: Experts Find Mixture of Causes," *New York Times*, January 24, 1979, p. A1 ff; Pranay B. Gupte, U. S. to Allow Shift of Some Gas Stocks to Urban Sections," *New York Times*, June 30, 1979, pp. A 1 ff. On the 3,000 pages of regulations and subsequent "clarifications," see the story by Rattner listed above. On the lack of gasoline shortages in the United States during the 1967 Arab oil embargo, see Thomas W. Hazlett, *TV Coverage of the Oil Crises*, pp. 14–15. On gasoline prices reaching an all-time low, see "Gas is Cheap. But Taxes are Rising," *Consumer Research*, August 1994, pp. 28–29. The firing of Montgomery Ward executives who urged expansion into suburban malls is mentioned on page 153 of *The New York Times Century of business*, edited by Floyd Norris and Christine Blackman and published in the year 2000 by McGraw-Hill. The big New York department stores' initial rejection of credit cards is mentioned on page 204 of the same book.

CHAPTER 6: THE ROLE OF PROFITS—AND LOSSES

Data on corporate profit rates in the American economy are from pages 46 and 49 of *The Illustrated Guide to the American Economy* by Herbert Stein and Murray Foss, third edition, published in 1999 by the AEI Press for the American Enterprise Institute, a Washington think tank. The statistic that the largest manufacturer of automobiles in the United States in 1896 produced just six cars is from *The American Car Dealership* by Robert Genat, page 7. The story of the microchip, including Intel's risking its corporate survival for the sake of research, is discussed on pages 247–248, 254, 259–262 of *Forbes Greatest Business Stories of All Time*, edited by Daniel Gross, et al and published in 1996 by John Wiley & Co. Data on economies and diseconomies of scale in the automobile and beer industries are from pages 76, 77, 131 and 145 of *The Structure of American Industry*, 9th edition, by Walter Adams and James Brock, published by Prentice-Hall. Data and comments on the efficiency of Soviet enterprises is from *The Turning Point* by Soviet economists Nikolai Shmelev and Vladimir Popov. Howard Johnson's pioneering in restaurant franchising is discussed on page 51 of *Fast Food: Roadside Restaurants in the Automobile Age* by John A Jakle & Keither A. Sculle, published by Johns Hopkins University Press in 1999.

CHAPTER 7: BIG BUSINESS AND GOVERNMENT

Data on the trucking industry are from pages 435 and 436 of an article by Thomas G. Moore titled "Trucking Deregulation" in *The Fortune Encyclopedia of Economics*. Data on airlines are from pages 380 and 381 of an article in the same book by Alfred E. Kahn titled "Airline Deregulation." Soviet enterprises' tendency to make things for themselves, rather than get them from specialized producers, is discussed on pages 160–161 of *The Red Executive* by David Granick.

CHAPTER 8: AN OVERVIEW

The historical information about the A & P grocery chain is from *The Rise and Decline of the Great Atlantic & Pacific Tea Company* by William I. Walsh. Lenin's estimate of how easy it was to run an enterprise was from his book *The State and Revolution*, written on the eve of the Bolshevik revolution. His later change of mind is from . The information on the McDonald's restaurant chain is from *Fast Food* by John A. Jakle and Keith Sculle, pages 58 and 146–147, and from *Masters of Enterprise: From John Jacob Astor and J. P. Morgan to Bill Gates and Oprah Winfrey* by H. W. Brands, published in 1999 by The Free Press 1999, page 222.

CHAPTER 9: PRODUCTIVITY AND PAY

The misleading claim that income quintiles divide the country into five equal parts was made on page 48 of *Economics Explained* by Robert Heilbroner and Lester Thurow. Data on household incomes are from a U. S. Bureau of the Census serial publication, *Current Population Reports*, P–23–196, with its individual title being *Changes in Median Household Income: 1969 to 1996*. The misguided remark from the *Washington Post* is from page 34 of *The Washington Post Weekly Edition*, September 7, 1998 in an article titled "The Rich Get Richer, and So Do the Old," by Barbara Vobejda. No doubt it was reprinted from a recent issue of the regular daily *Washington Post*. Data on people's changing incomes between 1975 and 1991 are from pages 8 and 22 of the 1995 *Annual Report* of the Federal Reserve Bank of Dallas. Earlier studies indicating similar patterns include *Years of Poverty, Years of Plenty* by Greg Duncan et al, published by the University of Michigan Press. The number of Americans working in the Soviet Union is from page 11 of *The Turning Point* by Nikolai Shmelev and Vladimir Popov. The fact that women who worked continuously earned slightly more than men who did the same is from page 103 of "The Economic Role of Women," *The Economic Report of the President, 1973* (Washington, D.C.: U.S. Government Printing Office, 1973). The difference between the earnings of women with and without children are from page 15 of a valuable compendium of data on women in the economy titled *Women's Figures*, 1999 edition, written by Diana Furchtgott-Roth and Christine Stolba and published by the American Enterprise Institute, a Washington think tank. Data on male predominance in work-related deaths are from the same source, page 33. Data on the average life of capital equipment in the Soviet Union and in the United States are from pages 145–146 of *The Turning Point* by Nikolai Shmelev and Vladimir Popov. The internally contradictory claim that people are "living below subsistence" has been made in remarkably numerous, including a book published by the Harvard University Press in 1981, *America's Struggle Against Poverty: 1900–1980* by James T. Patterson, page 42.

CHAPTER 10: CONTROLLED LABOR MARKETS

The effect of minimum wages in reducing the employment of workers in general in various countries, and the employment of younger and less skilled workers in particular, is discussed on pages 33, 34, and 335 of *What Future for New Zealand's Minimum Wage Law*, based on a study done by ACIL Economics and Policy, Pty. Ltd., and published by the New Zealand Business Roundtable. Similar conclusions for the United States are found in *Youth and Minority Unemployment*, written by Walter E. Williams and published in 1977 by the Hoover Institution Press. The effect of informal minimum wages in West Africa are discussed on pages 18 and 19 of *West African Trade*, written by Professor P. T. Bauer of the London School of Economics and published in 1954 by Cambridge University Press. The use of minimum wage laws to promote racial discrimination is discussed on page 14 of *Youth and Minority Unemployment* by Walter Williams and on page 50 of *The Japanese Canadians* by Charles H. Young and Helen R. Y. Reid. Data on American automobile production and employment are from *Motor Vehicle Facts & Figures: 1997*, published by the American Automobile Manufacturers Association and from pages 19 and 20 of an article by Christopher J. Singleton titled "Auto Industry Jobs in the 1980s: A Decade of Transition," which appeared in the U. S. Department of Labor's *Monthly Labor Review* for February 1992. Data on the decline of unionization is available from many sources, one being an article by Richard A. Ryan titled "Labors Gains Undercut by Lingering Problems," which appeared in *The Detroit News* of July 265, 1999.

CHAPTER 11: AN OVERVIEW

Data on employees' share in national income are from page 39 of *The Illustrated Guide to the American Economy*, third edition, written by Herbert Stein and Murray Foss, and published in 1999 by the AEI Press.

Data on the movement of individuals from one income bracket to another over time are from pages 8 and 14 of the 1995 *Annual Report* of the Federal Reserve Bank of Dallas. Data on the income levels that mark the beginning of various quintiles were downloaded from the U. S. Bureau of the Census web site. Data on the hours worked by people in the top one percent of the income distribution is from page 31 of *A Portrait of the Affluent in America Today* published in 1998 by the U. S. Trust Company.

CHAPTER 12: INVESTMENT AND SPECULATION

The disastrous speculation in silver by the Hunt brothers is covered on pages 249–250 of *The New York Times Century of Business,* edited by Floyd Norris and Christine Bockelmann and published in the year 2000 by McGraw-Hill. The buying up of future payments due to accident victims in installments by paying a lump sum is discussed in an article beginning on the front page of the *Wall Street Journal* of February 25, 1998 titled "Thriving Industry Buys Insurance Settlements from Injured Plaintiffs." Twentieth century energy consumption and the growth of know reserves of various metals are discussed on pages 40 and 41 of an article by William J. Baumol and Sue Anne Blackman titled "Natural Resources" in *The Fortune Encyclopedia of Economics.* See also Section II, Table 1 of the *Basic Petroleum Data Book,* vol. XX, No. 2 (July s2000), published by the American Petroleum Institute.

CHAPTER 13: RISKS AND INSURANCE

Information on the current value of a dollar invested in gold, stocks, and bonds in 1801 is from an article titled "Now What?" in the September 21,1998 *Forbes Global Business & Finance,* pages 20–21. The comment on academic institutions losing money in the stock market is from the *Wall Street Journal* of October 13, 1998, page C1. Information on the number of insurance companies in the United States and their assets is from page 2 of a 1994 publication of the Insurance Institute of America titled *How Insurance Works,* written by Barry D. Smith and Eric A. Wiening. The use of global positioning systems by insurance companies looking for their policy-holders in the wake of natural disaster is from the *New York Times* of January 18, 1999, section, C, page 8. The title of the story is 'Media; Sweetheart, Give Me a Reboot" and it was written by Dylan Loeb McClain.

CHAPTER 14: AN OVERVIEW

California motorists' reactions to heavier fines for traffic violations were reported in a story beginning on the front page of the *San Francisco Chronicle* of July 23, 1992. The story is titled "Revolt Against Steep Traffic Fines" and was written by T. Christian Miller. The comment on the negative effects of anticipations of land reform is from *Development Without Aid* by Melvyn B. Krauss.

CHAPTER 15: NATIONAL OUTPUT

Data on the unemployment rate during the Great Depression of the 1930s is from page 196 of an article titled "Great Depression" by Robert J. Samuelson, published in the *Fortune Encyclopedia of Economics*. Data on the fall in prices of various corporate stocks from 1929 to 1932 are from page 76 of *Since Yesterday: The 1930s in America* by Frederick Lewis Allen, published in 1986 in the Perennial Library edition by Harper & Row.

CHAPTER 16: MONEY AND THE BANKING SYSTEM

The fact that a hundred-dollar bill in the 1990s had less purchasing power than a twenty-dollar bill in the 1960s is from page 47 of an article titled "Going Underground," written by Peter Brimelow and published in the September 21, 1998 issue of *Forbes Global Business and Finance*. The fact that Chinese money was once preferred to Japanese money in Japan is from page 150 of a book titled *Money* by Jonathan Williams. The fact that most savings accounts in Bolivia were in dollars during that country's runaway inflation is from page 210 of an article titled "Hyperinflation," written by Michael K. Salemi and published in *The Fortune Encyclopedia of Economics*, where the German hyperinflation of the 1920s is also discussed on page 208. The fact that German workers were paid twice a day during this period is from pages 450–451 of *Germany: 1866–1945* by Gordon A. Craig. The haste of Russians to spend their rubles during that country's inflation is in a news story from the front page of the *Christian Science Monitor* of August 31, 1999. The reporter was Judith Matloff and the title of the story was "Russians Replay 'Bad Old Days'." Data on the 1921 inflation in the Soviet Union is from page 6 of *The Turning Point* by Nikolai Shmelev and Vladimir Popov. The remarkable agreement of both liberal and conservative economists on the confused and counterproductive monetary policies of the Federal Reserve during the Great Depression of the 1930s can be found by comparing the accounts in *The Great Crash* by John Kenneth Galbraith and in *A Monetary History of the United States* by Milton Friedman and Anna J. Schwartz, where this point is discussed on pages 407–419. President Herbert Hoover's admonition to President-elect Franklin D. Roosevelt is quoted on page 16 of *The Great Depression* by John A. Garraty. The collapse of hundreds of American banks during the Great Depression is mentioned on page 11 of *A Monetary History of the United States* by Friedman and Schwartz.

CHAPTER 17: THE ROLE OF GOVERNMENT

The comment on the changing role of government in economies around the world is from page 10 of a 1990 book that goes into that subject at length—*The Commanding Heights,* written by Daniel Yergin and Joseph Stanislaw and published by Simon & Schuster. Complaints about the confiscation of the profits of Soviet enterprises by the government of the U.S.S.R. are from page 261 of *The Turning Point* by Nikolai Shmelev and Vladimir Popov. The comment on bribes in China and Japan is from by Angelo Codevilla.

The story of how unscrupulous landlords exploit and destroy rent-controlled apartment buildings is told in *The Ecology of Housing Destruction* by Peter D. Salins. The particular comment quoted is from page 93 of that book. The story of the genesis and consequences of President Nixon's wage and price controls is from page of *The Commanding Heights* by Daniel Yergin and Joseph Stanislaw and from an essay by Herbert Stein in the *Wall Street Journal* of August 25, 1996, page A 12. Examples of private market ways of taking externalities into account are found in an article titled "Public Goods and Externalities" by Tyler Cowen in *The Fortune Encyclopedia of Economics,* edited by David R. Henderson. Franklin D. Roosevelt's use of presidential powers created during the First World War to take the United States off the gold standard is mentioned on page 86 of *The New York Times Century of Business.*

CHAPTER 18: AN OVERVIEW

The argument that government policy worsened, rather than alleviated, the Great Depression can be found in *A Monetary History of the United States* by Milton Friedman and Anna J. Schwartz, pages 407–419, in Paul Johnson's *A History of the American People,* pages 737–760 and in *Out of Work* by Richard K. Vedder and Lowell E. Gallaway, pages 89–97, 137–146.

CHAPTER 19: INTERNATIONAL TRADE

The comment from the *New York Times* about whether the United States was a "job winner" or a "job loser" from freer trade was from an article by Louis Uchitelle titled "Nafta and Jobs," which appeared in the November 14, 1993 issue, on the first page of section 4. Congressman Bonior's warning and the facts to the contrary are both from page 3 of a study titled *Trade Liberalization: The North American Free Trade Agreement's Economic Impact on Michigan,* published in December 1999 by The Mackinac Center, a think tank in Michigan. The Estimate of economies of scale in automobile production are from page 76 of *The Structure of American In-*

dustry, ninth edition, by Walter Adams and James Brock, published in 1995 by Prentice-Hall. Pages 97 and 104 of the same book discusses job losses in the American steel industry and the job losses in the U.S. economy as a whole from trying to protect jobs in the steel industry. Information on automobile production in Australia is from pages 59 and 81 *Ward's Automotive Yearbook*, 59th edition, published in 1997 by Ward's Communications in Southfield, Michigan. Reports on the Dutch and Swedish international retailers is from "Shopping All Over the World," in *The Economist* of June 19, 1999, page 60. An example of how job shifts abroad lead to production changes domestically can be seen in a *Wall Street Journal* story by Joel Millman titled "Job Shift to Mexico Lets U.S. Firms Upgrade," which appeared in the November 15, 1999, page A 28.

CHAPTER 20: INTERNATIONAL TRANSFERS OF WEALTH

Data on imports and exports between affiliates of the same company are from page 272 of *The Illustrated Guide to the American Economy*, third edition, by Herbert Stein and Murray Foss, which also has capital inflow data on pages 274 and 275. Statistics on foreign investment in the United States are from the an official Commerce Department publication, *Survey of Current Business*, Volume 79, Number 4 (June 1999), p. 16. The fact that a balance of payments surplus preceded the 1992 recession is also from *Survey of Current Business*, Vol. 79, No. 2. (December 1999), page D–20. Data on foreign ownership of American railroads in the nineteenth century are from page 195 of *The History of Foreign Investment in the United States to 1914*, Data on foreign ownership of American railroads in the nineteenth century are from page 195 of *The History of Foreign Investment in the United States to 1914*, written by Mira Wilkins and published by Harvard University Press. Information on Americans producing more on than one-third of all the manufactured goods in the world in 1913 is from page 142 of the same book. Page 68 of Myron Weiner's 1995 book, *The Migration Crisis* is the source of the statement that remittances from citizens living abroad exceed all the foreign aid from all the government agencies in the world. Professor P. T. Bauer's comment on foreign aid is from page 102 of his 1981 book *Equality, the Third World and Economic Delusion*, published by Harvard University Press. J. P. Morgan's comment on gold was quoted on page 41 of *The New York Times Century of Business*.

CHAPTER 21: AN OVERVIEW

The counterproductive effects of recycling have been shown by many studies. See, for example, John Tierney, "Recycling is Garbage,' *New York Times Magazine*, June 30, 1996, beginning on page 24.

CHAPTER 22: "NON-ECONOMIC" VALUES

Comparisons of delivery times the Post Office, on the one hand, and Federal Express and United Parcel Service, on the other are from an article titled "Special Delivery" in the December 1998 issue of *Consumer Reports*, page 15. Data on how many people buy cameras from discount houses, rather than camera stores, is from *The 1997–1998 PMA Industry Trends Report* published in Jackson, Michigan, by the Photo Marketing Association International.

CHAPTER 23: PRICES AND PURCHASING POWER

The quotes from Adam Smith are from the Modern Library edition of *The Wealth of Nations*, page 128 and 250. The quote from David Ricardo is from page 123 of Volume III of *The Works and Correspondence of David Ricardo*, edited by Piero Sraffa and published by Cambridge University Press. The fact that the bulk of agricultural subsidies go to big corporations, rather than to family farmers, can be verified from many sources, including *The Structure of American Industry* by Walter Adams and James Brock, 9th edition, page 29. The same book also has data on losses in the computer industry on pages 166–167. Business support for President Nixon's wage and price controls is mentioned on page 149 of *The Suicidal Corporation* by Paul Weaver. Data on air fares and better use of plane capacity after airline deregulation are from an article by Don Phillips titled '20 Days, 18 Flights," which appeared on page 8 of the *Washington Post National Weekly Edition* of July 5, 1999—and which probably appeared shortly before that in the regular daily edition. For an example of the old federal "fair trade" laws in action, see Thomas O'Donnell and Janet Banford, "Jack Daniels, Meet Adam Smith" in the November 23, 1961 issue of *Forbes* magazine, page 163. Information on fees charged by non-profit organizations is from an interview with Peter Drucker that was published in the March/April 1999 issue of *Philanthropy* on page 11. The controversial practice of non-profit organizations selling the right to use their logos to commercial businesses is discussed in a *New York Times* story beginning on page A1 of their May 3,1999 issue under the title, "Sales Pitches Tied to Charities Draw States' Scrutiny," written by Reed Abelson.

INDEX